music 4.0

music**PRO** guides

music 4.0

A Survival Guide for

Making Music in the Internet Age

Bobby Owsinski

Hal Leonard Books
An Imprint of Hal Leonard Corporation

Published in 2014 by Hal Leonard Books
An Imprint of Hal Leonard Corporation
7777 West Bluemound Road
Milwaukee, WI 53213

Trade Book Division Editorial Offices
33 Plymouth St., Montclair, NJ 07042

Printed in the United States of America

Book design by Stephen Ramirez
Book composition by Bill Gibson

Library of Congress Cataloging-in-Publication Data

Owsinski, Bobby.
 Music 4.0 : a survival guide for making music in the Internet age / Bobby Owsinski.
    pages cm. -- (Music pro guides)
 ISBN 978-1-4803-5514-9 (alk. paper)
1. Music trade--Technological innovations. 2. Music trade--Computer network resources. 3. Music and the Internet. 4. Internet marketing. I. Title.
 ML3790.O9683 2014
 780.68'8--dc23
                    2014006752

www.halleonardbooks.com

Contents

Introduction

elcome to the third edition of *Music 3.0: A Survival Guide for Making Music in the Internet Age*. As you've probably noticed, it's now called *Music 4.0*, and that's because the industry has continued to change at a record pace and has now evolved to the next level of evolution.

I originally decided to write this book precisely because the music world was changing so much. Oh, it's always been evolving, but the speed of the industry's remodeling has increased at a rate previously unimagined. It would be nice to say that this change is brought about by a leap in musical creativity, but that's not the case. This metamorphosis has been caused by technology.

The Internet has brought us so many conveniences and so many new ways of living our lives, having fun, and communicating with those we know and don't know that we sometimes don't appreciate how quickly it's all come about. It's also brought us so many choices in the way we make music and ultimately make it available that, unfortunately, it's also left most artists and music makers dazed and confused with all the seemingly endless options. What should I do? How can I do it? Who are my customers and fans? What do they want from me? How do I reach them? How do I take advantage of all these choices? How am I going to make money? These are all questions that an artist might have had previously, but the relevancy and urgency have only increased with the current times.

I came up with the concept of the original Music 3.0 edition after writing a post on my production blog (bobbyowsinski.blogspot.com; there's now also music3point0.blogspot.com) in which I discussed the current woes of not only the music business, but especially the artists who are just trying to do the thing they love most—play music. I know that some artists have grand ambitions to be the next Justin Timberlake, Christina Aguilera, Jay-Z, Coldplay, or any number of best-selling acts. Sometimes artists crave fame a lot more than they yearn to make the kind of music that will attract and keep fans for the long term. These musicians seem to be the ones that burn out of the business the fastest, once they realize how much work they really have to put in.

The vast majority of artists aren't like that. They love what they do and are supremely happy when they find others that love what they do too. For them, just being able to make music without having to work a job on the side is considered a success. If that describes you, I hear you and feel you. Reading this book might not get you there, but it can set you on your way. Knowledge is power—and that phrase has never been truer than in the current music stage that I call "Music 4.0." The possibilities for what can happen to your music are endless, but you've got to know how to take advantage of those possibilities before you can put them into action.

Throughout this book I'll refer to Music 4.0 as M4.0, or "M four oh." It has a nice ring and rolls off the tongue well. But you're probably wondering, "How did we get to M4.0? What were M1.0, 2.0, and so on?" While we'll go over all that in depth in Chapter 1, here's how I briefly delineate the various stages of the music business.

Music 0.5: The embryonic stage of the music business predating recorded music, where the product was limited to sheet music and piano rolls, and the song was much more important than the artist.

Music 1.0: The first generation of the music business as we know it today, in which the product was vinyl records, the artist had no direct contact with the record buyer, radio was the primary source of promotion, the record labels were run by record people, and records were bought from retail stores.

Music 1.5: The second generation of the music business, in which the product was primarily CDs, labels were owned and run by large conglomerates, MTV caused the labels to shift from artist development to image development, radio was still the major source of promotion, and CDs were purchased from retail stores.

Music 2.0: The third generation of the music business, which signaled the beginning of digital music and during which piracy ran rampant due to peer-to-peer networks. The industry, however, took little notice, since CD sales were still strong from radio promotion.

Music 2.5: The fourth generation of the music business, in which digital music became monetized thanks to iTunes and, later, others such as Amazon MP3. CD sales plunged, the music industry contracted, and retail stores closed.

Music 3.0: The fifth generation of the music business, in which the artist could communicate, interact, market, and sell directly to the fan. Record labels, radio, and television became somewhat irrelevant, and single songs were purchased more often than albums.

Music 3.5: The sixth generation of the music business, where YouTube and other online video platforms became the new radio, and the digital side of the business began to slowly morph from one of downloads to streaming.

Music 4.0: The generation of the music business that we're now entering, where streaming becomes the preferred music delivery method for the consumer, which makes it profitable on a wide scale and increases revenue for artists, songwriters, publishers, and labels.

This book is an aggregation of concepts about the new music business in the so-called Internet age, which I've been following for some time. It contains the guiding insights of some of the brightest minds in the music industry about where the industry has been, where it is now, and where it's going. With so much information currently available, I wanted to do what I do best—collect it, organize it, and present it in a way that everyone can understand.

As in my other books, I've sought out the help of some of the most respected voices that are on the cutting edge of different aspects of the music business, and I've included their interviews at the end of this book and incorporated selected quotes along the way. The interviews are fun and informative, and conducting them was one of the most enjoyable aspects of writing this book.

Let me briefly introduce these respected experts to you:

Dae Bogan has considerable experience in both music and social media marketing, starting out in event production for major brands such as Chipotle, Dell, Blackberry, Virgin Mobile, and Def Jam, then as vice president of marketing for Shiekh shoes and their Shiekh music artists program. His current company, Chazbo Music, provides in-store video music entertainment services by programming custom-curated channels for businesses, music, and lifestyle.

Richard Feldman has been a very successful songwriter and producer who has Platinum and No. 1 records and a Grammy award to his credit, and now leads a publishing venture focused on evergreen music compositions, a music library serving Time Warner Cable and Fox Sports, and a successful music placement agency, Artists First Music. As a past president of the American Association of Independent Music Publishers, Richard brings a unique perspective to publishing as seen from the point of view of a musician, producer, songwriter, and businessman.

An expert on entertainment analytics, **Larry Gerbrandt** advises his clients on the economics of media and content on traditional and emerging technology platforms. Formerly a senior vice president with research giant Nielsen Analytics, Gerbrandt provides a wealth of experience in entertainment market research that we're pleased we could tap for this book.

Shan Dan Horan is the director of the New Media Department at Century Media Records as well as the head of Social Media at Standby Records. He's also a talented music video director and photographer for his own company (ShanDanVideo.com), a skill set that's quite in demand these days when YouTube is the king of music distribution and discovery. Shan Dan provides some insight as to what's required to get the online presence together for a newly signed band.

Bruce Houghton started his highly influential Hypebot blog because he wanted to better understand the changes in the music business in order to help educate the clients of his Skyline Music agency. Since then, Bruce's blog has become a must-read for anyone at any level in the music industry. His keen observations come from being not only a highly prominent blogger but also a booking agent working in the industry trenches every day.

Ariel Hyatt and her socially based Cyber PR agency have been guiding artists, bands, and musicians through the world of Facebook, YouTube, Twitter, and social media since the birth of each of those platforms. As you'll see, Ariel was one of the first publicists to incorporate those tools into her skill set, and she's one of the few true experts in the field of online publicity and social media.

One of the pioneers of search engine optimization (SEO) and marketing, **Gregory Markel**'s company Infuse Creative touts major entertainment clients such as Gibson Musical Instruments, New Line Cinema, the National Geographic Channel, Led Zeppelin, The Rolling Stones, the television show *24*, and many more. As a recording artist and great singer formerly signed to Warner Brothers, Markel has a deep empathy for the plight of today's artist and provides an abundance of good advice in his interview.

One of the most respected and beloved executives in the music industry, **Rupert Perry** held a variety of executive positions with EMI for 32 years. He went from vice president of A&R at Capitol to president of EMI America to managing director of EMI Australia—and, later, of EMI Records UK—to president and CEO of EMI Europe to, finally, the worldwide position of vice president of EMI Recorded Music. Rupert is well up on the latest technology and trends within the music business, and he shares some surprising contrasts between the old business and the one we're in right now.

Jacob Tell founded Oniracom, a new breed of company that provides a full line of digital media services to artists, labels, and management. Helping artists in the digital space before there was a YouTube, MySpace, or Facebook, Jacob has watched the development of social networking and learned how an artist can best take advantage of it along the way. Now 12 years old, Oniracom has branched into branding and design as well as their core business of web development, social media marketing, and community management for artists.

Michael Terpin is the founder of SocialRadius, a social media marketing company focusing on social media outreach and strategy. The projects that his firm has worked on include the outreach for recording artist Will.i.am's "Yes We Can" video for the Obama presidential campaign (which won Emmy, Global Media, and Webby Awards), and social media event marketing for music events such as Live8, LiveEarth, the Green Inaugural Ball, and the David Lynch Foundation. Terpin also founded Marketwire, one of the world's largest international newswires.

Dan Tsurif is head of digital strategy and an artist manager at Mercenary Management, where he handles the day-to-day management for The Casualties, Nekroantix, and Black Label Society. He'll describe how management now utilizes social media to promote artists.

When reading this book, be aware that there is one basic concept that it subtly follows. It's an idea I've lived by for some time, and it helps to clarify an artist's intent (which is now more important than ever) if kept in mind.

> Art is something you do for yourself.
> A craft is something you do for everyone else.

You'll see as you read this book that it's really important to know whether what you're doing is really an art or if it's a craft, since that will determine your level of involvement in the many jobs required to advance your career as an artist. If you're making music for yourself (as compared to for someone else), all the rules change—as does your level of commitment to the muse itself!

As said before, the music business is changing rapidly and, although painful, will ultimately change for the better. There will be a lot of the old guard who will fall by the wayside, but it's probably time that happened anyway (perhaps it's long overdue). Consumers are more selective and sophisticated in their tastes and about technology, and that's something that everyone in the industry should not only be aware of but also cater to. It's the only way to survive in today's music world.

Keep in mind that there are many, many issues that reach out to us in M4.0, but things change so quickly that this book would be obsolete before it even got on the retail shelves if it were too specific in certain areas. I won't discuss the legal issues of copyright, I won't evaluate individual distributors and social networks beyond some generalities, and I won't discuss the relative merits of a particular website or service. Once again, things could all change so quickly that you'd get no value from the book if it were that detailed. I'll look mostly at the big picture, but drill down where it's appropriate.

This book looks at how to utilize Music 4.0 to its utmost. If you're an artist, you've got to be aware of all your options—both traditional and online. This book will tell you who controls today's music industry; who the new movers and shakers are; how to grow, market to, sell to, and interact with your fan base; how to utilize the new concepts that power M4.0; and what you need to do to harness the potential of M4.0, all without spending so much time online that you aren't left with time to make music.

It seems like a lot of information, but if you want to control your destiny in the new music industry, this book will show you how.

This third edition of this book includes new interviews and the latest updated info whenever possible. There's some philosophy, some how-to's, and some predictions, but it's all based on some excellent information provided by a variety of expert sources, some of whom you'll meet in this book.

Keep in mind that this book is not only for the musician but also for other members of the music industry. Everyone must understand his or her options and challenges in order to survive in this new business environment. Hopefully, you'll find this book to be an invaluable tool as you go forth into this new world.

Other Books by Bobby Owsinski

Of particular interest to readers of this book:

Social Media Promotion for Musicians (ISBN 978-0-9888391-1-3—
BOMG Publishing)

The Mixing Engineer's Handbook, 3rd Edition (ISBN 128542087X—
Course Technology PTR)

The Recording Engineer's Handbook, 3rd Edition (ISBN 1285442016—
Course Technology PTR)

The Audio Mastering Handbook, 2nd Edition (ISBN 978-
1598634495—Course Technology PTR)

The Drum Recording Handbook, with DVD (with Dennis Moody)
(ISBN 978-1423443438—Hal Leonard)

How to Make Your Band Sound Great, with DVD (ISBN 978-
1423441907—Hal Leonard)

The Studio Musician's Handbook, with DVD (with Paul ILL) (ISBN
978-1423463412—Hal Leonard)

The Music Producer's Handbook, with DVD (ISBN 978-1423474005—
Hal Leonard)

The Musician's Video Handbook, with DVD (ISBN 978-1423484448—
Hal Leonard)

Mixing and Mastering with T-RackS: The Official Guide (ISBN 978-
1435457591—Course Technology PTR)

The Touring Musician's Handbook (ISBN 978-1423492368—Hal
Leonard)

The Ultimate Guitar Tone Handbook (ISBN 978-739075357—Alfred Publishing)

The Studio Builder's Handbook (ISBN 978-0739077030—Alfred Publishing)

Abbey Road to Ziggy Stardust (with Ken Scott) (ISBN—978-0739078587 Alfred Publishing)

The Audio Mixing Bootcamp, with DVD (ISBN—978-0739082393 Alfred Publishing)

Audio Recording Basic Training, with DVD (ISBN—978-0739086001 Alfred Publishing)

You can get more information and read excerpts from each book by visiting the excerpts section of bobbyowsinski.com.

Bobby Owsinski Online

. . . .

Bobby's website–bobbyowsinski.com.

Bobby's Music Production Blog—bobbyowsinski.blogspot.com.

Bobby's Music Industry Blog—music3point0.blogspot.com.

Bobby on Facebook—facebook.com/bobby.owsinski.

Bobby on Twitter—@bobbyowsinski.

Bobby on YouTube—youtube.com/polymedia.

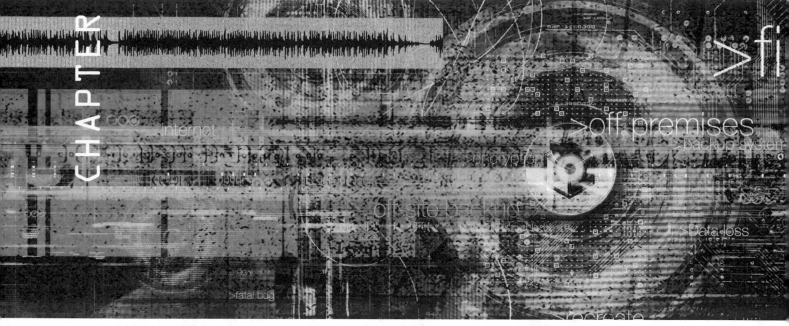

ONE

The Life Stages of the Music Industry

The history of the music business can be broken down into distinct stages. Each stage is readily apparent once you know what to look for, although the exact beginning and ending points may not be. In order to understand the significance of the stage termed "Music 4.0" (we'll call it M4.0, pronounced "em-four-oh," from now on), it's important to look closely at the other stages to spot the changes, and the opportunities, that present themselves.

One thing to remember is that what we all have come to think of as the "music business" is mostly based around popular ("pop") music, meaning music that's aimed at reaching the largest number of people possible. This popularity used to be measured exclusively by sales activity, but now even the charts of unofficial industry bible *Billboard*

1

magazine uses digital streaming and YouTube views in generating its rankings.

In fact, new charts such as *Billboard*'s Social 50 and the Ultimate Chart (ultimatechart.com), which go a step further and take all social media into account as well, are now becoming a serious force in determining the true popularity of an artist.

This means that as you read about the following stages of the music business, keep in mind that the way success was determined has changed through the years as new products, sales, and measurement technologies were introduced.

Music 0.5—The Precursor Business

In the days before recorded music, the music business was a different animal indeed. This was an industry centered around sheet music, which is how music was disseminated to the public. Thus, the only way music was heard was to buy sheet music and perform it live in your home, so the original music industry promoted the song, not the artist.

Although this industry really started in the 18th century, by the late 19th century, the center of this industry was based around the music publishers of New York's "Tin Pan Alley" district. When player pianos, the first big leap in music delivery, were introduced, the publishers created the system of what we now call "promotion" to get their songs included on player rolls, the mechanism that allowed the pianos to play by themselves. Promotion soon became an essential part of the music business that exists to this day.

NEW TECHNOLOGY DRIVES THE BUSINESS

Various new music technology delivery systems were soon created, changing the focus of the industry more the artist. The first record player, the gramophone, was introduced in 1890. In the 1920s the radio was introduced, and music delivery quickly grew as new popular songs and the artists who recorded them could now spread to a wide audience rapidly. The late 1920s then gave us motion pictures with sound ("talkies"), which soon became another source of music dissemination. In 1932, the first record store in the US came into existence ("George's Song Shop" in Johnstown, PA), and in 1941, the first store of what would become the largest chain of record stores ever, Tower Records, was opened. With the rise of the distributor known as the "rack jobber," department stores all over the country now dedicated a portion of the store just to record sales. During this time period, entrepreneurs worldwide began to recognize the new opportunities of the music business, as nearly 200 record labels were created in the US alone and retail record stores began to pop up in every town.

The music business had been formed. There was now a delivery format (vinyl records), a delivery system (record stores), and a promotional system (radio and movies) in place. The opportunity for profits had not escaped many corporations though, and by 1930, the long, slow road to industry consolidation had begun.

In 1929, Radio Corporation of America (RCA) acquired the largest manufacturer of phonographs and records, the Victor Talking Machine Company, to become RCA-Victor. In 1931, their British affiliate, the Gramophone Company, merged with the Columbia Graphophone Company to become EMI, a music industry powerhouse for years to come. RCA went on to sell its interest in EMI in 1935, but both companies were now in position to become major industry players in the future. The business was still in its infancy, however, and would have more than a decade to grow before it started to gain major traction with consumers.

Music 1.0—The Original Music Business

· ·

The music business as we know it today really started in the stage called Music 1.0, a period that lasted from the 1950s to the early 1980s. During this time, the music business mostly experienced unprecedented yearly growth, except for a brief period around 1980 when it experienced a major recession. Year-to-year sales and profits surged upward until they caught the attention of Wall Street, which turned out to be one of the industry's defining moments (more on that later). For historical purposes and to educate younger readers about how business was conducted during those times, here's an overview of the business structure of Music 1.0.

For almost 50 years, the way the music business worked remained the same. The artist (usually after submitting his or her demo tape) was signed to a recording contract by the record label, which then assigned an A&R (Artist and Repertoire) person to be the liaison between the artist and the record company product manager for the record releases by the artist. In the beginning, the A&R person would also assign a producer, who was responsible for making the record, although how this was accomplished eventually became a mutual decision with the artist over the years. Many times the producer would be on staff, and in other cases, the A&R person also served double duty as the producer.

The structure looked like this:

In the early days of the record business, the artist usually had minimal control over the end product, as that was the domain of the producer. As the business developed, and more and more artists demanded and received artistic control, the producer assigned to help the artist record was often an independent contractor from outside the label who was amenable to the musician's artistic wishes, as long as they fit the vision of the label. After some success (that is, hit records), many artists even bore responsibility for production as well.

After the song or album was recorded, the label pressed the vinyl record (and later, the cassette and CD) and distributed it to dedicated retail record stores either through the label's own distribution network or via an independent network of distributors, rack jobbers, one-stops, and wholesalers—which, under the right circumstances, placed the record in every record store, diner, car wash, department store, and anywhere else where floor space could be rented.

The structure now looked like this:

The record label was also responsible for the marketing of the record, which centered around radio airplay. If you could get a record a lot of airplay, you would probably sell a lot of records (as long as the record was in the stores and available to buy).

The other thing is how people consumed content in those days, which was that people mostly listened to the radio. Then the Japanese came up with the transistor radio, which was portable. Suddenly portability meant that the consumer didn't have to sit in their living room in front of that radio. That was the start of something else from a distribution point of few. You can look at all the things that changed, but then you look at the transistor radio and think, "Gosh, the portability was so important."
—Rupert Perry

Airplay was crucial to the success of a record and resulted in large promotion departments within the record labels dedicated to getting radio airplay. Competition for airplay became so fierce that promotion departments began to resort to using gifts of cash, prostitutes, vacations, and anything that would influence a radio station's program director to place a song in rotation. This was known as "payola," a practice that eventually was outlawed and subsequently resulted in several scandals and investigations of the record and radio industries and the way they did business together.

The structure now looked like this:

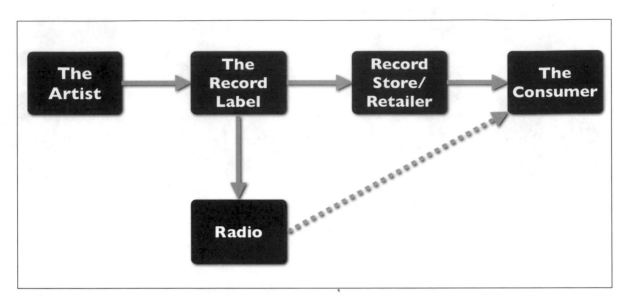

In order to avoid being prosecuted for payola, record labels decreased the use of their in-house promotion departments and instead began to use independent promoters, on the theory that anything a third-party promoter offered to a program director essentially eliminated the label's legal responsibility (the courts eventually found this to be illegal anyway). Regardless, radio airplay was the key to a hit, and promotion was the key to radio airplay.

The structure for the Music 1.0 way of doing business finally evolved into this:

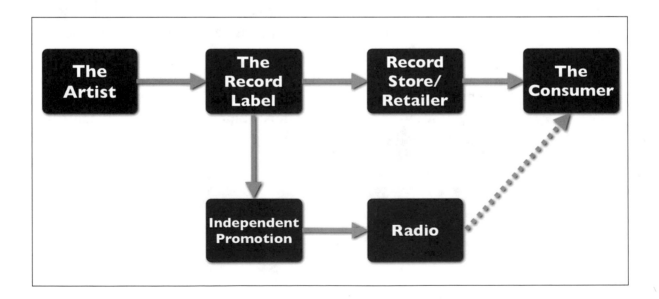

With the exception of limited exposure to the consumer via fan clubs and in-store album signings, the artist was segregated from the consumer and distribution chain. The artist might do some occasional promotion on radio, but his or her connection with the music consumer was limited. Luckily, interaction and communication with the fan wasn't needed much at this time, thanks to the overwhelming influence of radio, the 800-pound gorilla in the room of Music 1.0.

Music 1.0 gave into lots of record-label foibles in addition to payola. In order to exaggerate chart position, labels would fudge sales by having record stores intentionally report that a record was selling even if it wasn't. This practice was later put to rest with the implementation of SoundScan technology, which would compute sales via the scanned bar code on each album or CD. Although it seems like a fair way to determine actual sales, SoundScan used a system that would weight a sale in each store differently, causing a sale in a large store in Chicago to have a greater determination on chart position than a small store in Grand Rapids—a point that caused heated debate throughout the industry.

Another standard industry practice of the time used to game the system was to hire college students to go to what was deemed an important record store and buy a particular record to make it chart higher. This technique proved to be successful in that it was much more difficult to police than other methods previously used.

Another interesting practice of the era was the "shipped Platinum" syndrome. To exaggerate sales, labels would ship huge numbers of records, and then state that the record "shipped Platinum" (meaning it sold enough to be certified as a Platinum-selling record, with sales over one million units), insinuating that the demand was so great that the units shipped were presold. It usually wasn't reported, however, when the records were returned to the label in Platinum numbers if the public turned a deaf ear to the product.

Music 1.0

The record label is all powerful.

The artist is isolated from fans.

Radio is the key to hits.

Artists are given multiple release opportunities for long-term development.

It's a singles world.

But the album makes more money.

Music 1.5—The Suits Take Over

The era of Music 1.5 produced the greatest level of business that the industry has seen or is ever likely to see.

When the CD was released in 1982, record companies got a boost to ever-greater profits in several ways. Because the technology was initially expensive, the labels increased the retail price on each CD while decreasing the royalty rate to the artist, supposedly because of the "technology expense" that was involved. While the retail price never decreased even after the technology was amortized (it increased, in fact), artists eventually saw this royalty charge eliminated, but they never saw another contract clause from the past terminated. "Breakage," a 10 percent charge against royalties—left over from the days when vinyl records would break in transit, and irrelevant in the new CD age—was never deleted from typical recording contracts during this period, giving the record labels an extra 10 percent piece of the sales pie.

Perhaps the biggest shot in the arm to record labels was the ability to resell their catalog to a public eager to switch to CDs and buy a copy of an album they already owned on vinyl. Catalog sales (sales of records from an artist before his or her most recent) increased profits because production costs were minimal (just the cost of pressing the CD), as were promotional costs. Consumers bought the new and better-sounding (to some) CD to supplement their newfound CD collections, thereby providing a financial windfall for the labels deep with catalog items.

Record companies now had a cash cow that shot profits through the financial stratosphere, which immediately gained the attention of Wall Street. Always the poor stepchild of the entertainment industry, the music business was suddenly every investment banker's darling, with the remaining four of the six major labels that were still independently controlled eventually sold to multinational conglomerates during this period. Columbia Records was bought by Sony (eventually becoming Sony Music), Warner Bros. Records by Time Inc. (becoming Time-Warner), Universal Music by Matsushita (later purchased by Vivendi), and EMI by Thorn Industries. Polygram was already owned by a conglomerate (the Dutch electronics company Philips), and BMG was owned by the German giant Bertelsmann AG. Now all six major labels were under conglomerate control.

> *The other big thing that happened was the compact disc. When it came along, there was a big upsurge in the growth of the business, and a lot of large corporations began to take notice. When CBS, who was the king of the business at the time, sold their record business to Sony—that was huge! It was a momentous happening because CBS decided they wanted to exit the music business, which they had been in for years.*
>
> —Rupert Perry

With conglomerate ownership came MBAs, accountants, and attorneys running the business—a major departure from the seat-of-the-pants, street-smart music men such as Mo Ostin, Ahmet Ertegan, Jac Holtzman, Berry Gordy, and Howie Stein, who could feel a hit in their bones. Where previously a label would nurture artists or groups through three, four, even five albums until they broke through, the new corporate structure demanded instant results "this quarter." Artist development, so crucial to the careers of the stars and superstars that we consider legends today, died—slowly at first, then faster and faster as bottom-line results became the mantra.

THE RISE OF MTV

About this time, another unexpected boost came to the music industry in the form of a small cable television network startup called MTV. Suddenly, music was on television, and a new avenue of exposure increased sales yet again. MTV soon had the power to "make" a hit, just like radio previously could, by the simple act of placing a music video in heavy rotation.

Although no one expected it at the time, The Buggles' song "Video Killed the Radio Star" (which was the first video ever played on MTV) actually came to pass. Image soon became much more important than musical ability. If you didn't look appealing, you weren't getting on MTV; and if you didn't get on MTV, your chances of having a hit diminished greatly. Quickly the newfound corporate culture began to shift gears to find good-looking "musicians" to fill the bill. Artistry became just one component of a new act instead of *the* component, as image became foremost in the label mindset.

To a non-record-industry executive, art doesn't make sense. Business demands repeatable outcomes, and art is not a part of that equation. Craft was a big part of the corporate hit-making formula though. First find an artist similar to whoever is the most popular at the moment, hire a successful songwriter to write the perfect generic (usually pop) song, add a producer with a proven track record, then record it all in a studio where big hits have been previously made and with the musicians who have played on those hits. The actual "artist" matters little in this corporate scenario. He or she had better look great though, because the music videos (put together by directors, choreographers, and stylists with recent hits on their résumés) must project the image that Madison Avenue deems necessary to sell product, since that's ultimately who's footing the bill.

THE FARM TEAMS DISBAND

Unfortunately, the passage of the drunk-driving laws in 1983 negatively affected long-term artist development in a real way. Prior to 1972, the legal drinking age ranged from 18 to 21, depending upon the state, but the war in Vietnam brought about the "If I can fight for my country, I should be able to drink" argument (which we're seeing again today). By 1972, most states agreed that if you were old enough to vote and fight for your country, then it should be legal for you to partake in an alcoholic beverage, and the drinking age was lowered to 18 years old countrywide. This opened the floodgates to clubs everywhere to accommodate a whole new set of thirsty patrons, and the way to get them in the door was to provide live entertainment.

Clubs sprang up everywhere, and live music thrived. If you were a half-decent band, you could easily find somewhere to play almost every night of the week, and get paid for it too ("pay to play" didn't exist at the time).

This was great for the music business, because it gave neophyte musicians a place to get it together both musically and performance-wise. Just like The Beatles did in Hamburg in 1962, a band could play five sets a night for seven nights a week and really hone their chops. Do that for a year or two, and you were ready to take the next step toward doing your own thing, if that's what you wanted to do.

Unfortunately, it was also easy to fall into the trap of just playing clubs forever because the money was so good, but those with ambition took their club days for what they were and moved on up. They had learned what they needed by constantly playing in front of crowds.

Since the drinking age was nationally raised to 21 in 1982, the excitement and diversity in music has steadily decreased. Music has become bland and homogenized, and there are longer periods between new musical trends. This is because of the large-scale reduction of the club scene due to the higher drinking age and the tougher DUI laws. Higher drinking age and more arrests meant fewer club patrons. Fewer club patrons meant goodbye to the many previously packed clubs that served as on-the-job training for up-and-coming musicians.

This musical support infrastructure is greatly diminished these days. A band that is considered to be working a lot today is lucky if it works once a week. That means it will take a group a lot longer, not only to get more comfortable in front of crowds, but also to become musically and vocally tight. The longer it takes a band to make progress, the more likely it is that it will break up or change its direction, which means that perhaps the next great trend in music has shriveled on the vine.

Musicians need the constant feedback and attention that only an audience can provide. The more you play live, the better you get at it, which leads to more experimenting, which means the more likely you are to find your own voice

Music 1.5

Major labels are now owned by conglomerates.

Quarterly profits take precedence over art.

Many album songs are just filler.

MTV is created and has a significant role in record sales.

The artist's image becomes more important than the music.

DUI laws kill the farm team.

Music 2.0—Enter the Digital Age

· ·

The day that the first MP3 music file was shared was the first day of Music 2.0 (sometime around 1994). Although no one knew it at the time, this became the disruption that would someday bring the music industry to its knees.

If we roll forward to the start of the Internet in 1993, people in the content industry didn't get just how monumental the change was. To have any form of content available through a computer

was a totally new form of distribution, but the difference was that the record label had no control over it. Up until that point, any of the media distributors (film, television, or music) were always able to control the distribution, and when you did that, you could decide where it went, who got it, and what people paid for it. With the Internet, that went out the window fast.

—Rupert Perry

Up until the MP3 arrived, a CD-quality digital file of a song was both large in size (a little over 5 MB for every one minute of a stereo song) and took a lot of bandwidth to play (1,411 kbps), which meant that it was just about impossible to play over the Internet given the severely limited bandwidth available at the time. The same file encoded with the MP3 format would be about a tenth of the file size if the bandwidth was between 128 kbps and 256 kbps, which would make the file easy to download even on the primitive dial-up network connections available during that period. Using an MP3 codec is like letting the air out of a bicycle tire: the tire becomes small enough to fit into a small box, yet it's the same tire. The MP3 codec "let the air out" of a digital file, making it a lot smaller. Although the audio quality of the MP3 wasn't as good as what was on a CD, consumers had previously shown when they heartily adopted cassette tapes that audio quality wasn't a major issue in their purchasing and listening decisions.

P2P MAKES ITS MARK

Peer-to-peer (shortened to P2P) networking was the second new technology that changed the music business during this era. In a peer-to-peer network, each computer on the network can supply and receive files without using a central server, with bandwidth and processing distributed among all members of the network. In other words, files live on multiple interconnected users' computers, with each user able to download a file (or pieces of the same file from multiple computers) from anyone he or she is connected to (see Fig. 1.1).

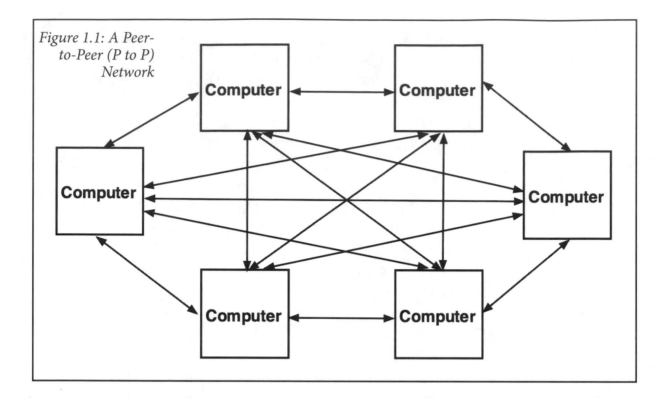

Figure 1.1: A Peer-to-Peer (P to P) Network

Napster was the first of the many massively popular peer-to-peer file-distribution systems, although it was not totally peer to peer, because it used central servers to maintain lists of connected systems and their files (a factor in their later legal undoing). Although there were already networks that facilitated the distribution of files across the Internet—such as IRC, Hotline, and UseNet—Napster specialized exclusively in music and, as a result of its enormous popularity, offered a huge selection of music to download.

Shortly after its inception, the company was presented with multiple legal challenges from artists (Metallica, Dr. Dre, Madonna), record labels (A&M), and the music industry itself (the RIAA) regarding copyright infringement, and was eventually shut down in July of 2001. Napster use peaked in February 2001, with 26.4 million users worldwide, which seems laughably low today but was enormous at the time.

MP3.com, started in 1999, was another similar service, although it primarily featured independent music instead of signed acts. Sued by Universal Music Group for copyright violations, the company settled for an out-of-court payment of $200 million to UMG and was essentially put out of business. At its peak, MP3.com delivered more than 4 million MP3 audio files per day to over 800,000 unique users and had a customer base of 25 million registered users. The company was eventually purchased by Roxio and renamed Napster, then again by big-box retailer Best Buy in 2011, then merged with streaming-music provider Rhapsody in June 2013. It now provides legal paid downloads and a subscription streaming service.

Although the original Napster and MP3.com were shut down by court order, they paved the way for decentralized peer-to-peer file-distribution programs such as Gnutella and Limewire (now discontinued), which are much harder to control. As a result, the RIAA aggressively prosecuted users who used those services, despite the outcry from the public and the industry. It has since backed off from prosecuting when it was determined that they were spending millions in legal fees only to recover paltry amounts in damages, not to mention the harm incurred to the overall industry's reputation

PIRACY TAKES ANOTHER FORM

Another major disruption of the traditional music business came as a result of the inexpensive CD burner, and its impact cannot be underestimated. In the days of vinyl, unauthorized manufacturing was almost unheard of because of the economics of a pirating operation. Pressing a vinyl record required large, costly, and specialized gear that was beyond that of even the most dedicated enthusiast. When the CD was introduced, the first CD recorders were found only in professional mastering studios because of their cost (about $250,000, with blank CDs costing $200 each). Economics kept the pirates and the casual traders at bay.

Of course the audiotape cassette, from its very inception in 1964, was a thorn in the music industry's side. Using the compact, relatively inexpensive (around $1.00 for a blank tape), and easy-to-use cassettes, home tapers could record a hit song off the radio with ease. Generally providing mediocre audio quality, the cassette was the first example where quality was a minor consideration when compared with price.

When the CD burner began to appear on just about every computer, and blank CDs fell below the $1.00 level, digital music rapidly became a runaway train going down a slippery mountain: you could try everything to stop it, but once it reached terminal velocity, there was no halting it. And so began the digital age of the record industry.

Music 2.5—Digital Music Is Monetized

Soon it became apparent that unless the music industry jumped onboard, it would be left behind in an ocean of digits. Ironically, it was the computer industry that threw the music industry a lifeline. While different digital music services presented alternatives to the labels for paid downloads, it was Apple Computer's iTunes that proved to be the business model that worked. Basically a closed system because iTunes initially required Apple's iPod digital music player (the platform choices were later expanded), iTunes was a winner with consumers for its ease of use (a trait Apple is known for) and the iPod's newfound place as a fashion accessory. Now the industry could finally monetize its digital offerings. But at $0.99 per track, there wasn't a lot left for profit (see Fig. 1.2).

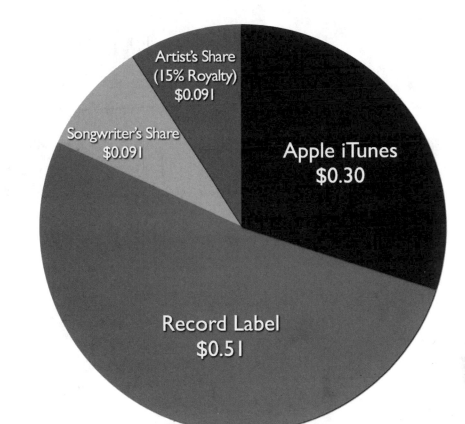

Figure 1.2: How the Money From an iTunes Song Is Distributed (in Cents)

Artist's Share (15% Royalty) $0.091

Songwriter's Share $0.091

Apple iTunes $0.30

Record Label $0.51

Released in January 2001, iTunes was an instant success that was followed by frequent and significant upgrades. In late 2001, iPod support was implemented, which started the snowball down the hill for the industry as digital music began to become the rage. In 2003, the iTunes store was introduced, and both the consumer and Apple have never looked back. In the years since, movies, television shows, music videos, podcasts, applications, and video games have been added to the extensive iTunes Store's catalog. In April of 2009, the iTunes store went to a tiered pricing structure after much prodding by the major labels. Songs are now available for $0.69, $0.99, or $1.29. At the time that this book was written, over 25 billion songs have been downloaded since the service first launched on April 28, 2003.

While iTunes is the monster of the digital-music industry, other worthy competitors have emerged. From Amazon MP3 to eMusic to the upstart Google Play, there are now numerous places online to buy songs, and even more places to listen to songs if streaming services such as Spotify, Pandora, and Rdio are taken into account. Of course, iTunes has also entered the streaming ranks with iTunes Radio, which threatens to shift the entire digital music paradigm once again. We'll go over these in more detail in Chapter 9, "The New Distribution."

Monetized digital music also brought about another big change with the return to the singles business that was similar to the '50s and early '60s. Rather than being forced to buy an album of ten songs in order to get the one he or she liked, the consumer could now buy only the songs that he or she wanted. Since the entire economics of the music industry had been centered around the album format and the money it generated, returning to the single-song purchase was a major blow to the financial model that had been in place for 40 years. Overhead had been set up for sales that were in $10.00 increments (the approximate wholesale price of an album). That was suddenly cut to sales that were in increments of less than $1.00 (the sale of a download), and the labels' financial structures were shaken to their cores.

ENTER THE 360 DEAL

To make up for the lost revenue, the major label had to have income streams that went beyond the sale of the CD, and the logical place to get that was from the artist. Since it's always been understood that 90 percent or more of an artist's income comes from touring, the record labels saw that as a potential income source and wanted a piece, and so they launched what came to be known as "360 deals." The term *360 deal* means that the record label shares in the income from all income streams available to an artist beyond just the music recordings, including things such as publishing, merchandise, and touring. The label would, in effect, become an artist's manager and share in everything he or she made.

While you can see why a record label would want to share in all of the income streams of an artist, you have to wonder why an artist would want to let them. The argument goes that if the label's expertise is in selling music (which currently isn't selling all that well), then what kind of management experience does it have? While this may be the only way to do business with a major label these days, it's yet another reason for an artist to ignore it under most circumstances.

In the meantime, traditional artist management was becoming even more powerful, because the manager was now required to make more decisions for the artist than ever before. With the influence of the record labels waning, it was now up to the manager to find new sources of income, deal with potential sponsors, handle social media, and make deals with online digital distributors, among other things. With much of the sales and marketing now in the hands of the artist, managers had incrementally larger responsibilities than in previous eras, and their guidance and impact became that much more valuable to the artist.

Music 2.5 Overview

Digital music is monetized.

Sales change from album to singles (no more album filler).

Major labels impose 360 label deals on artists.

Management becomes more important than ever.

Music 3.0—The Dawn of Artist/Fan Communication

The biggest change that came with Music 3.0 is that the structure of the business was reshaped. In M3.0 the middlemen can be cut out of the loop. The artist and the fan can keep in touch directly on any and every level they choose to, from creation to promotion to marketing to sales. But merely staying in touch with a fan can be as fleeting as it sometimes is with friends or family. True fans, just like friends and family, want regular communication, and whether artists know it or not, so do they. The structure of M3.0 looks like this:

Music 3.0 allowed the artists to promote and market directly to the fans. If they can reach the fans, they can make them aware of their products (music, event tickets, and merchandise). If they can reach the fans, they can sell directly to them (although "offer them a product" might be a better way of putting it). Most importantly, Music 3.0 allowed the artists to have dialogs with the fans in order to help the artists with sales and marketing. What do the fans want? Just ask them. Do the fans want to be alerted when the artists come to town? Do the fans want remixed versions of songs? Would fans be interested in premium box sets? By the artists just asking, the fans will gladly let them know. And this is the essence of Web 3.0—communication between the fans and the artists.

Another factor in M3.0 is that the audience became niche oriented. From Swahili polka to Mandarin madrigal, if an artist searches long enough, he or she can find an audience. But although stratification of the audience means more opportunities for more artists, it also means that the possibility of a huge multimillion-selling breakout hit diminishes as fewer people are exposed to a single musical genre than ever before. Nearly gone are the days that a television appearance, heavy-rotation radio or MTV airplay alone can propel an artist to Platinum-level success.

Music 3.0

The middleman can be eliminated.

Direct artist-to-fan communication pervades.

Direct sales can be made to the fan.

Direct marketing approaches can be made to the fan.

The audience is stratified.

Music 3.5—YouTube Becomes the New Radio

. . . .

As Music 3.0 progressed into 2012, music consumers gradually transitioned their music consumption to where a new medium somewhat replaced an old one. Although traditional terrestrial radio continues to be the principle way that all age groups combined discover new music (primarily thanks to the car radio), the crucial teen demographic prefers not only discovering music on YouTube but actually listening to it there as well. According to Nielsen's annual Music 360 report, two-thirds of all American teens use YouTube as their major source of music consumption, and that number continues to grow.

It's a fact that YouTube has evolved into a major music destination site, and has grown to become No. 1 in music discovery online, as well as in music search, both of which are critical to the health of the industry. Music has become the No. 1 content category in YouTube globally, partially because YouTube is available for free in web browsers and most smart phones, and the music there is easily accessible and can be simply shared with friends in social media.

Part of this came from the fact that the major labels were initially reluctant to authorize streaming services like Spotify, and YouTube proved to be an easily available alternative to hear the latest songs that Spotify couldn't get. Plus many streaming services didn't have the songs of some of the major stars like The Beatles, The Eagles, Pink Floyd, and Metallica, but you could find just about anything you wanted from any artist on YouTube.

While major labels continue to place a good deal of their faith and marketing money in traditional media like print and radio, indie artists such as Psy, Gotye, Macklemore, and Baauer ("Harlem Shake") finally began to break out from their YouTube plays to the point where it was now possible to reach the top of the charts propelled by video views as the major marketing tool. This was the fruition of the promise that Music 3.0 held, where an unknown artist could actually have a hit without being signed to a major label, at least in the beginning. The fact of the matter is that these artists eventually signed a version of a distribution deal with their record labels instead of the standard recording contract that used to be a prerequisite before a recording could hit the charts.

Perhaps the best thing about YouTube is that it's color blind when it comes to genres, providing an opportunity for exposure to some that would not have had a chance in a previous musical era. Take the case of Ukrainian classical pianist Valentina Lisitsa, who began uploading her performance videos after her stage career stalled. Now with more than 55 million views and 77,000 channel subscribers, her career has not only revived, but is flourishing. Then there's Gummibar, the brain child of German producers Moritz Bad and Christian André Schneider, who have created one of the most successful acts of all time in terms of children's music, with channel views of over 3 billion!

Although it might seem that the public is focused on pop music, YouTube is proving to be surprisingly musically democratic, which again speaks to the changes brought about after Music 3.0.

STREAMING CATCHES ON

One of the byproducts of listening to music on YouTube is that the public became used to streaming, and with that comfort level came a gradual flourishing of streaming services, led by the proliferation of Pandora and Spotify's introduction in the United States. Music consumers began to see that having access to tens of millions of songs at any time was preferable to purchasing a few a month and clogging your hard drive. The idea behind a streaming or "access" service is that you pay a set monthly fee to be able to listen to as much music as you want during that time with no limitations. The music is streamed, so you don't actually own it, but since it's available at any time, there's really no need to keep it on your computer, phone, or mobile device anyway.

Most of these services work on a "freemium" basis, where usage is either free with ads or capped after a certain number of hours per month. The difficulty is not getting consumers to adopt, but to upgrade to the paid tier. That coupled with the fact that the majority of a streaming company's revenue is paid out as royalties to labels, publishers, and performance rights organizations makes the future of some of the services (even some of the larger ones) somewhat tenuous.

That said, record labels dream of a paid subscription service that the majority of music consumers participate in because they like the idea of a more-or-less fixed monthly revenue stream as a result of their license agreement with the service. The artists aren't as keen, however, since much of the money collected by the labels is not passed on in what they feel is an equitable fashion (see Chapter 9). Publishers are dubious as well, noting the high cost of administration versus the income generated (see Chapter 11). Regardless, although the number of registered subscribers is expanding, music subscription hasn't reached anything near critical mass yet.

But artists see streaming another way, since millions of streams at fractions of a cent each (we'll cover the subject more in Chapters 9 and 11) result in such meager payouts that they can't help but feel exploited. Which brings us to Music 4.0.

Music 3.5

YouTube replaces radio for teens.

Music becomes the top content category for YouTube globally.

YouTube becomes the top place online for music discovery and search.

Indie artists break out big from YouTube views.

Streaming picks up speed.

Artists complain about meager royalty payouts.

Music 4.0—Streaming Becomes Profitable

Music 4.0 is the era that the music business is on the cusp of entering as this book is being written. It's an era where a tipping point is reached, and streaming (or more accurately, the ability to "access" music) becomes profitable for the entire musical supply chain, from songwriters to artists to publishers to labels to the streaming services themselves. Let's look at how this happens.

While the streaming market has been limited to Spotify, Pandora, Slacker, Rdio, Deezer (outside the US), and a number of smaller services, they accounted for 29 million paying customers at the end of 2013, worth around $2 billion globally. A study by ABI Research predicts that figure will rise to 191 million, worth a whopping $46 billion by the end of 2018. Considering that the total worldwide music revenue for 2012 was $67 billion (including touring and publishing), this is a huge increase, and since more than two-thirds of this amount goes back to the rights holders in the form of royalties, that means that the music industry can be back at or beyond its highest revenue levels of 1999.

This may seem like a pipe dream, except for the fact that the major new entrant into the market is Apple's iRadio, which has 575 million users worldwide, each with a credit card on file. Even prior to the introduction of iRadio, iTunes users spent an average of $12 a year on music (according to Apple), and $43 per account on software, apps, music, books, and video combined. iRadio will be free with ads or ad free for $24.95 a year.

Other major entrants with significant financial backing include Beats Music, which differentiates itself by professional music curators supplying playlists, Google Play Music, and YouTube's new music subscription service. And these services are all global, which means that there are far more potential consumers that will be reached than ever before.

Couple that with the fact that consumers have already seen the light when it comes to streaming and are adopting it faster than previously anticipated. The first time a music fan runs out of room on a hard drive or storage device because it's filled to the brim with music files, the value of streaming music becomes very apparent. After the consumer tries a service and realizes that 10 to 20 million or even more songs are at her fingertips anytime and anywhere, she's sold.

What that means is that although each individual royalty stream might be small, there will be many more of them to make up the difference, much like music publishing experienced with the rise of the 200-channel cable television universe. Simply put, more users plus more streams plus more distributors equals more revenue, which every artist, musician, and songwriter (labels and publishers too) should love. In Music 4.0, the "access" model revives the music business.

Music 4.0

Major new streaming services
are introduced.

Streaming reaches a tipping
point with users.

More revenue streams come from
different sources.

A higher global revenue
pool is created.

While remnants of the old Music 1.0 structure still exist (record labels, brick-and-mortar record stores, terrestrial radio, MTV, and so on) and can even be useful to the Music 4.0 artist, they will probably never again be the primary driving factor in the success of any artist. In a roundabout way, they never really were (the music is always the defining factor), although their influence was admittedly higher in the past.

It's said that a record label never signed an act because of its music; the label signed the act for the number of fans it either already had or had the potential of developing. If you had lines around the block waiting to see you play, the music didn't matter to the label, because you had an audience that was willing to buy it. And so it is with Music 4.0, only now you can develop that audience in a more efficient way and actually make a living with a limited but rabid fan base (see the section "The 1,000 True Fans Theory" in Chapter 10).

The rest of this book is about how to make use of the benefits that Music 4.0 affords an artist.

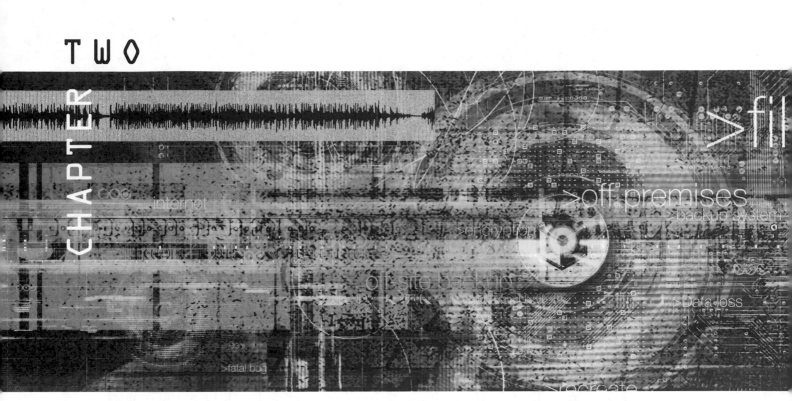

CHAPTER TWO

How the Music World Has Changed

Just like everything else technological, the music business has changed considerably in the past few years, and it continues to change at a rapid pace. Although we've seen industry evolution before, never has there been one as dramatic as what started in M3.0. Although the phrase has been overused, the paradigm had truly shifted, and many of the traditional players in the industry now had new, less prominent roles. Let's look at some of them.

Who's In Control?

· ·

Although it may not be readily apparent, Wall Street and Madison Avenue indirectly control what remains of the M2.5 music industry through their tremendous influence on the financial bottom lines of record labels, record stores, concert promotion, radio, and television. If you're owned by a publicly traded conglomerate (as most major labels, major concert promoters, and radio and television stations are), then you're in the business of selling stock, not servicing the consumer. What that means is that nothing matters more than quarterly earnings. To keep those earnings as high as possible, Wall Street turns to Madison Avenue to devise the best marketing strategies to sell to its customers. Madison Avenue (in the form of the major advertising agencies) can bring in the big ad dollars, but only under certain content conditions (such as programming that is tailored around the advertising), and the process repeats itself over and over. The advertising industry (Madison Avenue), not the music industry, therefore drives the music cycle in the United States.

In M2.5, it's all about passing focus-group tests, which have separated listeners into the distinct demographic groups that advertisers are then able to tell stock analysts they have micromarketed their products to. As a result, radio, television, and live performances are no longer about aggregating and entertaining large audiences, but rather just a group of market niches. The bright side to this fact is that there's one heck of an opportunity opening up for folks who don't get hung up on trying to sell via traditional advertising.

Wall Street and Madison Avenue have tried to redefine what music means to people, but most people have voted with their wallets by refusing to buy any new recordings on the scale that was previously expected. The view of the vast majority of consumers is that fewer new recordings are worth buying compared to those released a couple decades ago, and this has become the dilemma of the industry. You have to sell product to survive, but it's impossible to develop that product while trying to please your corporate masters. It might work when selling soap or clothing or any other consumer product, but a creative endeavor like music just doesn't work the same way. It's too personal, both to the artist and the consumer, to be a mass-market product.

Control in Music 2.5

Wall Street and Madison Avenue
control the media.

Record labels need to keep stock price
and quarterly profits high.

Radio and television only play what
appeals to advertisers.

Consumers are divided into demographic groups.

Music becomes devalued.

Where Did the Record Stores Go?

Although sales of physical product such as CDs are way down in
the music business (off by more than 78 percent since 2000, according to RIAA statistics), a major reason is that consumers often can't
find the product when they want to buy it. It used to be that almost
every town had some kind of store where you could buy recorded
music, but now even major shopping malls around the country are
CD-barren wastelands. Since 2003, 3,500 music retailers have closed,
according to the Almighty Institute of Music Retail, an industry
research group. There are now fewer than 2,500 dedicated retail music
stores left (although there are around 12,000 retail outlets that sell
music).

So where did the music retailers go? Just like so much else in M1.0
through M2.0, music retailing was once a thriving business that had
no shortage of customers, but several factors throughout the years
delivered a knockout blow from which the retail part of the industry
now finds it difficult to recover. First up came the closing of the large
music retail chains such as Tower (93 stores), the Wherehouse (320
stores), and Sam Goody (1,300 stores), all now defunct. While initially

good for business, these chains began to put price pressure on the small independent retailers that were the backbone of the industry. If you can buy it cheaper from the chain store, that's where you'll go, and so the buying public did.

But soon the music retail chain stores got a taste of their own medicine. In the '90s, Best Buy, Target, and Wal-Mart began to stock CDs as a loss leader in order to get customers in the door to buy their pricier merchandise. This combination of the music-buying experience along with traditional shopping proved hard to beat. Soon these three megaretailers were responsible for more than half of all CD sales, and their leverage hit home with record labels and traditional record retailers alike. The music retail chains, finding it impossible to compete with CDs priced at wholesale prices and below, soon closed, leaving only a dwindling number of independent stores. Ironically, all three megaretailers have now decreased their in-store inventory to only Top 40 selections, and are looking to trim that even more in the future.

Then came the rise of M2.5, as digital music files (MP3s) penetrated the consciousness of the consumer, and soon CD sales began to drop year after year. Digital piracy, online CD sales, CD copying via CD burners, paid digital downloads, and the lack of new music trends and blockbuster product caused the number of music retailers to fall to unprecedented low levels. Even the highest-grossing record store in the country, Virgin Records in New York's Times Square, closed in 2009—not because it was losing money, but because more money could potentially be generated from the same square footage with another business. So even when a new blockbuster music product that everyone wants exists, you can't buy it if you can't find it.

Many of the indie record stores that are left have been forced to diversify in order to keep the doors open, concentrating more on hard-to-get box sets, books (yet another industry in flux), and music accessories and merchandise. While vinyl records have been a temporary boon to indie retailers, with sales in 2012 increasing by almost 29 percent (according to the RIAA), they represent a minute part of the business, with a total of only 7.1 million units sold (not counting used sales). But the used vinyl market, even though it's small, continues to thrive.

What does the future hold for the record store? No less than Sir Richard Branson, whose initial fortune came from his string of Virgin

Megastores in the UK, predicts that there will be no record stores left anywhere in the world by the year 2020. That assessment may be a bit radical, but we can be pretty sure the number will continue on a downward spiral in the future.

Reasons for Record Store Decline

Online purchasing

Loss-leaders from Best Buy, Wal-Mart, and Target

Digital pirating

CD burners

Fewer blockbuster releases

The rise of the MP3

Why Traditional Radio Is No Longer the Factor It Once Was

Broadcast radio was once the lifeblood of the music industry. Even moderate airplay of a song could be enough to establish an artist, while heavy rotation of enough of his or her different songs could almost guarantee the artist's long-term career success. Today, radio is just a shell of its former self, far less relevant in its impact on the success of an artist, thanks to limited and homogenized playlists and the rise of music discovery on YouTube and social media.

So how has radio gone from Holy Grail to dirty coffee cup? Radio has undergone its own version of technological morphing paralleling that of the music industry. Back in the early days of radio, each station was locally owned and reflected the tastes of the community and region, including the music. Much of the great music from the '50s through the '70s came about as a result of these local tastes;

from Philadelphia to Detroit to Memphis to Cleveland to Chicago to Houston to Los Angeles, each region had its own distinct sound.

Another factor in radio's rise was the relative freedom that disc jockeys had, being able to play just about any record that they liked. In the late '60s and '70s, this freedom hit its apex on FM radio, as people tuned in specifically because they trusted the taste of the DJ. You could hear back to back a raga from Ravi Shankar, hard rock from Led Zeppelin, jazz from Miles Davis, and acoustic folk music from Richie Havens. With the air of discovery high and listeners flocking to the major FM stations in each region of the country, your DJ was your personal music guide, who could take you to new musical destinations if you just let him or her.

During this period, FM radio was considered a poor stepchild to AM, because the proliferation of FM radio was just beginning and its advertising revenues were still relatively low, so large ownership groups generally overlooked the format as a potential source of revenue. But money always follows listeners, and soon FM radio was raking in big advertising dollars, which attracted major players from both Wall Street and Madison Avenue looking for a new income stream. Soon local AM and FM stations were purchased by station groups, and the station groups by conglomerates. In an effort to maximize profits, radio "consultants" were hired to review the stations' playlists and make them more listener friendly. When this happened, the DJ lost all his or her freedom of what to play as the playlists were tightened. The consultants even picked the time when the songs they chose could be played. Since the same consultant was determining the playlists for the entire station group, stations using the same formats were playing the same songs virtually everywhere in the country, regardless of the region. Radio became homogenized and stale.

Worse still was the fact that what had always been a localized media soon became anything but, with some stations turning to automated broadcasting with no live on-air personnel or even local news. Soon came the endless commercial spots from national advertisers, since few local advertisers could now afford the service.

For the listener, radio went from a point of endless music discovery, where listening all night could be considered a reasonable leisure activity, to a sonic clump of audio goo designed to be as inoffensive as possible. In an effort to grow their profits, big corporations turned radio into a supplier of background music, rather than the aural companion that it used to be.

Prior to the influx of big-money ownership, radio couldn't afford demographic market research, and each station decided what to play by noting the calls they received from their listeners or by calling the local music stores to see what customers were buying. Although the possibility of overhyping a particular record existed, this information bore more of a relationship to what the people in the area were actually buying and listening to. Now, because focus-group results take precedence over the preferences of listeners, we have more "turntable hits" than ever before, in which a recording gets massive exposure but no one is willing to purchase it.

Advertisers want to control what's being played around their advertising dollars, and the need to please the advertiser (instead of the listener) is one of the reasons that radio is where it is today. No advertiser is willing to take the risk of being associated with new music when, for the same money, they can be associated with a known quantity. Yet listeners have proven over and over that they are more than happy to embrace something new.

Arbitron ratings between stations continue to be important, but far less so than when there used to be competition between stations as opposed to station groups.

COLLEGE RADIO ON THE BRINK

For many years, college radio has been the beacon of hope shining brightly across the wasteland that is commercial radio. As radio has become more and more homogenized, thanks to group ownership and consultant-led playlists, the only place for many indie acts to break has been the local college radio station. But now college radio sadly faces extinction as more and more colleges either close their stations down, sell them off, or convert them to online only. This is due to a couple of reasons:

▶ Fewer on-campus listeners. Students just don't listen to radio much anymore, opting to discover their music online. Ironically, studies by the stations themselves have found that most of a college radio's listenership is off campus. That being said, college broadcast courses will remain in place as university radio stations move to the

Web, but the traditional college broadcast radio station may soon be gone.

▶ Budgetary shortfalls. Thanks to the recession, college administrators everywhere are faced with the prospect of making cuts, and frequently the first item to get the axe is the radio station with its expensive upkeep, especially if it can be sold off.

Realistically though, college radio had been infiltrated by big business more than a decade ago, after record labels discovered that it was the last bastion of open playlists. That being said, at least the consultants (who are largely responsible for homogenized radio) have been kept out of it, hence the continuing local flavor that each remaining station maintains.

Just like the music business, radio isn't what it once was and probably never will be again. In the end, it might not matter much if college radio ceases to exist, since in many ways it's been gone for while; just not many have noticed.

Broadcast Radio's Decline

Loss of local control.

Local stations bought by station groups.

The rise of the consultants.

Market share loss to Internet and satellite radio.

The slow death of college radio.

Why Television Is No Longer a Factor

. . . .

It used to be that an appearance on television could give an act a pretty good sales boost. During the 1970s and '80s heyday of *Saturday Night Live,* an act could count on at least 100,000 unit sales (usually more) the week after an appearance, and of course MTV made acts into bona fide stars and superstars. For the most part, those days are over.

Today, an appearance on a late-night talk show such as David Letterman's will probably go unnoticed, since the demographic watching is falling off to sleep and may not be interested in buying new music anyway. A new act might get some small amount of traction on Conan O'Brien or Jimmy Kimmel's show, but probably won't sell many units because of it. Daytime TV can help sales though. An appearance on Ellen DeGeneres's afternoon show can be sales gold, but the demographic is narrow (mostly women age 25 to 45), so this type of appearance can't be utilized by every artist.

That said, the Disney Channel and Nickelodeon are the only major star-making venues on the television airwaves today, although they're limited by their demographic as well (kids between the ages of 6 and 14). An act appealing to prepubescents can truly move product, but the time window is small because the audience grows up, which usually makes for short careers. Disney and Nickelodeon sell cute, not art, and there's only room for a few acts.

In the end, television is much like the Internet, with so many vertical avenues that have sucked viewership from the major networks. If you have an eclectic viewing taste, there's probably a channel for you, but there's less and less space for music instead of more. MTV and its sister stations are now more about lifestyle than music, and any music show on an outlying cable network has an already limited viewership. The fractured demographic and viewing habits mean that fewer and fewer eyes see music on television, which translates into fewer sales being made.

What's happening is that the numbers for traditional broadcast television are dropping dramatically. In a five hundred channel universe, viewers simply have a lot of choices, and a lot of the programming is simply not compelling enough.

—Larry Gerbrandt

Music on Television

Daytime television helps sales more than nighttime.

Disney and Nickelodeon become the main outlets for star making.

Disney and Nickelodeon sell cute, not talent.

Most music shows have small audiences.

TV appearance no longer ensures a sales bump.

The Trouble with Labels

The record label used to be the be-all, end-all to the music business. It was the gatekeeper, the taste maker, the banker, and the sales and publicity engine that the music world revolved around. While on the superstar level all that's still true in M4.0, a record label, especially a major label, holds much less influence in virtually all facets of the music industry than ever before.

WHERE DIGITAL MUSIC HAS FAILED

When the music industry was at its peak, all of its revenues and projected revenues were based around the album. The retail price for a CD was anywhere from $10.00 to $18.00, which, although the margins were thin at many points of the supply chain, still provided enough of a return to drive industry revenue to new heights, thanks to the volume of CDs that were being sold. With sales of physical product in double-digit decline year over year, the industry held out hope that revenues of digital product might take the place of the CDs.

According to Soundscan, digital download sales were actually down by 5.7 percent in 2013, so they certainly weren't enough to offset the decrease in physical sales, which were down by about 78 percent from 2000. This illustrates the big failing of digital music until now in that you can't take a product that sells for $10.00 to $18.00 and replace it with one that sells for $0.99 and expect the industry to remain healthy. Plus, you can't sell fewer products than you did in the past and expect everyone in the business to remain smiling either.

A full 59 percent of record-label revenues in the US came from digital sales in 2013, and total album sales were down by 8.4 percent from the year before. Much of this has to do with purchasing habits changing from the album to the single as we actually consume more music digitally, as well as consumers using streaming services more and more. So why have album sales failed to catch on in a big way in the digital age?

▶ It once was a visual experience. During the vinyl record age, the album form had the advantage of that wonderful piece of cardboard known as the album jacket. The album jacket contained the cover art (still found on CDs), and most importantly, the liner notes on the back, which we'll get to in a second. But one thing that everyone either forgets or has never experienced is the fact that millions of albums were purchased completely on impulse because of the album artwork alone!

It may be hard to believe, but it was quite common to come across an album cover that was so cool that you'd buy it without knowing a thing about the artist. Sometimes it would be a total loser, but you still had the liner notes to read, and occasionally that would still make it a worthwhile purchase.

▶ It was an informational experience too. Those too young to have experienced the age of vinyl don't know how much the liner notes meant to nearly everyone who bought an album (see Figure 2.6). You could spend hours reading a well-written gatefold jacket, checking out every credit, wondering about where these exotic studios where the album was recorded were, and generally soaking up any info you could about the artist. Of course, this was in a time before the Internet, so the liner notes were sometimes the only place to find any info on the artist at all.

To say the least, the visuals and information along with the music made buying an album a total experience that today's album doesn't some close to.

▶ Too much filler. Most vinyl albums are between 35 and 45 minutes long. This was out of necessity because of the physics of a record. Make it any longer and it starts to get noisy, the frequency response suffers, and it won't play as loudly. But 40 minutes or so turns out to be the perfect amount of time for listening. There's a time commitment you have to make, but it's well within reason, especially if you like the music.

The average CD is capable of containing a bit more than 76 minutes of music. Unfortunately, artists began to think that it was a really good idea to include on the CD all the secondary material that they normally would've tossed from a vinyl record. Now instead of having 40 minutes of great music, we had 55 minutes of mediocrity. Even if the artist had some great songs, they were frequently buried under another 50 minutes of filler. Now not only was the fan paying more money, but he or she was paying more money for less quality. Something had to give.

When MP3s came on the scene, the music business was eventually pushed from an album-oriented business into the singles business that it has now become. Ironically, popular music started with as a singles business, to whence it now returns.

IT'S THE MUSIC, STUPID

Overlooked in all this is the effect that the actual music has on consumer buying habits. If consumers can't relate to or identify with the music, they won't buy it. Some industry critics feel that the release of safe music guided by the hand of Madison Avenue (like the boy band One Direction or Justin Bieber) is as much a factor in the decline of music sales as anything else, and indeed, they may have a point.

THE DEATH OF ARTIST DEVELOPMENT

For the most part, the music industry has been slow to develop a new generation of major artists capable of filling stadiums, instead relying on so-called "heritage" artists such as The Eagles and Madonna for large sales numbers. True, there are always new stars that quickly attain popularity, but it's surprising how poorly many do when it comes to sustaining careers. The fact is that with fewer record labels and less artist development than ever before, the music industry may be fighting the artist discovery battle with one arm tied behind its back.

Artist development has always been the lifeblood of the industry, even as far back as M1.0. A good example of this is Geffen Records (now owned by the Universal Music Group). To build his label, David Geffen signed three of the biggest stars in the world at the time (1980): Donna Summer, Elton John, and John Lennon. Donna Summers's and Elton John's first albums for Geffen stiffed outright. John Lennon's was also headed for the dumper prior to his unfortunate passing, which caused his entire catalog's sales to spike. It wasn't until the label signed new acts that it truly became successful, with Whitesnake and Guns N' Roses leading the way. As always, if you want to get rich in the music business, you've got to invest in the new.

The nature of artist development has changed through the years, going from being one of patience to that of instant win or lose for the artist. In the music business's so-called glory days of the late '60s and '70s, it was not uncommon for a record label to stay with an artist for three, four, or even five albums (as was the case with megastars David Bowie, Fleetwood Mac, and Tom Petty) as the artist built an audience and eventually broke into the mainstream music consciousness. This is because the most successful labels such as Warner Bros., Atlantic, and Elektra were run by music visionaries instead of large corporations worried about their quarterly bottom lines. As the conglomerates gradually took over the major labels, that patience grew less and less until it reached today's "the first record must be a hit or you're dropped" mentality. Luckily, M4.0 finally provides an alternative to this way of thinking within the corporate music industry.

THE DEATH OF A&R

The job of A&R isn't what it used to be, as the major record labels continue to feel that they can get by with fewer and fewer A&R executives. According to former Arista Records A&R man Rich Esra (one of the publishers of *The Music Business Registry*, a quarterly publication that tracks A&R people and provides their contact information) there were only 55 A&R execs hired in 2012, while 27 were let go without a single one of them being rehired. Contrast that to 2008 when 80 were hired, and you can see a definite trend.

Rich recently posted the reasons that he thought A&R was dying in the excellent *Digital Music News* newsletter. According to Esra:

1. The major labels are hiring fewer and fewer A&R executives because the volume of acts (and more importantly, the types of acts) being signed have dramatically decreased.

2. The A&R process used to be about the discovery, signing, and nurturing of the act. Today, A&R executives are not looking for talent per se. They are looking for an ongoing business.

   An artist who has developed some kind of traction and awareness on his or her own is what I'm talking about. Today, acts need to be "developed," or at least be developing in a business sense, for any label to have even the slightest amount of interest. The *idea* that today's A&R executives will discover an unknown act/artist and develop that artist is an illusion. They currently have neither the desire, time, or the money, for that matter.

3. This is why from an A&R perspective, only the most generic, ubiquitous type of acts get any attention from labels today. There is only a certain type of act these days that major labels are willing to sign.

We've all heard the stories about the meddling A&R guy who knows nothing, yet demands that an artist change his or her music or direction for reasons known only to him, but the fact of the matter is that there were far more good A&R people employed than bad ones. Someone has to find the next generation of talent just to keep these companies alive, and without A&R, it's more likely than ever that the major labels will die along with the position.

THE PIRACY ARGUMENT DISSIPATES

Until recently, illegally downloading songs was a way of life for many consumers. Now subscription services have essentially rendered piracy moot, since it's far easier and more convenient to obtain music legally.

The exact amount that piracy impacted sales was always debatable, but the fact of the matter is that it certainly existed before digital downloads (especially in M1.5 and M2.0), going back as far as when recording devices first became commercially available. While piracy's impact cannot be underestimated, it shouldn't be overestimated either. For many years, the music industry has used piracy as a convenient excuse to cover its many other ills and shortcomings.

> *But what really people forget is that by the end of the '70s, the recorded music business was in deep, deep trouble. There was a recession and a couple of years of downward trends, and a lot of people thought, "This is the end of it." There was a lot of piracy, thanks to the cassette player and that issue of that "Record" button, and people just weren't buying vinyl records anymore. The issue of people making their own copies was a pretty big issue even in those days. People were copying music for free off the radio or from another cassette or record. We reckoned that we were losing at least 25 percent of our business to home taping. So when people talk about "free" today, there's nothing particularly new about it, it's just a different version of the same thing.*
>
> —Rupert Perry

While music industry sources such as the RIAA and IFPI often floated claims that every 9 out of 10, to 19 out of 20, files downloaded were illegal, it was always difficult to know what to make of these statistics. As difficult as it is to get precise numbers on real sales that aren't being reported (anything outside of SoundScan usually isn't taken into consideration, such as direct downloads from artist's websites, or CD purchases either from distributors such as Tunecore or CD Baby or directly from acts at concerts), what makes anyone think that the piracy numbers were or are now anything more than a number pulled out of thin air?

In fact, a study conducted at Carlos III University of Madrid in Spain, in collaboration with scientists at the IMDEA Networks Institute, the University of Oregon (USA), and the Technical University of Darmstadt (Germany), found that illegal file sharers tended to be either organizations such as record labels that put up fake or malware-infected files to discourage piracy (called "fake publishers"), or "top publishers" that earn profits from advertising and subscription using pirated content as bait.

In the end, the study concluded that "since BitTorrent's popularity is tied to a small group of users who engage in illegal file-sharing for 'economic benefits,' if the same users lost interest or simply disappeared, BitTorrent's traffic would be 'drastically reduced.'"

A more recent study (2013) called "Copy Culture" by two researchers at Columbia University found that copying and online file sharing were actually mostly complementary to purchasing product. In other words, copying or sharing had no significant impact on music purchasing. The study also found that file sharers were heavy media consumers and purchased as many legal physical products and services as their non-file-sharing counterparts. Not only that, they also displayed a marginally higher willingness to pay.

The bottom line is that piracy hardly seems to be the issue that it once was, for a variety of reasons. It undoubtedly still exists, and always will to some extent, but the problems of the music industry now lie elsewhere.

The Trouble with Labels

Less artist development.

Safe artist signings.

No new music trends.

Longer time period between trends.

Decline in album sales.

No replacement format for the CD.

Fewer A&R executives, with limited signing power.

Piracy problems have somewhat dissipated.

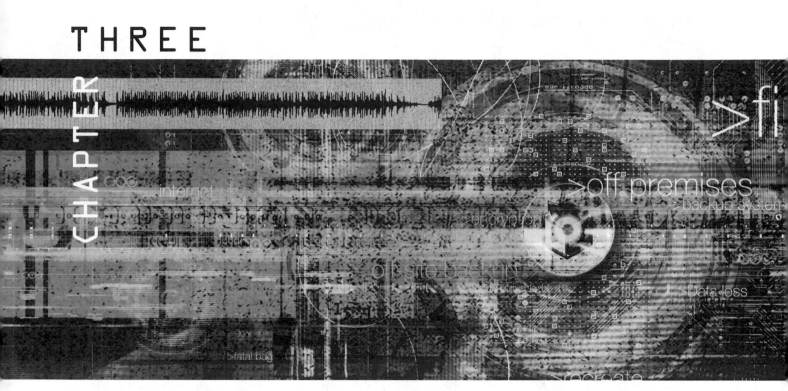

THREE

CHAPTER

The New Music Industry

f you've read the previous chapters, it's evident that the music industry is entering some uncharted waters. There are remnants of the old
that will probably always survive, but what we're seeing is a reset from
the old way of doing business to a new, still partially undiscovered
method. This makes the new music industry both exciting and a little
scary at the same time, but only if you've experienced the previous
business version. Let's take a look at what the new music industry
looks like.

The Music Industry Is Not Dying

Despite the doom and gloom that you hear from the many industry pundits, anyone who thinks the music business is really dying is absolutely wrong. It's evolving, morphing, transmuting, adjusting, adapting, reconfiguring, transitioning, and progressing; but it's not in any danger of dying.

Consider these figures:

▶ While it's absolutely true that CD sales are down 78 percent from 2000, that still means that 165 million were sold in 2013 in the US alone that could be counted (direct sales on artist and band websites or distribution services are not). That's still a lot of physical music product being sold.

▶ 2013 also saw 1.26 *billion* digital downloads purchased. Again, a huge amount.

▶ Internet radio service Pandora has over 175 million registered users and 65 million active users a month.

▶ As of the beginning of 2012, more than 278,000 artists sell their music at CD Baby, and over 5 million of their CDs have been sold online to customers.

▶ The 2013 report by Nielsen reported almost 118 billion music streams, up 32 percent from the same time the previous year. This was before the introduction of iTunes Radio, Beats Music, and YouTube's new streaming service.

There are still a lot of people out there willing to part with their hard-earned money for the music they love.

For better or worse, more and more people make music than ever before, thanks to powerful yet inexpensive tools that go way beyond what an artist, producer, or engineer could even dream about during the Music 1.0 era. The good part is that if you'd like to make your own music, it's easier than ever. The bad part is that there is more and more mediocre music available than at any other time, mostly because the built-in filters of the A&R departments of the record labels are extremely diminished in their clout or just bypassed completely.

Although consumers' listening habits have changed dramatically, there's proof everywhere that they're still willing to pay for music they like, as evidenced by British singer Adele, who sold over 28 million units of her album *21* over a period between 2011 to 2013, a figure that many industry observers predicted could never be approached again. This shows that people are willing to pay for quality music; they just haven't seen or heard enough of it to get really excited with their pocketbooks in the numbers they used to. And there's more competition for those dollars and the listener's attention than ever before. If anything, music today has to be better than ever to compete.

Remember, the music industry only dies when people stop listening. See any evidence of that lately?

The Music Industry Isn't Dying

Huge numbers of CDs are still sold.

More people than ever before listen to music.

More people than ever before make music.

People are always willing to pay for quality music.

The New Radio

As outlined in chapter 2, traditional radio has gone from being a cultural juggernaut to almost a media has-been, but new flavors of radio have significantly energized the medium to the point of rebirth. Let's look at some of the ways today's radio listeners consume its product.

INTERNET RADIO

Radio is said to have gone through its own version of the music generations, with Radio 1.0 being the early, startup days of AM, R1.5 being the age of the Top 40 formats of the '60s and '70s, R2.0 being the rise of FM, R2.5 being the rise of talk radio, and R3.0 being the era of Internet radio. You can say that we've entered into R3.5 as Internet radio has matured and now moves into the car.

Internet radio has risen in popularity quickly as a whole new set of online-only virtual stations have appeared along with Internet counterparts of many of the terrestrial stations as well. In fact, Internet radio has radically changed our listening habits, according to Arbitron/Edison Research, a leader in media opinion and marketing research used by the radio industry. In their *Infinite Dial* 2013 report, they state:

▶ Approximately 120 million people a month listen to radio online.
▶ 45 percent of all radio listeners have listened to radio online.
▶ 33 percent listen to Internet radio while working.
▶ They listen to Internet radio because of the control and variety it provides.
▶ Pandora is the clear leader in top-of-the-mind awareness at 69 percent.
▶ Users listen to online radio three times longer than they watch online videos.

Most independent Internet radio stations differ from their terrestrial cousins in that they utilize the vertical nature of the Internet to provide very specific targeted programming to their listeners. But while terrestrial stations have a sales staff with a host of customers used to advertising, their independent Internet counterparts require a different business model to survive, as they are somewhat relegated to traditional Internet sales support, such as banner and contextual ads, paid search, and pay-per-click, if they don't utilize on-air advertising.

Pandora, MOG, iHeart Radio, iTunes Radio, Slacker, and similar services are successful because they solve the filter problem. You program your own music channel, and your choices are analyzed and some additional recommendations given. This is the antithesis of traditional broadcasting, where the programming choice is made for you via consultants, focus groups, advertiser requirements, or in the good old days, by the DJ himself. It's also one of the reasons why these services will continue to gain support, as the various services try to outdo one another with better recommendations.

One of the biggest problems for Internet radio is the issue of performance fees, which broadcast radio does not pay (although this might change soon). Currently, an Internet radio station pays on a sliding scale, depending on the type of station and number of listeners, but the rates gradually rise each year until 2015, jeopardizing one of the truly great resources to new artists. As the cost of doing business for Internet radio rises, many stations will have to resort to the advertiser-supported model of their terrestrial cousins to survive. This also brings with it the same problems that their terrestrial counterparts now endure, meaning outside pressure on the makeup of their playlist. The bottom line remains that the fans are out of the loop in advertising-supported entertainment, other than their passing interests in something like chart statistics.

In the end, technology doesn't change the lessons of broadcast history or the fact that there is always intense competition for advertising dollars. There is very little difference between electronic distribution and broadcasting once you peel away all of the hype.

THE CONNECTED CAR

The real revolution in radio is the connected car, and that journey is only just beginning. With WiFi, 4G (fourth generation), and LTE (Long Term Evolution) mobile data technologies becoming more and more available, any Internet radio station is capable of being streamed or cached. With Pandora, Spotify, Rdio, and iHeartRadio the current heavy hitters, new apps such as iTunes Radio and Beats Music may change the driving experience forever. How? Until the recent introduction of satellite radio, listening to radio in a car was a geographic experience, since you were limited to the local stations around you. With the connected car, this limitation is breached for good, as you can now access any station from any spot in the world. You can access any format, music genre, or personality that you desire.

Most auto manufacturers have already added Internet radio capabilities into their latest cars, with Ford, Mercedes, BMW, Chrysler, Chevrolet, Toyota, Buick, Lexus, Honda, and Hyundai leading the charge. Indeed, the race is clearly on to capture this huge audience, with the prize goal of 70 to 80 percent of in-car listeners for one lucky service.

But could the advance of Internet radio be the last nail in the coffin of local radio? Already suffering from corporate homogenization, local radio has been severely criticized in recent years for not attending to the needs of its immediate community. It's just not local enough anymore.

With its listener base further fractured by yet more choices for the listening consumers, Internet radio could either be a death blow or a new beginning, as corporations decide that radio is no longer a contributor to their bottom lines and sell the stations back to the locals. It could be one situation where more diversity actually leads to greater listener selection.

SATELLITE RADIO

Satellite broadcasting was once thought to be the next revolution in radio, and while providing a superior listening experience to the consumer in many ways, it has run into many more snags than expected. The two original competing services, XM and Sirius, merged in the face of staggering startup costs and overhead, and while Sirius XM's current subscriber base is a healthy 25 million listeners as of the writing of this book, program licensing costs with the NFL, MLB, and especially the latest $80-million-per-year deal with shock jock Howard Stern continue to be a huge impediment to profitability.

But despite these large cost burdens, Sirius XM provides programming unlike any found on terrestrial radio, with more than 165 digital channels coast to coast, including 72 commercial-free music channels and original music and talk channels created by the company's XM original programming unit and by leading brand-name content providers such as Martha Stewart, Oprah, John Madden, Tom Petty, and Bob Dylan. Sirius XM is now available in over 60 percent of new car models (cars being the main target of the service), and with new car sales showing a healthy increase, Sirius XM projects to add a million users a year to its subscriber base.

Some wonder whether Sirius XM can survive despite its die-hard following, since the eventual replacement of its satellites will require a large influx of cash that the marketplace seemingly can't support. This calls into question the subscription model for programming versus the age-old advertising model, which, as we've seen, eventually leads to controlled playlists. And while Sirius XM has solved the problem of endless radio commercials, it still hasn't solved the problem that many of their stations sound just as much like the dreaded terrestrial ones, just without the ads.

WHAT IS RADIO'S FUTURE?

While we can easily see what radio is like today, it's much more difficult to look into a crystal ball at its future, but a study by Edison Research/Arbitron called "The Infinite Dial 2013," which examined the media and technology habits of Americans, may give us some insight as to what to expect. The first part of the study looked at the music discovery and consumption habits of this group and produced some significant findings:

► Americans that listed themselves as "heavy radio users" listen to more than six hours per day, which is twice as long as they spend online or watching television.

► Heavy radio use is very even across all adult demographics, with only a 6 percent difference between categories.

► One in five Americans have used their cell phone to listen to online radio in their cars.

► Americans still listen to radio an average of 12 hours per week.

► Online radio reaches 120 million listeners a month (more than a third of the population).

► Broadcast radio has over 240 million listeners per week, with an average listen time of two hours.

► Surprisingly, radio continues to be the medium most often used for music discovery, with 72 percent of 12-to-24-year-olds reporting that they "frequently" find out about new music by listening to the radio. Other significant sources include friends (79 percent), YouTube (77 percent), and social networking sites (57 percent).

Providing that none of this data is skewed (no guarantee there), radio is currently listened to more, and has a greater influence, than most people believe. While it may be true that local radio is on the serious decline, and Internet may be its future, good old-fashioned terrestrial radio has some life left in it yet.

THE NEW TELEVISION

As with just about all media, television is in the middle of a huge transition. Where cable television dominated for the last 30 years with one of the most desirable business models of any business, that subscription business is showing signs of deterioration as more and more video is being consumed online. Indeed, some of that content may be restricted in the future in an effort to stop the cannibalization of the broadcast audience, and to keep the connected viewers from "cutting the cord" by dropping their cable service and viewing strictly online.

THE EFFECT OF YOUTUBE

In many ways, YouTube can be considered the new television. Consider the following numbers for 2013:

▶ YouTube has over 1 billion unique viewers each month.
▶ 6 billion hours of video are watched each month on YouTube, or almost an hour for every person on earth.
▶ There are 100 hours of video uploaded every minute.
▶ YouTube is the No. 2 search engine behind Google (although it's owned by Google), bigger than Bing, Yahoo, Ask, and AOL combined.
▶ YouTube is 28 percent of all Google searches.
▶ The average user views 186 videos a month.
▶ 90 percent of Internet traffic is video.
▶ People now consume more music by watching it than by any other means. Fifty-seven percent have watched music videos on computers in the last three months from sites such as YouTube.

As far as music is concerned, YouTube has become the top music discovery site online, with music accounting for 31 percent of the site's visits every month, which is by far its largest category. What's more, it has now become a major source of income for record labels, as half of the 25 billion views each month that contain music generate around $1.3 billion in advertising revenue. As we enter into M4.0, YouTube has morphed from strictly a major music delivery platform to one that makes money as well.

THE BROADCAST ALTERNATIVES

Traditional over-the-air or cable television is taking a hit from alternative forms of television consumption such as Netflix and Hulu. With DVD sales declining even more quickly than CD sales, there's now a 61 percent chance that any given legal movie stream or download comes from Netflix, thanks to its inclusion in newer television and set-top boxes. In fact, Netflix subscribers can stream videos to practically every popular device currently available, including iOS devices, Android devices, Roku boxes, Apple TVs, Xbox 360s, and more. And with a huge library of movies and television shows, it has quickly become the service of choice of many consumers.

With 36 million monthly users that access over 260 million content streams, Hulu is already big, but it has become much more influential in recent years thanks to original content good enough for a host of Emmy nominations in 2013. Hulu boasts 627 advertisers and 250 content partners as of the writing of this book, which represents meteoric growth over the last three years. When the site launched, it had only 2 content partners and a dozen advertisers.

What does the change in television have to do with music? Where once upon a time, a performance on television could insure a boost of sales and some new fans, that's not the case any longer, as television becomes just as fragmented and stratified as music. Indeed, a performance on a late-night television show is for fans only (if that), resulting in few new fans and a negligible sales bump. And with the new on-demand nature of television instead of the "television by appointment" of the past, a television appearance or show underscore can no longer be counted on to be fresh and up to date.

THE CONNECTED TV

With most major consumer electronics manufacturers now offering some sort of connected TV, watching videos is no longer relegated to the computer. What is a connected television? It's a TV that connects directly to the Internet like a computer, allowing the viewer to access content from YouTube, Hulu, NetFlix, Amazon or any other video distributor so you can watch it on that big 55-inch screen instead of your 15-inch laptop.

But the connected TV means much more—potentially. It now lends itself to true interactivity, allowing the viewer to discover information on the characters, actors, and back story, and even socially connect with friends and other viewers in real time. Until now, you'd need a computer or tablet to be able to do at least some of that (known in the industry as "the second screen").

The connected TV is also a new means for marketing and sales, allowing you to buy products as you see them onscreen, respond instantly to discount offers, and even browse while watching a program. The new tablet computers also open up new avenues of viewership as the screens are optimized for video. In fact, in the future the kids may prefer iPads to televisions in their rooms. They're more personal.

The New Television

The future television viewer will be increasingly connected.

The "second screen" becomes part of the viewing experience.

YouTube is the new television in many ways.

YouTube is now a major music consumption and discovery site.

Television performances no longer add fans or sell product.

While sales of connected televisions to date have been primarily of customer unfamiliarity, connection confusion, and customer support, they're clearly the wave of the future. With them opens a wide range of creative, marketing, and sales opportunities to the M4.0 musician.

The New Players

Control of the music industry has slowly drifted from the power days of the record label executive to the new power base of today—management and the promoter. That said, a new generation of record label entrepreneurs could someday change that balance.

MANAGEMENT

Managers of talent have always been powerful (especially with a big-selling act in the stable) and have, for the most part, stayed behind the scenes. After all, it's the acts that should have the most attention. But as the music industry transitions into Music 4.0, managers are more powerful, and more needed, than ever. The reason is that the fortunes of the manager are directly tied to the act. If the act makes money, so does the manager; if the act tanks, the manager starves. As a result, the manager has to truly believe in the act and represent it with a passion. The manager's singular vision must be to make that act successful. Any other member of the artist or group's team, from producer to attorney to record label to publicist and so on, will not have his or her fortunes tied so directly to the artist's success, and, as a result, his or her passion can't be expected to ever be as high. With most service contractors that an artist employs, you can never be sure where their loyalty actually lies. Is it with the record label, distributor or promoter, or the artist? With a manager, the answer to that question should never be in doubt.

So why has the manager's role become more profound in M4.0? Because as the choices for the artist have expanded, so has the manager's influence. In M1.0 through 2.5, the manager's main focus was on dealing with the record label and getting the act booked. The label was the 800-pound gorilla in the room, and the manager was the keeper. With the record label's influence now decreased to that of a chimpanzee, the manager has ascended to become the giant in the act's life.

As we'll see in later chapters, there are far more possibilities for every aspect of the act, and that means far more decisions are required.

An interesting trend is that management is now adapting to M4.0, bringing multiple talents in-house for instant access and attention by the artist. These talents include concert promotion, Internet promotion, dedicated social networking, the handling of street teams, and where it's legal, even acting as a booking agent.

Not every artist is able to connect with forward-thinking management of this type, or even any kind of organized management, but that's okay. Personal management is ineffective unless the manager is passionate about you, since passion can overcome inexperience. Passion is something that you can't buy or contract—the manager has to truly believe in you or you're wasting your time. And as the act gets bigger, it's easier for a less powerful manager to plug into a larger management company and "four-wall," or get the best of both worlds: the power of the larger management company with the attention of the smaller.

THE PROMOTER

The second most powerful entity in M4.0 is the promoter. Regardless of whether he or she is booking a coffee house on a community-college campus or a 10,000-seat arena, the promoter is needed to keep the act doing what it should do best, which is playing in front of people. Promoters have always been important, since despite what you might think, most artists have always derived the majority of their income from touring rather than from record sales. In M4.0, promoters are an even more crucial link in the chain than before. No longer do acts tour to promote their records as they once did in M1.0 to M2.5. Since M3.0, the record promotes the tour and is often relegated to being an additional piece of swag for the onsite vendors to sell. In M4.0, it's more important than ever that the artist's tour be successful, and the promoter's influence has risen appreciably as a result.

It used to be that promoters relied on SoundScan numbers to determine the ticket-selling potential of the act. These days, they could care less where a record sits on the charts, because ticket sales are the only figures that matter. In the promoter's M4.0 world, success begets success. If you sell tickets in one region or venue, a promoter in another is more likely to work with you than if you have a release in the current No. 1 chart spot.

Thanks to changing tastes and leaner economic times, the promoters' general approach to talent has changed. Back in the M1.0 to M2.5 days, the promoter was willing to lose money on an act on its way up in the clubs in order to reap the rewards in the arena later. Unfortunately, there's little of that these days, since there are fewer indie and regional promoters than ever before, having been rolled up in numerous industry consolidations into what has become the Live Nation and AEG behemoths. As a result, most of the middle- and upper-tier promoters are large corporations with deep pockets (sound familiar?), which leaves the smaller indie promoter unable to roll the dice on an act in fear of losing money. While a promoter might take a chance in the past in the hopes of gaining some loyalty from the artist, this scenario has become less and less likely.

That being said, today's promoter is more willing to think outside the box. Paperless tickets (which are hated by some and declared the future by others), multitiered pricing, and coupons and promotion tie-ins to other entertainment such as restaurants are all the things that the promoter is now willing to try.

But promoters still hold the keys to a successful career for an artist. Financially successful recorded music is very much a reflection of people's experiences in enjoying live music. The more they experience it, the more they are likely to buy it. The promoter is an integral part of that success.

THE NEW RECORD LABEL

Record labels both large and small are transforming before our very eyes in order to adapt to the new music-buying audience. Where once the record label was the gatekeeper to talent and a filter that separated the worthy from the worthless for the masses, today's label is in many ways struggling to find its way in the M4.0 world.

While major labels are excellent at exposing and exploiting mainstream-oriented acts, they're no longer in the business of much else. And as outlined before, talent development and A&R have largely fallen by the wayside. The problem is that it's a numbers game, and the numbers are no longer on the side of the majors. If only one out of ten acts makes money, but only makes one-tenth of what it made during the good old days, that's not much of a value proposition.

The M4.0 record label is no different from the record label of the '50s in spirit. It's built by people who love music and are more concerned with exposing talent than making money. Their overhead is low, the execs don't draw hefty salaries (or any salary at all in many cases), and they're willing to keep putting out releases by artists they love regardless of the sales figures.

Their marketing consists of mostly social media and online promotion because that's all they can afford, and that's all their audience responds to. And they're willing to try different approaches. Labels such as Kill/Hurt, Not For Fun, Bridgetown Records, and Burger Records print limited runs of cassettes and vinyl, two formats long ago given up for dead, and they not only stay alive but manage to grow.

The major labels of tomorrow are the indie labels that are a mere blip on the radar screen of the industry today, and those labels wedded to the past will be engulfed by it.

The New Players

Managers have more power and influence than ever.

Management has brought many traditional artist services in-house.

To a promoter, only ticket sales, not chart sales, matter.

Promoters are less willing to take a chance on a new act.

Record-company influence has decreased.

The new indie labels are more concerned about music than money.

And they're willing to think outside the box.

The New Audience

. . . .

Today's audience is a combination of a stratified vortex of special tastes and ultratargeted desires, which still has a profound fancy for all things Top 40 oriented. Regardless of whether your taste lies in electronic Bantu music or alien space music, if it's out there you can find it. But finding the music that moves you is both the key and the dilemma.

> *I see more and more niche markets finding more coherent audiences. You can be into Hungarian Death Metal or Central Canadian Bluegrass and easily fill your iPod with songs of that particular genre, then in your spare time you can read blogs pertaining to only that subject.*
> —Bruce Houghton

One of the main attributes of the new M4.0 audience is how it likes to receive and play the music it loves. More and more of the current audience chooses to listen to its music in a digital streaming format from YouTube, Pandora, Spotify, or any number of alternative sources. With more than 86 percent growth in streaming and subscriptions and 1.26 billion digital downloads purchased in 2013, digital music has become a major distribution method, as 59 percent of all music purchased in the United States is now in a digital form (according to the RIAA). Digital music has indeed caused listening and buying habits to change.

The new digital demographic has become a consumer of the single song (or "single"), opting for buying only one or two known and liked songs, as compared to the ten or twelve normally found on an album. While full-length albums were the cash cow of the industry until M2.5, the music buyer from M3.0 onward has returned to the habits of the '50s, when the single was the main point of interest. The M4.0 consumer still wants to discover new music and is willing to sample songs from any of the music distribution or discovery sites, but he or she is no longer compelled or required to purchase an album that has only one or two good songs on it. As a result, according to the RIAA, CD sales in 2013 fell 14.5 percent from the previous year, a trend that began in 2002.

The new audience also has many more entertainment choices than ever before, and it's only natural that music is going to suffer for it, just as network television has suffered in the face of the expanded cable universe. Social media, video games, YouTube, and a host of other on- and offline activities now occupy the time that used to be reserved for listening to music.

The tastes of the new audience are different from their predecessors as well. A shorter attention span and proficiency in multitasking has taken its toll on the album. While in the late '60s and the '70s (M1.0 and M1.5) an album release would be an event (usually followed by a listen front to back without a break), that rarely happens today. The current audience wants to taste a little from everywhere rather than take a long sip of just one drink.

The New Audience

Singles are more important than an album.

Album filler material is rejected by
the music consumer.

The audience has a shorter music attention span.

Ultratargeted demographics are developed.

Stratified tastes arise.

There are more entertainment choices than ever.

Enter Music 4.0

Music 4.0 is the natural evolution of the music business. It allows the artist to take into account the current deficiencies of the business entities that were prevalent in previous music generations and provides the ability to bypass them completely in the course of building an audience and career, until those entities can be used to the artist's advantage. In M4.0, the artist has the ability to directly engage the fan with no one in between, and the fan has the ability to engage back. Assuming that the artist creates music that can capture an audience in the first place (however small it might be), the opportunity to build an audience is more available than ever before, providing that the artist has the skills to take advantage of social media. Let's take a closer look at Music 4.0 and the best way to develop those skills.

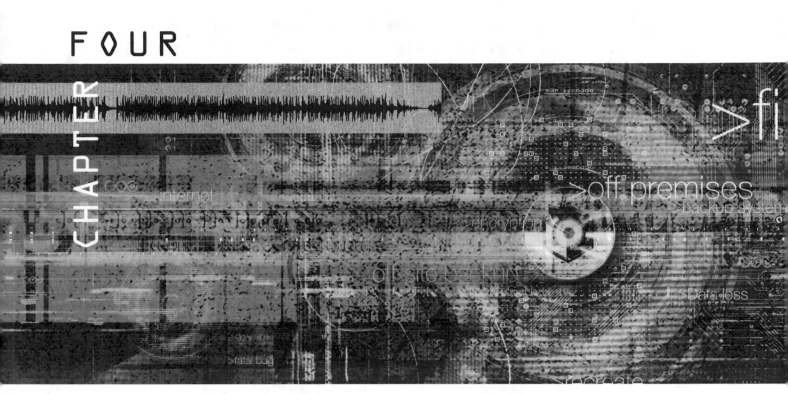

FOUR

The New Masters
of the Domain

To understand Music 4.0, you have to understand its major influencers. M4.0 (and beyond) has been shaped by the following people and the concepts they bring, so it's important to grasp the significance of their contributions. They set the guidelines for the future of music and the way the artist interacts with it.

Seth Godin's Tribes

Seth Godin has been one of the most influential voices in marketing for some time now. He has written 12 best-selling books on marketing, and his marketing blog (sethgodin.typepad.com) is one of the most read on the Internet. His most significant contribution in terms of M4.0 comes from his book *Tribes: We Need You to Lead Us*. *Tribes* illustrates a concept that is at the core of M4.0, which is that an artist's fan base is his "tribe," and the artist is the tribal leader.

A tribe, in the context of M4.0, is a group of people who are passionate about the music of an artist (although it could be about an entire genre or subgenre of music too). The artist is the most passionate (since she's the creator) and is therefore the leader. That said, what the tribe craves most is communication and direction from the leader, which is the key component of the concept.

A tribe can have a large number of members or be very small, but it must have at least three members to exist. It's different from a typical fan base, special-interest group, or community, in terms of the intense passion it presents. A fan base usually has one thing, such as a person or product (or both when it comes to music), which draws people to the group, while a special-interest group is built around a shared interest or value, such as C++ programming or voluntourism. A community involves a special-interest group that has some form of group communication, such as a newsletter or a phone call, to keep the members informed. Thanks to email, blogs, chat, and Twitter, these groups become a tribe when its members gain the ability to interact with each another and a leader comes forward.

Some leaders create the tribe, while some tribes find their leader. The leader sets the direction and facilitates a way for tribe members to interface with each other.

How is a tribe different from a brand? A brand is a promise of quality and consistency. No matter where in the world you go for a McDonald's hamburger, you know what to expect. No matter what product you purchase from Apple, you can expect sleek high-tech design and an easy-to-understand user interface. Brand management is protecting the image of the brand and carefully selecting how to best exploit it. Tribal management looks at its brand in a different light.

Whether the tribe is a brand, a person, a service, or music, people want to interact with other people, not with a company or the "brand" itself. If someone in the Killers' Brandon Flowers's tribe hears from Island Records in company-speak rather than from Brandon directly, that satisfies no one and defeats the principle of the tribe. Now if a real person who happens to work for Island interacts with the tribe, that can work. The tribe wants a story to tell and something to discuss, but only if it comes from another tribe member. Or if Brandon's assistant communicates with the tribe on behalf of Brandon, that can work as well. The idea in M4.0 is to feed and grow the tribe and not the brand. You don't look for a customer to sell music to; you look to provide music that the tribe will want. The M4.0 artist should be aware that people will form a tribe with or without him or her (if he or she is popular enough already); the idea for the artist is to be a part of the tribe to make it better.

Here's how a tribe works in M4.0. Let's assume that you're a big fan of singer/songwriter Fiona Apple. As a member of her tribe, what you want most (besides her music) is communication directly from Fiona herself. If she's touring near where you live, you want an email from her asking you to come to the show. If she's planning to record a cover song on her next album, you want her to ask you for suggestions (see the two-way communication?). If she's coming out with a limited box set, you'd love to hear from her about the chance to buy it before anyone else can. Maybe Fiona is trying to raise some money to record her next album and asks you to prebuy a copy. If you're a big fan, you might buy five just to make sure that the album comes out in a timely fashion.

But being the leader of a tribe takes a lot of work and some expertise. Many artists justifiably prefer to spend their time making music, or maybe they just can't get their arms around the tech portion of the job. Some artists are afraid of interaction with fans on such an electronically intimate basis. That's why an external tribal management source is so important. This is what a record company should be doing in M4.0: either helping to manage or directly managing the tribes of their artists. (A few third-party companies do this already; see the interview with Jacob Tell of Oniracom in the interviews section of the book).

While we're illustrating a tribe in the context of music, remember that brands, products, services, and even experiences can all have tribes. For instance, Disney, Virgin, and Apple Computer are brands that have their own tribes, while services such as Greenpeace and Wikipedia do too. Products such as Kleenex, Sharpie pens, and Harry Potter have tribes, while leaders such as Al Gore, Nelson Mandela, and Malala Yousafzai have founded tribes that have a much larger impact than the individual himself.

Perhaps the best illustration of the ultimate leader of a tribe is an example that we'll get to in a little bit—Trent Reznor of the group Nine Inch Nails.

> ## A Tribe
>
> A tribe is group of people passionate about the music, the artist, or both.
>
> The artist is the leader.
>
> Members crave interaction with the leader and each other.

Radiohead's Grand Experiment

On October 1, 2007, the highly respected British alternative-rock band Radiohead announced that its seventh album, entitled *In Rainbows*, would be released in ten days (see Fig. 4.1). Normally, an album-release announcement wouldn't be anything special; it's been happening somewhere almost every day for the past 70 years or so. But *In Rainbows* was different in that it was to be available only as a digital download, and the band would allow its customers to pay *whatever amount they liked*. While it's still unknown whether this strategy was part of a grand master plan or was just a simple salute to the band's fan base, the move paid off handsomely as a public-relations coup, with press from all over the world running with the story, and the album and band receiving much notice within the music industry. In the ten days running up to the album's release, Radiohead reportedly received 1.2 million prepays for the album (the band's management never released the official figures). Little did they know at the time that this would be a much heralded and studied test case.

With a Website that stated "It's up to you" in the payment box, the *In Rainbows* experiment yielded some interesting statistics. According to the Internet marketing-research company comScore, 62 percent of the album's buyers in their focus group did not pay a single cent for the album. In other words, they downloaded it for nothing! Four percent of the band's fans paid between $12.00 and $20.00 (about the retail cost of a CD), while 12 percent paid between $8.00 and $12.00, which comScore determined to make up 52 percent of the band's profits.

In the end, those that paid forked over an average of $6.00, with the buyers from the United States paying about $8.05 per purchase and those from the United Kingdom paying about $4.64. According to comScore senior analyst Andrew Lipsman, Radiohead was estimated to have made a profit regardless of whether they intended to or not. "If [Radiohead] is getting $6.00 on average, and it's basically going straight into their pockets and their costs are minimal, it could be economically viable," Lipsman told *E! Online.* The band needed to make about $1.50 per download to break even, he estimated, so at $6.00 per buyer, the group seems to have made out pretty well.

But having the fans decide the amount they wished to pay accomplished something else that was perhaps more important. By giving *In Rainbows* away, Radiohead actually strengthened the sales of the CD when it was released later that year. Going directly to No. 1 on both the US's *Billboard 200* and the UK *Album Chart*, the disc box set (including a second disc and a hardcover book of artwork) went on to sell more than 3 million units worldwide.

By allowing the customer to set the price, Radiohead exercised what was then a new business theory called "The Economics of Free" (or EoF). EoF encourages content owners to give some of their products away for free, because if done correctly, you can increase your market size greatly, as seen in the case of *In Rainbows.* Shortly afterwards, both Franz Ferdinand and Arctic Monkeys unofficially leaked their initial releases for just the same reason, with great results.

You can't just start giving away your precious content without thought though. It has to be the center of a larger marketing plan. In terms of M4.0, an EoF campaign means the following:

▶ You, the artist, have two types of products: infinite products and scarce products. Infinite products would be your music, especially in digital form. Physical products such as CDs don't fit in here, because it actually costs you money to produce them (the CDs, not the music on them). Digital music is easy to copy and steal, and just as easy to give away.

▶ Scarce products are tickets to live shows, access to musicians, signed merchandise, backstage passes, private concerts, custom CDs, CD box sets, time spent with you, writing a song for a fan willing to pay for it, and anything else that has a limited supply.

So to take advantage of the Economics of Free, the artist must do the following:

1. Set the infinite products (or just some of them) free. Put them on a Torrent site, Facebook, YouTube, and anywhere you can. The more you get it out there, the greater the publicity and the wider the visibility. This makes the scarce products more valuable.

2. **Because of the free infinite products, you can now charge more for the scarce products.** Before number 1 is implemented, access to the artist or backstage passes might not be worth anything, but now they are. Before number 1, maybe no one wanted your CDs or vinyl albums, but now they're valuable as a collector's item, as are the box sets.

Setting your infinite products (your music) free expands your core audience (your tribe) by making your music your marketing tool. As your core audience expands, the demand for your scarce products grows. In M4.0, the artists that stick to the belief that their songs are their product will be relegated to a small audience forever.

The EoF theory is perfectly illustrated by Trent Reznor and NIN, the next example in this chapter. Radiohead and *In Rainbows* took the concept one step further by giving it away for free but asking their fans if they'd like to pay for it, and many did. It's interesting to note that the band did not return to the pay-what-you-want method on the next album, *King of Limbs*, instead employing a multitiered pay product offering like we'll look at next.

The Economics of Free

Give away infinite products (digital music).

Sell scarce products (CDs, merch, tickets, and so on).

Giving a product away can increase audience size.

Giving away infinite products makes scarce products more valuable.

You can now charge more for scarce products.

The Wisdom of Trent

Taking the Radiohead pay-what-you-want experiment one step further, and totally taking advantage of his relationship with his tribe, was Trent Reznor and his Nine Inch Nails project *Ghosts I–IV* (see Fig. 4.2). After splitting from Universal Records' Interscope imprint in 2007, Trent decided to take advantage of his passionate fan base and the new online consumerism with his first release that was post–major label.

Having an innate feel for dealing with his tribe even before the theory was articulated in Seth Godin's book, Reznor modeled his first release after the Radiohead experiment, with two important exceptions: he would give away some of the new album *Ghosts I–IV* for free, and he would provide products of the same release at different price points ranging from $5.00 to $2,500.

FREE DOWNLOAD includes the following:
- The first nine tracks of the album.
- DRM-free MP3s encoded at 320 kbps.
- A 40-page PDF book covering the album.
- A digital extras pack with wallpapers, icons, and other graphics.

$5 DOWNLOAD includes the following:
- 320 kbps encoded MP3 files.
- FLAC lossless files.
- Apple lossless files.
- A 40-page PDF book covering the album.
- A digital extras pack with wallpapers, icons, and other graphics.

$10 2-CD SET includes the following:
- 2 CDs in a six-panel digipak with a 16-page booklet.
- 320 kbps encoded MP3 files.
- FLAC lossless files.
- Apple lossless files.
- A 40-page PDF book covering the album.
- A digital extras pack with wallpapers, icons, and other graphics.

Ghosts I—IV Cover

$75 DELUXE EDITION includes the following:
- A large fabric slipcase containing two embossed, fabric-bound hardcover books.

Book 1 contains
- *Ghosts I—IV* on two audio CDs.
- A data DVD that can be read by Mac and Windows computers containing multitrack sessions for all 36 tracks in WAV-file format allowing easy remix.
- A Blu-ray disc containing the stereo mixes of *Ghosts* in 96 kHz, 24-bit audio, plus an exclusive slide show that plays with the music.

Book 2 contains

- 48 pages of photographs by Philip Graybill and Rob Sheridan.
- 320 kpbs encoded MP3 files.
- FLAC lossless files.
- Apple lossless files.
- A 40-page PDF book covering the album.
- A digital extras pack with wallpapers, icons, and other graphics.

$300 LIMITED EDITION includes the following:

- A 4-LP set of *Ghosts I—IV* on 180-gram vinyl in a fabric slipcase. Only available in the Limited Edition Package.
- A large fabric slipcase containing three embossed, fabric-bound hardcover books:

Book 1 contains

- *Ghosts I—IV* on two audio CDs.
- A data DVD that can be read by Mac and Windows computers containing multitrack sessions for all 36 tracks in WAV-file format allowing easy remix.
- A Blu-ray disc containing the stereo mixes of *Ghosts* in 96 kHz, 24-bit audio, plus an exclusive slide show that plays with the music.

Book 2 contains

- 48 pages of photographs by Philip Graybill and Rob Sheridan.
- 320 kpbs encoded MP3 files.
- FLAC lossless files.
- Apple lossless files.
- A 40-page PDF book covering the album.
- A digital extras pack with wallpapers, icons, and other graphics.

Book 3 contains

- Two exclusive Giclee art prints of imagery from *Ghosts I—IV*.
- These can be displayed in the book or removed for framing.
- Only available in the Limited Edition package.

Each Limited Edition package is numbered and personally signed by Trent Reznor.

The release was a smashing success, as the NIN servers were knocked offline with the massive interest in the project. The $300.00 limited-edition package completely sold out of its 2,500 unit run as Reznor transacted nearly 800,000 total units within the first week. A grand total of $0 was spent on the marketing of the record, since Reznor announced it only on his blog. Even more impressive was the fact that *Ghosts* was an instrumental album!

By year end, *Ghosts* became the best-selling album on Amazon's MP3 Store and was nominated for two Grammy Awards.

In an attempt to move beyond the industry's old pricing model of one product, one price, this is a perfect example of giving something of value for free (in this case, a free nine-song download) in order to make the music easily accessible to fans and as a sample for potential fans. The massive publicity generated, plus the multiple price points, meant that there was something for every economic and interest level. It also proved that fans are willing to support artists they really care about even if their music is offered at no cost.

Ghosts was licensed under a Creative Commons Attribution Non-Commercial Share Alike license that allows noncommercial redistribution. Creative Commons provides easy and effective ways to publish your content without abandoning all rights to its use—free distribution might be allowed, for instance, but only as long as the author is attributed and the distribution is noncommercial. For more information go to creativecommons.net.

Besides the sales, Reznor gained something else equally valuable with each transaction: email addresses. This allowed him to expand his fan base by simply reaching out to them personally, an act seen as unusually generous by most casual fans.

While Reznor was very successful as a DIY act, he and NIN returned to the major label fold in 2012, signing with Columbia Records, which goes to prove that the responsibilities of DIY can overwhelm even artists that are particularly good at it and who have built their own DIY infrastructure. That said, the practical knowledge obtained by being successful as an independent provides a level of oversight not available without that experience.

Another artist who has used the multitiered product offerings with great success is Josh Freese, who uses the tactic with an interesting and amusing twist. Freese, a Los Angeles-based drummer for Devo, Perfect Circle, and others (including Guns N' Roses), doesn't have the high visibility of an artist like Reznor, but makes up for it with a huge dose of humor, which becomes a marketing tool in itself.

Here are some of the package offerings for his *My New Friends* EP (taken from his website at joshfreese.com).

$5
- Digital Download

$12
- CD of *My New Friends*
- $50
- CD of *My New Friends*, CD/DVD of *Since 1972* CD
- A thank you call from Josh for purchasing his record.

$125—Limited Edition Box Set
- 1 of 100 Box sets of all 3 of Josh's CDs
- Thank you phone call
- Set of Signed Drumsticks
- Copy of Josh's 5th grade report card
- 1 of Josh's boarding passes from a past flight
- Bumper Sticker "I ♥ Josh Freese's New Friends"

$350—The Lunch Date
- Take Josh to lunch at P. F. Chang's in Long Beach
- 5 copies of both "My New Friends" and "Since 1972" (Pass 'em out to friends. A perfect way to tell someone "I love you" or "You are very special to me")
- Copy of Josh's 5th grade report card
- Bumper Sticker "I ♥ Josh Freese's New Friends"
- Signed drumhead
- Signed sticks
- Signed photo (can't promise what the photo will be . . . but it will be signed)

$7,500 (limited to 1)—Evoke Spirits with Tommy Lee, Danny Lohner and Josh
- Engage in light "80's hair metal/pinup girl gossip" w/ Tommy, Josh and Lohner while a 'C List Porn Star' applies 'corpse paint' to your astonished face. Next you'll be escorted to the opulent gardens of Castle Renhold'r, where the four of you will be Throwing Bones under the midnight moon in a blasphemous attempt to evoke the spirit/entity of YOUR CHOICE! (BYOB)
- 10 Copies of "My New Friends"
- Get a diddy written about you for next record (not necessarily a full on song but definitely a "diddy")
- $50 gift certificate to P. F. Chang's
- "Since 1972" CD
- "The Notorious One Man Orgy" CD
- Copy of Josh's 5th grade report card
- Bumper Sticker "I ♥ Josh Freese's New Friends"
- Signed drumhead
- Signed sticks

$10,000 Limited To 1
- 100 Copies of My New Friends
- Take home Josh's now infamous Volvo 940 Station Wagon (Perfect for hauling drums, plenty of room for getting busy in spacious back-seating area. Good for trips to Good Will or disposing bodies.)
- Make Josh's next record for him
- Josh joins your band for 2 days (quick book some studio time!)
- "Motorboat" Sarah for a minute or so (Josh's wife's friend...couples welcome, discreet parking available)
- Oh yeah...$100 gift certificate to PF Changs and a bumper sticker that says something funny on it.

$75,000 Same As It Ever Was
- Josh joins your band for a month (or becomes your personal assistant)
- Take home one of Josh's drumsets
- Josh writes and records a 5 song EP entirely about YOU.
- Take Shrooms and cruise Hollywood in Danny from TOOL's Lamborgini.
- 500 copies of "My New Friends" (start your own online CD store...specializing in just this one CD)
- Go get matching outfits at Tommy Bahama's and make everybody very sad.

One of the things to note is the similarity of sales package tiers to crowdfunding tiers (which we'll cover in depth in Chapter 11), the difference being that a sales tier offers a currently available product while crowdfunding offers one available in the future if the funding goal is reached. In either case, the success relies on having enough tiers to satisfy the majority of fans' price comfort levels.

The bottom line is that multitiered offerings work, and the more exclusive they are, the more you can charge for them. Sometimes the offering itself (especially if it involves being in close proximity to the artist) is more interesting than the music itself.

The Wisdom of Multitiered Offerings

Offer multitiered products, from free to very expensive.

Make the music easily accessible to fans and potential fans.

Harvest email addresses from free offerings.

Fans find exclusive offerings interesting.

Sometimes an offering that involves close proximity to the artist is more interesting than the music itself.

Have the leader directly communicate with the tribe.

Expand the fan base by personally reaching out.

Chris Anderson's Long Tail

· ·

The "Long Tail" is a concept first put forward in an article by Chris Anderson in the October 2004 issue of *Wired* magazine. The Long Tail basically puts the old 80:20 rule on its ear. For those of you who aren't into sales, the longstanding 80:20 rule refers to the fact that you usually get 80 percent of your business from 20 percent of your customers, or in the case of the music industry, 80 percent of the sales came from 20 percent of available albums (in other words, the current and recent hits). Because of limited shelf space, most retail stores would carry only the current hits and a limited number of catalog albums, since the hits are the products that quickly sell. This becomes a self-fulfilling prophecy, since if only the hits (the 20 percent) are available, there's hardly a possibility that much of the other 80 percent will sell, because they're not available.

The Long Tail turns the 80:20 rule around by stating that most of your sales will come from that other 80 percent of products if they're made available and *are easy to purchase* (the key phrase). A customer may buy the hit, but then buy another two pieces from the artist's catalog (or even from another artist's catalog) while he or she is at it. This concept was originally only able to be implemented in a few brick-and-mortar megastores such as Amoeba Music stores in California or the now-defunct Tower Records chain, but that all changed with online stores such as Amazon and iTunes and the movie site Netflix. Now an artist's entire catalog is more than likely available online, and subject to the Long Tail rules as a result.

As Chris Anderson points out in his book called *The Long Tail* (derived from the original *Wired* magazine article), half of the products that Netflix rents are ones that a retailer would never have the space to carry. Over half of Amazon's book sales are unavailable at the retailer Barnes and Noble. Most of what you can buy on iTunes is not available in any record store. It turns out that when customers are given a huge number of choices in every genre possible, they start looking down the "tail" to find what else might be interesting to them, and sales increase accordingly. As a result, where the attention used to be focused on the Top 40, now there's much more attention given to other titles in the catalog (the Long Tail), and because they're immediately available, consumption goes up.

A word of caution: the Long Tail doesn't work if all of your products are considered "Long Tail." You must have the hits as well to offset the catalog. Likewise, it doesn't work if only hits are available. The Long Tail needs the balance to operate effectively.

So how does this affect the music in M4.0? Anderson has the following three Long Tail rules that aptly apply:

Rule 1: Make Everything Available

Members of an artist's core audience want as much of the artist's music as they can get. Rehearsals, outtakes, different versions—they want it all and they want it now. While it was impractical to make everything available in the past, that's no longer the case online. Put it on every music site or limit it to your personal website; just make it available to your fan base.

Rule 2: Cut the Price in Half, Then Lower It

Many of the items that a tribe most adores are the ones that an artist spends the least time and money on, such as rough mixes, rehearsal and live recordings and videos, and original song demos. If it doesn't oppose the artist's artistic integrity, make it available to the tribe. Since the production costs are low, the prices can be low too. For older catalog items (especially those in a digital format), prices can be lowered if a service such as Kunaki (kunaki.com) is used for CD pressing. Kunaki will press and drop-ship CDs on demand for prices as low as $1.00 each.

Rule 3: Help Me Find It

It does no one any good if the customer can't easily find the product to buy. The Long Tail works only when the catalog items are easy to find. You must do everything in your power to make the experience of finding your catalog products as easy as possible.

There have been many rebuttals from economists and bloggers claiming that the Long Tail theory is full of holes, and it's true that generally it hasn't lived up to its original promise in terms of vastly increasing catalog sales. In fact, one study by Nielsen SoundScan of the tracks sold in the iTunes store in 2011 found that 94 percent of the tracks sold had sales of fewer than 100 units, and an astonishing 32 percent sold exactly one copy. On the other end of the scale, 102 tracks sold more than a million each, which accounted for 15 percent of the sales.

If you look at those figures you're bound to think that the Long Tail is a joke. While it might not be as effective as originally outlined by Anderson, I believe that the premise is basically sound, and the under-performance has been one of poor execution in most cases. Customers will buy or consume your older products (this goes for digital products like videos as well) if they are available and *easy to find*, and they'll consume more of these products if they're less expensive than the newer products, but all three of these principles must be in play in order for the Long Tail strategy to be effective. When you look at iTunes, or any digital music service for that matter, you can't exactly say all of the points are followed.

Follow the three rules of the Long Tail on your website, store, and merch table. I'll bet you'll be surprised how effective it can be.

The Long Tail

More of your sales come from older products (catalog) than newer.

It doesn't work unless you have hits to balance the catalog.

Customers can't buy older products if they're not available.

They'll buy more of these products if they're cheaper than newer products.

Make everything available as a product.

Sometimes the most valuable products are the ones that the artist spends the least to produce.

Make all products easy to find.

Irving Azoff's Steel Fist

The most powerful man currently in the music business is Irving Azoff. Actually, he's been one of the most powerful men for in the business for decades, but what he currently represents is a model for M4.0 and beyond, because of the large scale he operates on.

With the innate ability to drive a hard bargain, Azoff rose to prominence in the early '80s as the head of Frontline Management, which represented musical heavyweights The Eagles, Steely Dan, Heart, Stevie Nicks, and Jackson Browne, among others. Azoff soon became the head of then-major label MCA Records (which later became what we now know as Universal Music Group), then later owned his own Giant Records (a Warner Bros. imprint) before selling out and returning to managing a few selected clients such as The Eagles and Christina Aguilera. In 2005, his reconstituted Frontline became the most powerful management company in the history of the music industry as a result of Azoff's buying some 60 smaller management companies.

As a former label head, Azoff understood the dilemma of the record labels, and realizing that he could do business without them, he went directly to the most powerful retailer on the planet, Wal-Mart, to distribute the Eagle's first album since 1979, the double CD *Long Road Out of Eden*, released in 2007. Azoff understood the power of the chain's 6,500 stores, their ability to reach their 140 million visitors a week, and the promotional value of Wal-Mart's weekly circular seen by 85 million potential customers. Even priced at only $11.88 (extremely low for a double-CD set), the set would reportedly net the band far more than it ever could have had the band been signed to a record label (reportedly near $50 million). Thus Azoff sent the first warning shot across the bow of the old industry guard.

Then, realizing how the concert-promotion business was tightly controlled and that artists make most of their money from touring, he merged with the giant Ticketmaster, and then again with their major competitor Live Nation, becoming executive chairman in the process—which means that Azoff was then able to manage talent, book concerts, issue tickets, and sell artist-related merchandise under one roof.

Azoff bailed as executive chairman of Live Nation at the end of 2012, only to merge his Azoff Music Management Group with

Madison Square Garden Company (MSG) in September 2013. What makes this venture interesting is that the company has four divisions: artist management, music publishing, television production and live-event branding, and digital branding. Couple that with the many venues owned by MSG that could host concerts for the company's artists, and you have a look at what the new-world major label possibly looks like, even though they're not calling it a label (we'll look at this more closely in Chapter 12).

Now this is great if you're already a legacy artist, because now presumably you'll receive a larger part of each ticket sale, but what does it have to do with an up-and-coming artist in M4.0? It shows that the new music industry is a business of talent (as compared with distribution in the old model), and he who controls the talent, and the means to best utilize it, wins. As for the talent, the most essential part of an artist's team is the manager.

The major labels have less and less to offer an M4.0 artist. They sell music, but that's not where the business is today. The real business lies with everything else that an artist brings to the table. The labels now offer 360 deals to new acts, but that benefits only them and not the artist. If they can't do the one thing that they're supposed to do well, which is sell music (as the sales figures show), how can you expect them to sell your merch, or get you gigs?

M4.0 is the music business without the record labels of the past. Irving Azoff sees it, and so should you.

The New M4.0 Reality

A record label is no longer necessary for success.

Management is more important than ever.

Talent, not distribution, is king.

Distribution is easily available for any artist.

The record label of the future looks more like a management company.

Sanctuary's Blueprint

· ·

In 1979, Rod Smallwood and Andy Taylor discovered and then managed the legendary metal band Iron Maiden. They subsequently named their management company after the band's song "Sanctuary" and expanded their roster to include similar bands of the genre.

Soon afterward, Sanctuary Management had a brilliant idea. As managers of "heritage acts," which had long-term appeal and large fan bases but no record deals, the company decided to independently finance CD releases for the bands themselves. After all, the audience was built in and rabid. They'd buy anything the bands would put out, so why not release it themselves if a major label wouldn't? The bands were going to tour anyway, so they might as well have a product to sell. Little did they know at the time, but this was the beginning of the new business model where the tour sells the record instead of the record selling the tour, as it did in M1.0 to 2.0.

In the past, if an act would get hot as a result of local radio play, they would then tour in that location to take advantage of the energized interest. The record sold the tour by virtue of the airplay it received. If the record flopped, there would be no tour.

But in the new Sanctuary model, since the act had a strong enough fan base to support a tour anyway, why not have some product to back it up? With these new economics of self-financing the release, the act could now make more money than ever on fewer units sold. And since it was cheaper than ever to create a release (since by then most musicians had studios at home that were more powerful than The Beatles ever had during their heyday), the stage was set for taking advantage of both the technology and the consumer environment.

For a time, Sanctuary Records and its artists succeeded wildly, to the point that the company expanded into a full-fledged record label (and a subsidiary of Universal Music) with traditional M2.0 staff and infrastructure. Soon afterward, however, it collapsed under the weight of that traditional infrastructure. The company had ventured beyond its original concept and comfort level, and eventually paid for it. Sanctuary essentially ceased to exist as a record label at the end of 2007, although its assets have since been sold to BMG.

Sanctuary started the trend of an artist self-releasing a record during M2.0, way ahead of the curve and way ahead of what's commonplace today. Without knowing it at the time, the company paved the way for artists living in our current music generation, where self-production, promotion, and distribution are not only commonplace but the norm.

The Sanctuary Model

The tour sells the recording, not the other way around.

The CD becomes just another piece of merchandise.

The artist markets and sells directly to his fan base.

Self-releasing can be more profitable than having a label.

The artist can make more money on fewer sales

Justin Bieber—The Socially Made Star

To many Justin Bieber is just another example of a short-on-substance teen idol, but if you forget about the artist and look at how he was discovered and how his career was built, you'll find the perfect example of how social media can work in a big way in the new music industry.

Justin Bieber was the first artist made by YouTube. He was discovered there, and has prospered there almost more than any artist other than Lady Gaga. In fact, Bieber's song "Baby" had more than 900 million views alone, and all of his official videos together equal nearly 4 billion total views as of the writing of this book.

His career began when he was captured on a cell-phone video as he was busking outside the Avon Theatre in Stratford, Ontario (population 32,000) hoping to get noticed, a moment that has since been shared some 7 million times on YouTube. In just a little over 9 months, Bieber went from playing to 40 people at an outdoor water park in Poughkeepsie to headlining sold-out arena shows, all this while moving over 13 million albums worldwide over 14 months, opening his first movie on 3,000-plus screens with box-office earnings that topped $98 million, and inspiring hundreds of licensed merchandise items.

More than that, Bieber is one of the first artists to use social media to achieve superstardom, utilizing all forms of social media to capitalize on his success with over 45 million Twitter followers and 57 million Facebook fans. In fact, he is No. 1 in the top 100 Twitters and accounts for about 3 percent of all Twitter traffic as of the writing of this book in fall 2013.

Bieber is not the only current superstar to fully utilize social media though; Lady Gaga, Rhianna, Eminem, and Shakira have more than 70 million Facebook fans, while Katy Perry, Linken Park, Beyonce, Taylor Swift, and Akon all top 50-plus million, according to Fanpagelist.com. Katy Perry and Lady Gaga have more than 40 million, while Taylor Swift, Britney Spears, and Rhianna all have more than 30 million Twitter followers, according to Twittaholic. All of these stars have more than 100 million YouTube views, with several near or over a billion.

It's a fact that the superstar of today cannot reach that level of success without a large social media presence. While Twitter and Facebook strengthen the connection with the fan, YouTube acts not only as the major music delivery system, but now plays a huge part in music discovery as well. Even though superstars have the resources to better craft a message and media campaign than a new act just starting out, social media is essential to artists at all levels in order to prosper.

Social Media: The Crucial Component

Facebook and Twitter engagement strengthen the connection with the fan.

Engagement is the key social media element.

YouTube is now the major music delivery system.

YouTube is a major music and artist discovery portal.

Amanda Palmer—The Social Celebrity

If you're in the music business there's a good chance that you've heard of Amanda Palmer, although there's an even better chance that you've not heard her music. Palmer represents a conundrum in social media where she's become a huge presence in the music industry thanks to her extremely effective social media and crowdfunding campaigns, yet that hasn't helped to spread her music much beyond a small, yet avid, following.

Palmer rose to a low level of prominence as half of the duo Dresden Dolls before going solo in 2008. Her cult following grew from there, thanks to her extremely hands-on relationship with her fans. In an interview with Techdirt in 2012, she gave her secret:

> *"I've been tending this bamboo forest of fans for years and years, ever since leaving Roadrunner Records in 2009. Every person I talk to at a signing, every exchange I have online (sometimes dozens a day), every random music video or art gallery link sent to me by a fan that I curiously follow, every strange bed I've crashed on . . . all of that real human connecting has led to this moment, where I came back around, asking for direct help with a record. Asking everybody . . . And they help because . . . they know me."*

Palmer's notoriety again grew, thanks to reports of big merch sales through Twitter campaigns (such as $19,000 worth of T-shirts in less than a day), to where it reached a peak with a massively successful Kickstarter campaign in which she raised $1.2 million (the goal was $100,000) from nearly 25 thousand fans in 31 days for the marketing of an album/art book/gallery tour. This was followed shortly thereafter by a riveting TED talk where she described her fan-first business model.

Considering the exposure that Palmer has garnered from the mainstream media thanks to these events, her music still hasn't gained much traction, and she remains very much a niche artist, though one with a fanatical following. Only three of her videos have barely cracked 1 million views; she has less than a million Twitter followers and just over 200,000 Facebook Likes. While these are really great numbers for an indie artist, Palmer hasn't managed to transcend that narrow category, despite generally positive and vast exposure and a supercharged fan base. Amanda Palmer proves that no matter what your social media connections are, star and superstar success still depends on your music. In order to gain a mass audience, it must connect with the masses.

There's More to Music Than Social Media

Social prominence won't automatically cause people to like your music.

But it can cause people to notice you.

Caring deeply about your fans builds an avid fan base.

An avid fan base is essential for crowdfunding.

Psy—The Viral Star

. . . .

South Korean pop star Psy broke on the world scene in 2012 with the catchy electronic K-Pop (Korean pop) song "Gangnam Style," complete with an irresistible dance that chalked up over a half-billion YouTube views in its first five weeks. The video went on to record over 1.7 *billion* views. (Yes, that's billion with a *b*.) What's more, his follow up, "Gentleman," eventually cleared a half-billion views as well. His entire channel has over 3 billion views, which is the sixth highest of any on YouTube according to statsheep.com. And if you keep up with the social media side of things, "Gangnam Style" has over 7.7 million thumbs up, and "Gentleman" over 2.5 million.

No one could have predicted that a pudgy Asian singer in his mid-thirties would have nearly that kind of massive worldwide success simply because of a clever YouTube video, but that's exactly what happened. As the viewership of the song began to snowball, Psy made the wise decision of connecting with Justin Bieber's manager Scooter Braun, which then led to high-profile personal appearances and television commercials all over the world, as well as distribution for his music with Universal Republic.

Psy already had some measure of success in Korea, with a number of hit albums and awards to his credit, as well as being the scion of a wealthy family with a large stake in the Korean semiconductor industry. It was this basic infrastructure that provided the means for "Gangnam Style" to initially take off, along with the persistent rumors that many of the initial YouTube views were bought in order to trigger the YouTube algorithm to sense virility.

Interestingly, it's estimated that Psy only made a bit over $10 million from YouTube even with the record-setting view count, and despite going to No. 1 in 30 countries, the song sold just 9.7 million units. This was good for only third place behind Carley Rae Jepsen's song of the summer "Call Me Maybe" and Gotye's "Somebody That I Used to Know," which were both products of massive radio airplay. Perhaps the most profit that Psy (and his family) made was from the 30 percent rise in stock value of their DI Corporation brought about by "Gangnam Style"'s success.

The fact of the matter is that we've seen viral YouTube hits both before and since Psy, like OK Go's "Here It Goes Again," Baauer's

"Harlem Shake," and Macklemore and Ryan Lewis's "Thrift Shop," but few are able to recreate a high level of commercial success unless they secure the help of a sophisticated management team and distribution of a major label. Virility is one thing, exploiting it is another.

One of the problems with a short burst of success is the ability to sustain it. Most successful careers are built over a lengthy duration, converting one fan at a time at one show at a time. Instant success tends to come and go quickly, as the next success story replaces the previous. When it comes to music careers, the long and slow usually beats the short and fast.

The Global Nature of YouTube

YouTube virility can make a hit almost overnight.

Global stars can now be made more easily than ever.

But you still need an infrastructure to get to the next level.

Instant success doesn't necessarily create a career.

Macklemore And Ryan Lewis— Turning The Record-Label Paradigm Around

When Ben Haggerty (stage name Macklemore) and producer/partner Ryan Lewis were readying the self-release of their 2012 album *The Heist* in their small 500-square-foot distribution office, the only thing they knew for sure was that they were determined to stay independent. After some moderate success with several singles and a 2009 album called *The Unplanned Mixtape*, there were several major label deals on the table, yet Haggerty and Lewis felt that retaining their independence was important enough to forego the huge publicity push that could only come with the help of a major.

When the album rose to No. 1 on iTunes with 78,000 copies sold the first week, the Seattle-based duo was so hot that the majors upped their offers. Of most interest was the offer from the management team at Epic Records, who came with a unique proposal. Since the duo had come this far without a label, they knew that the chance of signing was limited. As an alternative, they suggested that Sony do the radio publicity for free in exchange for the band signing with them for the next album.

Haggerty and Lewis were distributed by Alternative Distribution Alliance (ADA), an independent-label service company that handles physical distribution and is a subsidiary of Warner Music Group. ADA was already working radio for free in an effort to boost sales. The duo, still determined to stay independent, went to Warners with a proposal. Could we use the publicity resources of Warners in exchange for a small percentage of *The Heist* only?

After initially rejecting the offer, Warners accepted, and thanks to their massive publicity efforts, pushed three singles to No. 1 and the album to No. 2 on the *Billboard* charts. Macklemore became a major worldwide star as a result, yet the duo still remain totally independent.

To cap off an incredibly successful year, the pair was nominated for seven Grammy awards at the 56th Annual Grammy Awards, winning four including Best New Artist, Best Rap Album (The Heist), Best Rap Song and Best Rap Performance ("Thrift Shop"). The pinnacle of musical stardom had been achieve that few could have predicted just a few years prior.

While many DIY (do it yourself) artists have met with small to moderate success, Macklemore and Ryan Lewis have proved that it's truly possible to become a superstar without signing a traditional record deal. You still need the infrastructure of a major label for that to happen, but it's now also true that alternative major label deals are possible to get that help in Music 4.0.

THE NEW WORLD OF LABEL SERVICES

Macklemore and Ryan Lewis started what very well may be a new trend in doing the business of music. Today with artists able to do so much of the work themselves, it's no longer necessary or desirable to sign such a traditional record deal. There still are some services that only a major label does well (like CD distribution and radio promotion) that are desirable, and now all the majors have developed their own "label services" divisions to make those services available to indie artists.

For instance, Sony Music provides label services through its Red Associated Labels, Warner Music Group through its ADA unit, and Universal Music has it's Caroline division, which handles Peter Gabriel and Korn. Plus BMG transitioned totally to label services when it sold its record label to Sony in 2008 and now handles Back Street Boys, Bryan Ferry and Anastacia, among others. Plus there's Kobalt (Pet Shop Boys and Prince) and in the UK, Cooking Vinyl (Madness and Amanda Palmer), as large indies getting into the arena.

While a brand new artist might not be able to afford these services, any artist with a small measure of success probably can—and should. Label services—truly a symbol of the new music business—are a rapidly rising revenue generator for the industry. It's a win-win situation for the artist and the label. The artist stays independent and gains the clout of the label, and the label gets added revenue without having to bankroll a new artist.

> ## DIY vs. Record Label
>
> DIY provides freedom.
>
> Major labels still have the publicity machine.
>
> Publicity is required for superstardom.
>
> It is possible to gain access to that infrastructure without signing a traditional record deal.

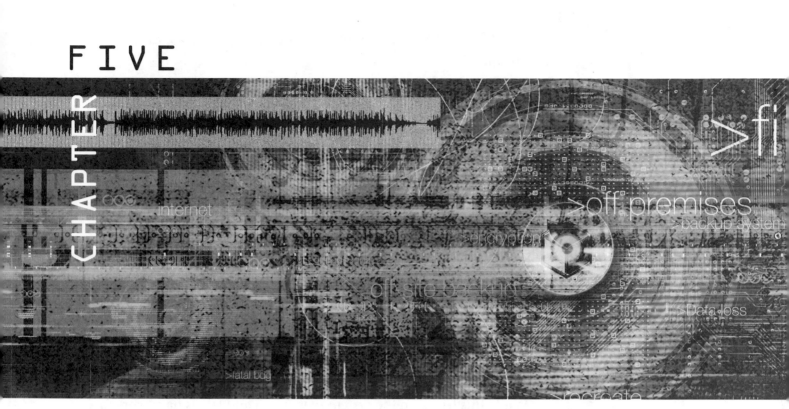

CHAPTER

The New Marketing—Part 1

An artist in Music 4.0 requires an entirely new marketing plan than in prior periods because the techniques commonly used in the past certainly won't work anymore, at least with the degree of success that they once had. Traditional media such as radio are no longer as much of a music-marketing factor, nor is television, unless you're an artist whose image counts more than your music.

Your Music Is Your Marketing

. . . .

The major marketing tool for the M4.0 artist is your music itself. It's no longer the major product that the artist has to sell, although it still is a product, so it has to be used differently and thought of differently as a result.

Perhaps recorded music was never the product we were led to believe it was. In the M1.0 and M1.5 days of vinyl records and CDs, the round plastic piece (the container that held the music) was the product. While the songwriter always made money when a song was played on the radio, the artist never did (although artists might soon get their due, depending on the status of impending Performance Rights Act legislation), and even when it was sold, the artist made only a small percentage of CD and vinyl sales (10 to 15 percent of wholesale, on average). In order for the artist to make any money from the recording, the costs involved in the production of the music product and the manufacturing of the container that transported the music (physical material costs, artwork, and so on) first had to be recouped. The fact of the matter was that the artist made most of his or her money on concert tickets and merchandise sales while touring, not in record sales.

While this has been the system that artists and labels have worked under for years, if you look at music in terms of the advertising world, you see it in a different light.

If you're selling a soap product, for instance, the production cost for a commercial to broadcast on television or the radio is trivial. It's the total ad buy (the agency purchasing the radio or television time for the sponsor) where most of the money is spent. Even then, it's considered part of the marketing budget of the product, which might be about 3 percent of total sales.

In M4.0, if you consider the music-production costs as part of the marketing budget in the same way as a national product, it takes on a whole new meaning.

Since the music is considered the major marketing tool for an artist, it could be considered a free product, a giveaway, an enticement. Give it away on your website, place it on the torrents for P2P, let your fans freely distribute it. It's all okay. Since most millennials already feel that music should be free and have lived in a culture where that's mostly so, don't fight it. Go with the flow! Just as it was during the past 60 years, the real money in the music business is made elsewhere anyway.

Further, just because you're giving it away doesn't mean that you can't charge for it, either at the same time or at sometime in the future.

There are numerous cases in which sales have actually decreased for an artist's iTunes tracks when the free tracks have been eliminated.

One such musician is Corey Smith. After six years, Corey has built his gross revenue to about $9 million, and free music has been the basic building block of his ever-increasing fan base. You can buy his tracks on iTunes (he's sold more than 1.2 million singles and 250,000 albums so far), but when his management experimented by taking the free tracks down from his website, his iTunes sales went down as well. The free music Corey offers allows potential fans to try him out. If they email and ask for a song that's not available for free, he just emails it back to them. He's tending his fan base!

Another example of reaping the rewards for giving it away for free is the electronic artist Moby, whose "Shot in the Back of the Head" became the best-selling iTunes track after being given away for free on his website for two months.

Of course, you can charge for your music with enhanced products such as box sets, compilations, special editions, and other value-added offerings. But to build a buzz, the initial releases for an artist on any level (except for the already-established star) must be free.

Your Music Is Your Marketing

Music is a your main marketing tool.

Give it away for free, but charge for it too.

Most of your income comes from elsewhere anyway.

Value-added products are your best revenue source.

The New Release Schedule

. . . .

M4.0 requires new thinking regarding song releases. If we go back to the '50s, vinyl singles had a notoriously fast manufacturing turn-around time, despite the labor-intensive process required to make a vinyl record. At that time, it was not uncommon to have a single (the small 7-inch "45" with a song on each side) on the streets within days of recording (and sometimes even writing) the song! Of course, the quick turnaround was helped by the fact that the song was usually recorded in a few hours, since there was little or no overdubbing, so it was possible to record a song on Monday and have it on the radio on Wednesday of the same week. Perhaps the last time a hit record turn-around happened this quickly was with the 1970 release of Crosby, Stills, Nash and Young's "Ohio," documenting the Kent State anti-Viet Nam war shootings within a few weeks of the event.

When the emphasis on releases turned from singles to albums, the length of time between releases increased accordingly, which was natural considering that more songs were being recorded. During the M1.0 days, there was a limitation on how many songs could be recorded for an album because there was the limitation of the vinyl itself. Twenty-three minutes per side was the goal to get the loud-est and highest-fidelity record. Any longer and the noise floor of the record increased as the volume decreased. As a result, artists were con-fined to about 45 to 50 minutes per album, but consumers didn't seem to mind, since they still felt they were getting value if they liked the songs.

The time limitation lifted with the introduction of the CD in M1.5. When first released, the CD had a maximum playing time of 74 min-utes (the number rumored to be chosen by the chairman of Sony at the time because it could fit the entire Beethoven's Ninth Symphony), which was later increased to a full 80 minutes. No longer saddled with the vinyl album's built-in time limitation, artists were able to stretch out and add more and longer songs to each album release. This soon proved to be a double-edged sword, since it now took longer to fin-ish recording each release because of the inclusion of all those extra songs.

But having more songs doesn't necessarily make a better record, and even backfired regarding the artist's popularity. While 40 to 45 minutes was a time bite easily digestible for a listener, 60 to 70 was not. The extra songs were not only little appreciated but, even worse, thought of as mere filler. The consumer began to think (sometimes rightfully so) that the songs were there just for the sake of being there, and they began to feel ripped off. Why pay for songs that you'll never listen to? Because you had to!

Over the years, the time between record releases gradually lengthened to the point that a superstar act might take several years. While this might have worked in M1.5 and 2.0, that strategy would never work in M3.0 and beyond, as the fans have an insatiable appetite for product. What's worse, the fan base can actually dissipate if the product does not come at regular intervals—the shorter the better.

And with CD sales way down, the album format itself seems to be going the way of the vinyl single of the '50s and '60s. Consumers in M4.0 buy only the songs they want, and therefore, they buy singles. Which brings about a new philosophy regarding recordings and how they are released.

In M4.0, artists record fewer songs but have more frequent releases. It's better to release a song or two every 6, 8, or 12 weeks than to wait a year for one release of ten songs. This benefits the artist in the following ways:

▶ The artist keeps his or her fans happy with a constant supply of new music. New music keeps the fans interested and keeps the buzz and dialog going.
▶ The artist gains increased exposure for every song. In a ten-song album release, it's easy for a fan, reviewer, or radio programmer to focus on just one or two songs while the others fall in priority. When releases are in twos, each song gets equal attention and has the ability to live and die on its own merits.
▶ All the songs can still be compiled into an album after having been individually released. At the end of the year, or at the end of the artist's creative cycle, the songs are then put into an album that can be released in any format. The advantage is that the album has much advanced exposure and publicity thanks to numerous single releases. Plus it can be treated as a marketing event, which is also to the artist's advantage.

Make no mistake, the album format is not dead in M4.0 (although sales are decreasing), but the emphasis has shifted to the individual song.

> ## The New Release Schedule
>
> Single or two-song releases every 6 to 12 weeks.
>
> Frequent new music keeps the fans happy.
>
> Exposure for all songs is increased.
>
> Singles can be compiled into an album later.
>
> Singles act as advanced publicity for the album.
>
> Each release can be treated as a marketing event.

Ten Music Marketing Ideas

It's easier to sell your music if you add extra value to it. Here are ten ways to think outside the box when it comes to distributing your music. Thanks to Bruce Houghton for numbers 7 through 10.

1. **Develop a package:** This could mean anything from a CD and a vinyl album, to a digital download and album with all alternative mixes, to a boxed set of CDs, or anything in between (see Trent Reznor's *Ghosts I–IV* or Josh Freese's offerings in chapter 4 for ideas). The idea is to go beyond just the typical CD and digital offerings.

2. **Sequential numbering:** Limiting the availability of physical products and numbering them (for example; number 7 of 500) gives it

the feeling of exclusivity. The product becomes a special edition and a must-have for the true fan.

3. **Tie it to merchandise:** Offer a physical product that contains the code for a free download of your album. Mos Def was so successful with the T-shirt release of *The Ecstatic* that *Billboard* magazine even began counting it as a music release on their charts. Prince did the same with an inclusion of his *20Ten* in the UK's *Daily Mirror* newspaper. Other artists have sold their music via codes on such items as golf balls, bandanas, and even canned food! You can use QR Codes on just about anything physical.

4. **Release a "double-sided" digital single:** Rhino Records' digital releases celebrating 60 years of the 45 RPM single set a fine example for this format. For between $1.49 and $1.99, Rhino provided the original hit song, its B side (the flip side of the vinyl record), and the original artwork. You can do the same by providing two songs for price of one—an A and a B side.

5. **Release on an old alternative format:** A number of artists such as The Decemberists, Jack White, and Radiohead have released vinyl-only physical products to great success. Cheap Trick did it on the old 8-track format from the '60s, and some bands have even recently released on cassette tape. Releasing on an older format can be good as a publicity tool (as long as everyone else isn't doing it), and who knows, maybe you can start a trend?

6. **Release on a new alternative format:** A new alternative format that's getting some traction is flash memory, or the common USB memory stick. Once again, Trent Reznor met with great viral success by planting unmarked memory sticks in bathrooms at NIN's concerts, and Sony even released the 25th anniversary of Michael Jackson's *Thriller* on the format. Everybody uses these things so you're bound to get at least a look, which you can't always say about other formats.

7. **Three sides:** Offer a song in an early studio version, the final mix, and then captured live.

8. **Radical mixes:** Offer two or three very different mixes of the same song, perhaps even done by the fans.

9. **Two sides of [your city]:** Two different bands each contribute a track to a series chronicling your local scene.

10. **"Artist X" introduces _____:** Add a track by your favorite new artist/band along with one of yours. This is similar to a gig trade-out with another band that many bands use as a way to play in new venues. The idea is that the band you feature will feature you on their release as well.

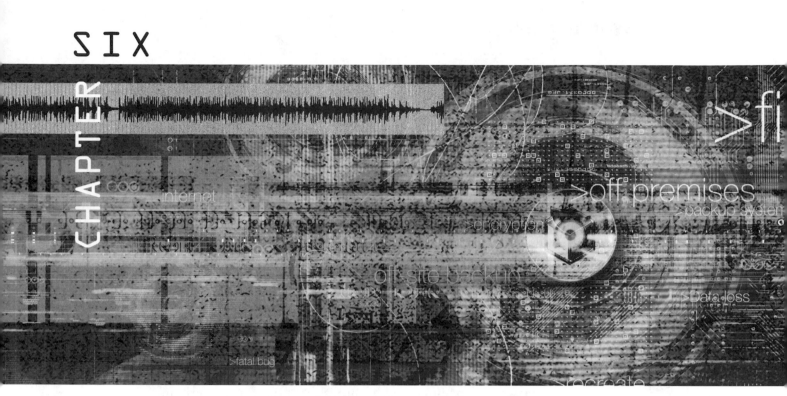

CHAPTER SIX

The New Marketing—Part 2

Where once an artist's major marketing thrust was directed at the traditional mediums of radio, television, and print, today it focuses more online to reach current and potential fans. While social networks tend to wax and wane in popularity, there are other aspects of an artist's online presence that can't be ignored. That said, it's not the social network or the online presence that's important. Those are only mechanisms to reach the most crucial element in an artist's success—the fan him- or herself.

The New Importance of the Fan

. . . .

As pointed out elsewhere in the book, prior to Music 3.0 the fan was treated differently. The artist wasn't able to easily come in contact with fans and, for the most part, didn't want to. Except for special releases and perks to the fan club, the fan was treated mostly as a consumer and kept at arm's length.

M3.0 has changed all that with Seth Godin's tribal concept, and now fan communication is a direct and integral part of an act's success. It's possible for an act to become hot for a while, but if the tribe of fans is not created and constantly enriched, any success will only be short term. Not only can the artist directly interact with the fan, but he or she also must interact in order to maintain the tribe!

That being said, fans know when they're being hyped, exploited, or taken lightly, and receiving anything less than total respect can prove disastrous to the fan base/tribe. Fans don't want to be marketed to, but they want to be informed of things that might interest them.

Fans want to know that the artist is listening to them. They don't need direct communication (although that's the best), but they want acknowledgement that they're being heard. Fans don't want to be talked at, but they want to be spoken to. They want to hear from the artist but not hyped or sold to, as that cheapens the experience. They don't want ad copy; they want it from the heart.

Going back to the email that Trent Reznor sent his fans:

> Hello everyone.
>
> I'd like to thank everyone for a very successful year so far in the world of Nine Inch Nails. I'm enjoying my couple of weeks off between legs of our Lights In The Sky tour and got to thinking . . . "wouldn't it be fun to send out a survey to everyone that's shown interest in NIN?" Well, that's not exactly how it went, but regardless—here it is. As we've moved from the familiar world of record labels and BS into the unknown world of doing everything yourself, we've realized it would benefit us and our ability to interact with you if we knew more about what you want, what you like, what you look like naked, etc. I know it's a pain in the ass but we'd truly appreciate it if you'd take a minute and help us out. As an incentive, everyone who completes the survey will be able to download a video of live performance from this most recent

tour (and I know what's going through your little minds right now: "I'll just grab this off a torrent site and not have to fill out the survey!!!" and guess what? You will be able to do just that and BEAT THE SYSTEM!!!! NIN=pwn3d!!!)

BUT

What if we were to select some of those that DO complete the survey and provide them with something really cool? I'm not saying we'll ever get around to it, but if we did maybe something like signed stuff, flying someone to a show somewhere in the world, a magic amulet that makes you invisible, a date with Jeordie White (condoms supplied of course), you know—something cool. See, you'd miss that opportunity AND be a cheater.

Do the right thing—help us out. You'll feel better.

Thank you and I've had too much caffeine this morning,

—Trent

Reznor treats his fans with respect, bidding them "hello everyone" and thanking them at the end. He tells you a little bit about himself with, "I've had too much caffeine this morning." He engages his fans to interact and help him, but most of all, you get the feeling that he's talking directly to you.

A fan that's treated well might not always stay a fan (though he or she probably will), but while a fan, he or she will remain loyal and an uberconsumer of anything the artist has to offer.

The New Importance of the Fan

Communication with the fan is now integral to an artist's success.

Fans know when they're being hyped, exploited, or taken lightly.

Fans want to know the artist is listening.

Fans want to be treated with respect.

Fans want to be informed, not marketed to.

Your Email List

By far one of the most, if not *the* most, important marketing tools that an artist has is his or her email list. It's the direct link to the artist's most rabid fans and one of the primary drivers of commerce in the artist's online arsenal.

Your email list is a major component for marketing to your fan base. It's widely overlooked, since most artists believe that their Facebook friends and Twitter followers are enough, but your email list allows you to reach out and personally connect with the fans and control your message while you're doing it.

A well thought-out email blast allows you to do the following:

1. Engage your fan on a one-to-one basis

2. Design the communication without the constraints of a social network

3. Add a call to action

Your email list makes it easier to inform, market to, and sell to your fans in a manner true fans (superfans, uberfans, tribal members—whatever you want to call them) enjoy, if you do it well. But execution is always key in the success of any venture, so here are some aspects of your email list to be aware of.

MAIL LIST SERVICES

Having an easy way to sign up for the list is essential, but having a way for the artist to maintain and control the list is just as important. Most artists just starting out rely on their own email client such as Outlook or Mac Mail to manage their lists, but these have built-in limitations that you'll soon outgrow. For one thing, you must manually clean the list of bounces and drop-offs, which is time consuming. Another major problem is that ISPs limit the number of emails that can be sent in a batch in order to eliminate spamming. This can mean that if your email list exceeds as few as 100 people, the email blast will get rejected by your Internet Service service Provider provider and you'll have to divide it into many smaller email groups.

A way around that is to use an email service provider (ESP) such as iContact, Constant Contact, Mail Chimp, or any of the other similar services to maintain your list. For a small monthly fee (as little as $10.00 depending upon the mailing list size), your email list can undergo a significant change for the better in the following ways:

▶ No limit on the number of subscribers in the email blast
▶ The list is automatically cleaned of bounces or invalid addresses
▶ Easily handles subscribers and opt-outs
▶ Extensive analytics as to who opens the email, how many click through, and how long they view
▶ Many professional email templates to choose from

Right now it's that combination of having a great email list and a great website that's constantly updated and gives the fans a reason to come back. In terms of growing an email list, I'm a big fan of the tools that Topspin and Bandcamp have, where it's something like, "Give us your email address and we'll give you this MP3," or "Here's an easy way to send this MP3 to your friends." I'm a big fan of anything that encourages viral growth.
—Bruce Houghton

Most email services have essentially the same feature set and prices, so the main difference between them is a user interface that suits the list owner—you. Most services offer a free try-out period, although some may limit the number of emails or addresses during this period.

SIX KEYS TO BUILDING YOUR MAILING LIST

Building an email list seems like an easy thing to do, but it's a lot more difficult than you'd think. Here are the six keys to building a successful list:

1. **Offer a high comfort level.** People don't like to give their email addresses out unless they're getting something in return. In other words, they use their email information as a form of currency. If they don't have trust in your site or they're unsure what you'll do with their address, it's really difficult to get them to register. If the

site is unprofessional and feels like it may disappear any day, chances are they won't sign up.

2. **Make the sign-up easy to find.** Make the registration prominent on not only your website but every marketing piece that you have. Most email services provide html widgets that both look good and work seamlessly without any programming on your part.

3. **Make it easy to register.** That means don't ask for too much information. It's easy to get their first name and their email address and maybe their city, but beyond that, many potential users begin to feel uncomfortable. Remember, you can always ask them for more information later after they sign up.

4. **Give them an incentive to subscribe.** They need a contest, a free download, or a promise of receiving something later as a reason to register. Remember, they're buying something with their email currency. They're thinking, "What's in it for me?"

5. **Cross-promote.** Promote your list through your social networks such as Twitter and Facebook, your blog, and even something as simple as on gig flyers or business cards. Every address is valuable, so don't let any opportunities for another registration go by the wayside.

6. **Use reminders.** Remind people in your videos, blog posts, podcasts, CD covers, and any other kind of content that you're producing about your email list. You don't have to be blatant about it; just make sure that the info is always present.

DESIGNING YOUR MAIL BLAST

There's no doubt that email is an important part of an artist's social strategy, but sometimes a poorly thought-out mail blast can be worse than none at all. Here are some important questions to ask yourself that will guide you in designing your email. These are questions you should know the answers to way before it's time to hit the send button.

► What's the purpose of this email? To inform? To sell? To entertain?
► Why should my subscribers care about what I'm sending?

▶ Why did the subscriber sign up to receive my emails in the first place? Does this email live up to that expectation?

▶ Did I include a call to action?

▶ Is my most important message above the fold (the point before the reader has to scroll down)?

▶ Have I run a test send?

While the first four points involve the conceptual part of the email, the last two are important design considerations. Keeping your most important message above the fold gives you the best chance of capturing readers' attention before they delete the mail and move on. Doing a test send or two to yourself is the best way to prevent an embarrassing oversight or glitch (like the links not working or a spelling or grammar mistake) from happening. Do it even if you're 100 percent sure you're ready to go. It's surprising how often you find that you're not.

BEST EMAIL PRACTICES

When it comes to emailing, there are good and bad ways to do it. Here are what you might consider "best practices" as revealed by Jed Carlson, founder and CEO of ReverbNation in his "Email 101 for Artists, Labels, and Venues" article on Music Think Tank.

1. **Always respect a person's desire to unsubscribe to your list.** *Immediately unsubscribe them* if your mailing list service doesn't do it for you.

2. **Always talk to them without swearing.** It may be part of your "persona" as a band, but some people don't like that language. Many Internet service providers (ISPs) such as Yahoo and Hotmail don't like it either, and your message will go directly to the junk box if it contains anything they deem "too colorful." You wouldn't talk to your grandma that way, would you?

3. **Always avoid "scam" words in the subject line.** Words such as *free* and *help* will land your message in the junk box 100 percent of the time.

4. **Always target them with messages that are relevant to them.** If you have a show in Seattle, don't message your fans in Miami. Keep your powder dry for a message to them later about something else.

5. **Always give them the basics about the information you are conveying.** Reporters call this the "who, what, why, when, where, how" model. If you have a show coming up, do your fans (and yourself) the service of providing dates, times, locations, ticket links, and lineup of the show. Over 75 percent of artists miss this essential piece when they email. If you want someone to respond and come to your show, for goodness sake, go so far as to give them driving directions if you can. Each ticket sold is money in your pocket.

6. **Always link them to some place to find out more info about the band:** This could be ReverbNation or a homepage or blog, but *always* give them a way to find out more.

So don't overlook the obvious. Your email list is your most important tool in Music 4.0 for reaching your fans, but you need a specialized application to use it to its utmost.

MORE IS LESS

In M4.0, "more is less" should be one of your main mantras. There's a limit to what fans can absorb, and exceeding that limit can alienate them. Too much communication can be counterproductive. Once a week is about the limit, although once a month can work too. More is okay if there's a real purpose.

> *Mailing list blasts have a definite point where it's too much. We like to limit those to a couple of times a month, or once a week at most if you're really doing something special or have unique content. If it's just announcing tour dates or trying to sell something, you shouldn't do it more than once a week, but we find once or twice a month works best. If it's unique content, that could be cool to blast weekly. On the other hand, if you're Twittering, the more the merrier because that's the kind of minutia that people are into. That platform is great for 3, to 10, to even 20 times a day.*
>
> —Jacob Tell of Oniracom

Just as 15 songs on a release are not necessarily better than 8 even if they all might be great, there is a tipping point for email blasts at which fans go from feeling informed to being intruded upon. It's just overload at that point and actually dilutes the effectiveness of your message and your marketing. The leader of the tribe must have a feel for where that point is and be sure to never cross it.

Your Email List

It's the most important marketing tool you have.

Professional email list-management services offer significant extra benefits.

Make your list sign-up easy to find and easy to do.

Think through your email blast before you send it.

Always observe best practices.

Fewer emails is always better.

The Eight Rules of Fan Communication

1. **Talk to your fans, not at them.** Don't try to sell them, but keep them informed. Anything that reads like ad copy might be counterproductive. Always treat them with respect, and never talk down to them.

2. **Engage in communication.** Communication is a two-way street. Fans want to know that they're being listened to. You don't have to answer every email, but you have to acknowledge that you heard it. The more questions you ask, polls you supply, and advice you seek, the more your fans will feel connected to you.

3. **Keep your promises.** If you say you're going to do something, do it in a timely fashion. Don't let your fans wait. If you promise you're going to email a link and post a song, sooner is always better.

4. **Stay engaged.** Even if you're only sending something simple such as a link, take the time to engage the fan. Tell him or her about upcoming gigs, events, or releases. Take a poll. Ask for advice. This is a great opportunity for communication, so take advantage of it. Some of the things that you ask might be:

The Eight Rules of Fan Communication (continued)

- Where do you live?
- Are there any venues nearby where you'd like to see us play?
- Do you prefer studio recordings or live performances?
- Would you like to obtain copies of our live performances?
- If we offered high-quality recordings of our shows, would you purchase them?
- Would you prefer personal updates or free music from our newsletter?
- Would you be interested in purchasing merch from us, and if so, what kind?
- Are you interested in seeing behind-the-scenes footage of our tour or recording sessions?

5. **Utilize preorders.** If you have a release coming out soon, take preorders as soon as you announce it, even if it's free. It's best to get people to act while their interests are high, and it gives the fans something to look forward to. To motivate fans for a preorder, it sometimes helps to include exclusive content or merchandise.

6. **Appearance means a lot.** Style counts when talking to fans. Make sure everything looks good and is readable. Spelling or grammar mistakes reflect badly on you. Try to keep it simple but stylish, but if you or your team don't have the design chops to make it look good, then it's better to just keep things simple and readable.

7. **Cater to uberfans.** All of the members of your tribe are passionate, but some are more passionate than others. Fans have different needs and wants, and it's to everyone's benefit if you can cater to them all. Try always to include a premium or deluxe tier for every offering, such as a free T-shirt or backstage pass as a reward for posting, a free ticket to an upcoming show, some signed artwork, some extra songs—anything to satiate the uberfan's interest.

8. **Give them a choice.** Give fans numerous ways to opt in, since not everyone wants to receive information in the same way. Ask if they would rather receive info by email, SMS, or even snail mail. Ask if they'd like to receive info on upcoming shows, song releases, video content, or contests. And ask how often they'd like be contacted.

Your Blog

A blog is essential to have for both communicating with your fans and having them communicate with you and each other. It's easier than ever to create a blog these days with either Blogger, WordPress, or Tumblr (which is less sophisticated and in a slightly different category as a micro-blog), which are priced the way most artists like—free.

You can design a fancy blog site if you want, but it's really not necessary. A generic one will do just fine as long as the look is somewhat consistent with your website and marketing materials to maintain your brand. If you can't do that or it will take too long to design, just make it plain vanilla. Since a blog is such a valuable tool, simply having one far outweighs how it looks.

Make sure that you update it regularly with photos, videos, and journal entries of your band's latest antics. Daily updates are best, but any interval can work as long as you stick to it. For instance, it's best if your fans always know that you post at 11 a.m. every Wednesday, but you better make sure that you don't miss a day or post at a different time, because that can lead to reader attrition.

You can also link with other musicians' blogs and sites, have fans subscribe, add a list of blogs that you like or suggest, and add widgets from other promotion sources. If you add keywords to your posts, they will be searchable through Google, and you can even set up Google AdSense to generate some additional revenue through adds on your blog or RSS feed.

A blog can do wonders for your communication with fans and general visibility, and all it takes is a little time on a regular basis..

OTHER MUSIC BLOGS

By using the general music blogs and the blogs relating to both your genre of music and similar-sounding artists, you can develop a very effective marketing strategy. Especially when you're first starting out, any review or mention that you get on a popular blog is an important step to spreading virally across the Web.

Everybody knows to set up a Facebook page and a YouTube Channel. Beyond that, regardless if you're offering your music for free or not, you want to utilize the rest of the Web that doesn't cost you anything, meaning all the social media stuff like personal profile pages, bookmarking and tagging, and an official Twitter channel. It's figuring out a way to broadcast to your fans and affinity groups, which are groups of people that like the type of music that you play. For example, if I sound a lot like John Meyer, then I want to reach out to John Meyer fans. You can do all that at no cost by simply putting the time in.

—Gregory Markel

So how do you get attention from a blog? Unlike the traditional media, where the attention of a magazine or newspaper editor is difficult to get, blogs are relatively easy, since they're typically not inundated with press releases and attention. Even the larger ones are pretty much open to stories or communication because of how difficult it is to fill blog space every day.

The best way to establish a relationship with influential music blogs that discuss music similar to your own is to post frequently so the blogger gets to know you, begin a relationship with the blogger via email, then send your music and ask for a review.

Here's some great info on finding the right blogs from the DIY (Do It Yourself) section of Bruce Houghton's ever-informative music blog, Hypbot.com:

> Most bloggers are true music fans who want to discover great new music and share it with the world . . . or at least their 37 friends who read them faithfully. If 10 percent of those 37 readers come to one of your shows, that's 37 fans that you didn't have yesterday telling their own 37 friends about you.
>
> Bloggers are also more approachable then most print journalists, who often can only write about what editors assign them. And bloggers have influence. Fans respect writers that are passionate about music and prove it by writing for love instead of a paycheck. One study from NYC's Stern School of Business even showed that blogs more than some social networks helped to sell new music.
>
> How to know which blogs to target? Two words: niche and location. Using a blog-specific search engine such as Google Blog Search or Technorati, type in "music + Chicago," or better yet a use specific genre, such as "heavy metal + Chicago." Think fans of Arcade Fire would like your band too? Try "Arcade Fire + [your city]." Try all kinds of combinations, including that obscure band that you think copied your style. If they wrote about them; why wouldn't they write about you? You can do the same thing nationally by simply searching under genres or similar artists.

Michael Terpin's Social Radius specializes in PR via blogs, and he suggests:

> Quite frankly, if you're trying to "court" a blogger who covers your space, the best thing to do is to first start reading them. The nice things about blogs is they all have RSS feeds, and most of them link their most important posts to their Twitter account, which is mobile and a lot easier to deal with than a large RSS aggregator. You can follow all these bloggers on Twitter, and it'll be on your iPhone, Blackberry or anything that has a Twitter client, and they'll sort of recognize you as you become a Twitter follower and are watching what they say. You can comment on

some of their posts, and all of a sudden, you have a bit of a relationship, so that when you come out, you don't come across as a salesman who's trying to spam 50 sites with the same information. It's better to come out and say, "Hey, I read your site frequently and here's what I'm doing."

Blogs

Great for direct communication with fans.

A fancy design isn't necessary.

Post on a regular schedule.

Marketing through existing music blogs is an effective strategy.

Establish a relationship with the blogger before asking for a review.

SEVEN

CHAPTER

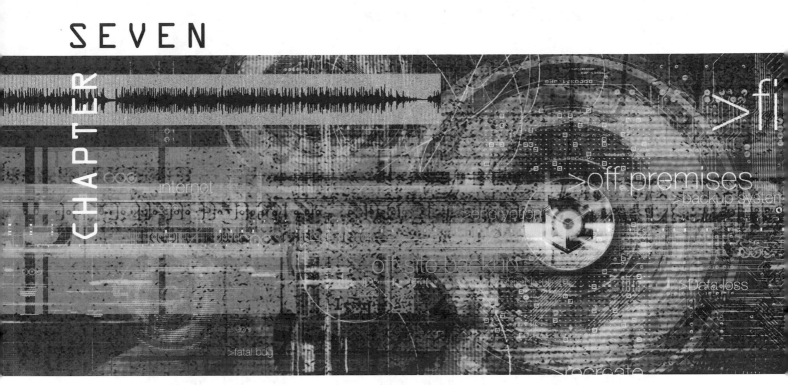

Marketing with Social Media

ne of the most powerful methods of marketing in M4.0 is by the use of social media, which means social networks such as Facebook, microblogs such as Twitter, video portals such as YouTube, and photo/video platforms such as Instagram. While Facebook and Twitter are primarily used for communicating with fans, their importance as marketing platforms should not be underestimated, and as noted several times before in this book, YouTube has become the primary means of music discovery and distribution today. Before we look at these networks more closely, let's look at a former online giant that's quickly moving toward irrelevancy.

The Death and Rebirth of MySpace

MySpace has been on a downward spiral since being purchased by media giant NewsCorp in 2005, mostly for not acknowledging what it was and focusing on what it wasn't instead.

At its core, MySpace was an entertainment site centered around music. It didn't perform that function well enough to maintain its audience though, and instead of improving its core value, it chose to try to be more of a general social network. That failed miserably, with Facebook coming from nowhere to dwarf its huge initial lead in both visitors and revenue.

While Facebook has become the dominant network of the social world, it's still not an obvious successor for music, since it still lacks many of the core assets that MySpace offers, despite some of the available music apps such as BandPage. The fact is that mixing a social network with a music network hasn't worked so far (e.g., iTunes Ping), and it remains to be seen if it will work in the future. That said, MySpace still has more than 36 million visitors per month as of the writing of this book, which looks to be rising slowly but steadily. After several years of rumors regarding its imminent closure, MySpace was sold at a fire-sale price to Specific Media in July of 2011, with singer Justin Timberlake as one of the investors.

In June of 2013 MySpace shut down the "Classic MySpace" in favor of a new updated version and, in doing so, created a scenario warned about elsewhere in this book by deleting years of user and follower data from every loyal member who had stuck with the service through the years. This created an uproar as everyone on the platform (even Timberlake) now started from the same place—zero.

With that, "new MySpace" also introduced several new features aimed directly at artists, such as a new user interface, a mobile app, integration with social networks, and more.

MySpace has essentially put all of the best tools from these other platforms together in one place, and they're more artist and user friendly today than they were in the past and probably more useful, in terms of suite of features, than other social platforms. You can post status updates on MySpace and then share them on Facebook and Twitter. You can upload and host a video on

MySpace and then build some nice-looking galleries. You can create video, music, and picture compilations, which is great when you're trying to tell a story with a multimedia campaign. You can have pictures from the tour, video from backstage, and the music video all in one "mix," which you can't do on any other platform. Every artist also has their own radio station, so you can curate your own music to show who you are as an artist. You can have a video that floats with the user as she moves around MySpace. There's also a lot of analytics, which are important for your strategy.

—Dae Bogan

Even with the new ownership and platform overhaul, there's little to indicate that the network will be able to reconstitute its once formidable user base. Despite its new features, the company has been ineffective at communicating its new abilities to artists, which along with the stigma of the MySpace of the past may have caused its slow growth.

MySpace held such promise, and delivered little of it. It's another example of a multinational company getting involved in the music business only to slowly run it into the ground. History repeats itself again.

Marketing with Facebook

In a few short years, Facebook has supplanted MySpace, not only as the most formidable social network, but also as an indispensable one for musical artists. According to Facebook's own stats (as of the time of this writing), the social network has more than 1.26 billion active users, 700 million that log into the service every day and spend an average of 20 minutes. The average user is connected to 80 community pages, groups, and events, and creates 90 pieces of the more than 30 billion pieces of content (web links, news stories, blog posts, notes, photo albums, etc.) shared each month. Plus it's truly international, with 70 percent of Facebook users outside the United States, and entrepreneurs and developers from over 190 countries build for the platform. And it's still growing!

With such a huge influence on almost any social happening, every artist should have his or her own page for promotional purposes. With numerous artist apps such as BandPage (Bandpage.com), Damn the Radio (damntheradio.com), My Band (facebook.com/rn.mybandapp), and utilities from artist platforms such as ReverbNation, it's easier than ever to design a custom page that perfectly fits the artist's needs. That said, it still comes down to regular posts for effective promotion, and many of the same rules that apply to Twitter also apply to Facebook.

EIGHT RULES OF FACEBOOK ENGAGEMENT

A white paper about Facebook engagement from the research site Buddy Media Platform provided a number of interesting points gathered in a report called *Strategies for Effective Facebook Wallposts: A Statistical Review.*

In the study they determined the Five Rules of Facebook engagement, which are:

1. **Keep your posts short and sweet.** Posts of 80 characters or less have 27 percent higher engagement rates.

2. **Think twice before using URL shorteners.** Engagement rates are three times higher using full-length URLs.

3. **Post when people are listening.** The highest traffic occurs midweek between 1 and 3 p.m..

4. **Some days are better than others.** Engagement rates are 18 percent higher on Thursday and Friday than the other days of the week, but Saturday and especially Sunday are good too. This can vary by industry though.

5. **Avoid the noise of Monday.** There's too much going on after the weekend.

You can add a few more to this list that exactly parallel the email and Twitter advice:

6. **Keep your posts relevant.** You're trying to promote your brand, so stay on topic.

7. **Don't post unnecessarily.** Too many posts can cause your fans to tune you out. It's been discovered that engagement decreases after two posts a day.

8. **Keep the interaction high.** Ask your fans for their opinions and advice. It will not only keep them involved, but you'll immediately feel the pulse of the tribe.

If you're posting to keep in touch with your friends or to let them know what you're doing, then the above data is of no consequence to you. But if you're posting strategically to promote your brand, then follow the eight points for better fan engagement.

BEST TIME OF DAY FOR FACEBOOK POSTS

While you might be writing the best, most engaging posts, they do you no good if there's no one reading, so the question then becomes, "When is the best time of day to post to Facebook so my readership will be high?"

A study from the social-media company Vitrue called *Managing Your Facebook Community: Findings on Conversation Volume by Day of Week, Hour and Minute,* which looked closely at the viewing habits of Facebook channels of selected companies and brands, found:

▶ The best times to post are at 11 a.m., 3 p.m., and 8 p.m. ET.
▶ Of those times, the absolute best is at 3 p.m. ET on weekdays.
▶ Wednesday at 3 p.m. is the best time of the week to post.
▶ Fans are less active on Sunday.
▶ Posts on the weekend can be more effective than during the week.
▶ Posts that occur in the morning tend to perform almost 40 percent better in terms of user engagement than those in the afternoon.

► Post at the top of the hour (:00 to :15 minutes) get more comments than other parts of the hour, with posts at the bottom of the hour (:30) getting the least.

► 65 percent of users only access Facebook in the evening.

UNDERSTANDING THE "LIKE" BUTTON

It's important to understand just what a "Like" means and not make too much or little of it. First of all, a Like is an endorsement by the fan. It has touched a nerve or a similar opinion or emotion, and it's an expression of that. It doesn't necessarily mean that you're especially clever, only that your post refers to something he or she wants to associate with. It's important to step back and look for a pattern of Likes or comments, then analyze them to see if there's a common thread. It's the best way to take the pulse of your tribe.

It's also important not to get too hung up with Likes, especially if you feel that you're not getting enough. An article by Robin Davey called "Only 10% Of Your Friends See Your Facebook Posts, And Only 1% Like It" on the Hypebot blog used the empirical evidence he received by a post on his personal wall asking his friends to Like it, and received about a 10 percent response. He determined the 1 percent portion of the article by looking at the following (an excerpt from the post—the total numbers are somewhat dated but the ratios still apply):

The Black Keys have 800,000 fans and they get around 800 likes per post, although they did reach 7,000 when they said "Lotsa Grammys."

Justin Bieber has 22,000,000 fans and gets between 25,000 and 50,000 likes per post.

Mumford and Sons have 1,300,000 fans and have recently pulled an impressive 17,000 likes on one post that simply said, "TOUR!!!"

But how impressive exactly is that?

The Black Keys, at 800 for the less popular posts, works out significantly below 1% of their fans choosing to like it, and just under 1% for their most popular post. Bieber's rampant fans achieve similar numbers. Mumford's impressive number is actually only just above 1%.

The flaw in this thinking is that if someone doesn't register a Like, then they're not actually reading the post, which is not the case at all. In fact many of us see and react to posts without ever registering a Like.

The reason an artist should continue to post without worrying about getting Likes is the same reason advertising works—it's all about the impressions. The more impressions, or views, the more likely the viewer will take some action, such as download some music, go to a show, or buy a T-shirt.

As long as the information you post is valuable to the reader in some way, it's worth doing, because you're reaching him or her in some way. In other words, it's nice to be "Liked," but it's not necessarily a sign of a successful post.

FACEBOOK ADS

One of the most useful marketing tools for an artist is Facebook ads, which can boost Likes, comments, awareness, and even sales. The beauty of Facebook ads is that you don't have to pay a lot, as you can set the price that you want to pay each day and the ad campaign duration. You can also target the exact audience, from either all your followers, the friends of all your followers, or people in a geographic location like a country, town, or zip code to even followers of a certain kind of music.

You're also able to promote a link to an outside website, a Facebook post, a video, or a photo, and you can select whether you want to display the ad in the newsfeed of your targeted audience (which is the most effective) or in the ad box on the right side of the page. While you can promote any post by selected "Boost Post," a much more precise way is to use the Facebook Ad Manager and Power Editor. This can take up an entire book by itself, but you can check out my *Social Media Promotion for Musicians* book for more details.

Now Facebook has added a new twist in that no one will get to see your post unless you pay, and now we have a problem. We've been saying for years that it's all about great content and engagement and keeping things interesting, and Facebook has come along and said, "Actually, no. If you pay us, we'll promote something that's not interesting to get you more eyeballs." This is detrimental because it's diluting the whole point of Facebook in the first place. That's why I find Facebook to be a necessary evil. There's still a huge number of active users so you need a strategy for it, but both the platform and the strategy are rapidly changing.

—Ariel Hyatt

Marketing with Facebook

Design a custom artist page using one of the many tools.

Keep your posts short.

Make sure to include a link back to your website or blog in your posts.

The best times to post are at 11 a.m., 3 p.m., and 8 p.m. EST.

A Like is a look at the pulse of the fan base.

Only 1 percent of your fan base will register a Like.

A post can be effective without receiving a Like.

Facebook ads boost Likes, comments, and awareness.

Google+

The latest major social network to be introduced is Google+, which is already making inroads toward Facebook's social dominance in terms of number of active users and penetration with Internet users, ranking second in both categories. In fact, Google+ now dominates Facebook in the number of monthly visits, but much of this has to do with the fact that other Google services such as Docs and Gmail are wrapped into each Google+ account.

Google+ has a number of interesting features that has caused users of other social networks to seriously consider it. These features promise to change the way we interact, socialize, and connect to others, and given the huge existing user footprint that Google already has, this could spell trouble for Facebook et al. in the long run. Here's a look at them:

1. **Circles:** The idea of Circles is to closely follow the way you organize your contacts in real life. Circles offers a simple means of organizing your social network by combining contacts into small groups such as family, friends, coworkers, and so forth.

2. **Stream:** Your stream is similar to your Facebook Newsfeed and allows you to receive instant updates from your friends and contacts in your Circles list, then lets you decide and choose which Circles and individuals you want to share your information with.

3. **Hangouts:** Hangouts is a video chat feature that allows up to ten people in a group to come together and video chat. This can be expanded by using Hangouts on Air, an extension of the feature that broadcasts your chat on YouTube for your fans to see. A Hangout is easy to set up, looks and sounds good, and is perfect for today's artist to visually keep in touch with the fan base via either an impromptu concert or an intimate look backstage, or to virtually join a meet and greet.

Google+ also has privacy features that go beyond what Facebook offers. This allows you to choose which Circles you want to share that content with, which can be a useful tool for communicating with your core fans while excluding your casual fans, or communicating just with friends or family.

Another big advantage Google+ has over Facebook is its "data liberation," which allows you to pack up and take your data away from Google+ should you decide to leave the service.

Marketing on Google+ is similar to that of Facebook, but its new features (especially Hangouts on Air) means that the marketing strategy for the network is at least slightly different than that of any other service. That said, uploading pictures is still the most popular activity on both platforms, which is still integral to an artist or band branding.

Marketing with Twitter

· ·

As for Twitter, if you're not using it, you should be. It's amazing how much you can say in 140 characters, and unlike email blasts, even with ten or more tweets a day, your fans never feel intruded upon.

The secret to successful twittering is to only tweet about relevant topics of interest to your fans. Keep the tweets informative and not so intimately personal that you lose people. Here's an example:

> "Playing at the Lone Star in Memphis tonite. 9:30 p.m. sharp. Meet and greet afterwards in the bar. Great place. Come and join us."

This is an effective tweet because it provides some real information for the fans, although only on a local basis. A tweet that's a bit more global yet informative might be something like this:

> "Great gig at the Lone Star tonite. You people ROK! Two girls jumped on stage and Jimmy boogied with them. Video at http://bit. ly/7GFjDq."

See how much info can be communicated in just 140 characters? Notice how it made people interested to go to the website to check out the video?

Here's an example of a tweet that doesn't work because it's a bit too personal to be effective unless your name is Prince or Bono:

> "Just had bacon and eggs and potatoes for breakfast. The bacon was greasy and the potatoes were burnt. The coffee was good though."

This isn't a compelling use of the medium because it's mostly irrelevant information. A way to take that same idea and make it work might be:

> "Just had breakfast after a great gig at the Lone Star last night. Met Sally B and Adrian there and they were at the gig. Thanks a lot guys!"

This gives a shout out to some fans and talks about the gig. The fans love it because they were acknowledged, and it makes other fans hope that you'll acknowledge them as well, all in exactly 140 characters.

The beauty of Twitter is that you don't have be "Friended" by somebody. You can follow anybody you want (thousands of people if you want) and they can follow you unless you're blocking your profile. And if you're following each other, that constitutes a friend relationship and that means you can direct message them. It becomes a very sophisticated way to search and have conversations with a wide array of thought leaders. It's a very sophisticated crowd now, but it's starting to expand to the masses. It's not real big in music promotion yet, but it will be.
—Michael Terpin

THE SECRET OF THE HASHTAG

One of the most egregious errors for an artist using Twitter is overlooking the use of hashtags (the "#" symbol before a keyword).

Using a hashtag is like including a keyword in your tweet. It's an unofficial feature of Twitter but now widely accepted and supported, and is an easy way for people to search for and find a particular topic.

Here's how it works, using some of my own tweets:

> "The Secret To The Merch Table. Want to sell more merch at gigs? Here's how. http://bit.ly/7GFjDq #merch #gig #bands"

This is a simple tweet regarding a post from my Music 3.0 blog (music3point0.blogspot.com), complete with a shortened URL link. At the end are the hashtags #merch, #gig, and #bands. How were they selected? First of all, both "merch" and "gig" appear in the tweet, but both were researched first to see if there were any searches for each by going to "search.twitter.com." On the site I searched for both "merch" and "#merch" and determined that there was enough search traffic to make it worth using, as was "gig." Since the post was aimed at bands and was a topic that they'd be most interested in, another search found that "bands" was also sizable, so that term was used as well.

Here's another way the hashtags could have been used in this tweet.

"The Secret to The #Merch Table. Want to sell more merch at #gigs? Here's how. http://bit.ly/7GFjDq"

In this case the hashtags are embedded directly into the tweet text. This method works, but it's sometimes too difficult to read, so the practice can quickly turn into a negative for less sophisticated users. Leaving room at the end of the tweet, especially for the hashtags, usually gets a better response.

Here's another example of a tweet from my Big Picture production blog (bobbyowsinski.blogspot.com).

"15 Steps To A Better Mix. A blueprint for better mixing. bit.ly/vjgIUQ #recording #musicians"

As in the previous example, a quick search discovered that #recording had more traffic than #mixing (there was some confusion with a food processor as well), and that many other tweets that contained #recording also contained #musicians, so it was a good match to include.

Using hashtags is the key way to help people find you, but don't forget to include a link to take them to your blog or website as well, since that's the real goal.

THE BEST TIME TO TWEET

If you're using Twitter for promotion, then the timing of when you tweet is critical. If you do it when most people are busy and not paying attention, then you have no hope of engaging them, since tweets generally have little shelf life.

According to a new study by Dan Zarrella, a researcher at Hubspot who looked at millions of tweets and showed their results in a webinar entitled "The Science of Timing," the later you tweet in the day, the better. The reason is that from 2 p.m. to 5 p.m. EST, your followers are more likely to see your tweet because there are fewer things demanding their attention. In fact, 4 p.m. was deemed to be the best tweet time of the day.

Zarrella also found that the weekends are great for tweet attention as people are more relaxed and aren't conflicted by work. He also found that tweeting the same link multiple times a day is an effective strategy, and unlike excessive emails, followers don't seem to mind.

It was also found that 92 percent of all retweets and 97 percent of all replies happen within the first hour of the tweet lifetime. After that, it's as good as gone.

TWITTER TOOLS

There are a number of websites that can provide keyword search, trending, and measurement information that are useful in maximizing Twitter as a promotional tool. Keep in mind that these were accurate as of the writing of this book, but websites frequently disappear, change names, or change focus without much warning.

1. Search.twitter.com is more of an all-purpose Twitter search site. If you're looking for any keywords related to hashtags, be sure to place one in front of your search term (such as #keyword). If you select "advanced search," you can make your search even more granular.

2. Twellow (twellow.com) is a Twitter yellow pages directory. It's interesting in that if you search for a keyword, you'll get the profiles of users with that keyword in their profiles based on who has the most tweets.

3. Tweetstats (tweetstats.com) and Tweetstats Trends (tweetstats.com/trends) are a good way to look at not only what your personal stats are, but also the latest trends on Twitter.

4. Twitter Counter (twittercounter.com) is an excellent way to keep track of your total follower count over time as well as future predictions.

5. Klout (klout.com) is unique in that it measures your online influence in terms of likes, retweets, mentions, and comments. The idea is to measure the size of your true Twitter audience, instead of just by followers alone.

6. Blast Follow (blastfollow.com) is indispensable for finding people in your niche (and beyond) and mass-following them with a single click. Good for research.

7. Tweepi (tweepi.com) allows you to Unfollow those who do not reciprocate. If you have to use this, you're using Twitter wrong.

8. Gremln (gremln.com) allows you to schedule your tweets in advance. Good app if you're using Twitter to broadcast blog postings. Not so good if used mostly for personal tweets.

9. Tweetdeck (tweetdeck.com) allows you to organize your followers and keep an eye on the really interesting ones in separate groups. It also allows you to post to Facebook and Linkedin at the same time, and to schedule your posts as well. I use this one all the time.

10. Tweetchat (tweetchat.com) allows you to isolate the conversation based on the hashtag.

11. TweetWhen (tweetwhen.com) analyzes your last 100 tweets and retweets and determines your best times to tweet.

Remember that you need to insert the hashtag (#) before your keyword when doing a keyword search. Also, a quick look at both the searches and trends before you select a keyword can make a difference in your Twitter traffic and ultimate attraction to new followers.

Marketing with Twitter

Start tweeting, but make sure you have something to say.

Always use hashtags to reach a greater audience.

Research the traffic a hashtag has before using it.

Make sure to include a link back to your website or blog.

2 to 5 p.m. are the best times to tweet during the day.

A tweet's lifetime is short, with most retweets or replies happening within the first hour.

Check multiple measurement tools to evaluate your progress.

Marketing with YouTube

YouTube has become much more than a site where you can watch amusing videos. It's also a major distribution point for music, and its value as a taste maker is now unparalleled. Why is the service so influential? Here are some staggering facts from YouTube's press section:

▶ Over 4 billion hours of video are viewed every month.
▶ 100 hours of video footage are uploaded to the site every minute, or over a decade of content every day!
▶ Every second there are more than 46,000 videos being watched around the world.
▶ YouTube has more than 800 million monthly users, or more than the entire population of Europe.

- Each month more than 6 billion hours of videos are watched.
- More video is uploaded every 60 days than the three major US television networks produced in 60 years.
- 2 billion video views per week are monetized, and that number is rapidly increasing.
- YouTube is localized in 25 countries across 43 languages.
- 70 percent of YouTube traffic comes from outside the US.
- More than half the videos on YouTube have been rated or commented on by users.

When it comes to music, YouTube has now become a major platform for music discovery. In fact, it's now the single most widely used website for music discovery and distribution, according to a September 2010 survey by Nielsen Music and Midem. The study went on to state:

- People now consume more music by watching it than by any other means.
- Age makes a bigger difference in consumers' music-video watching preferences than gender. The younger the consumer, the more likely he or she is to have consumed music videos via either of the media.

That's why it's so important to an artist's development to create a YouTube channel and start uploading videos. If you want someone to discover you, you have more of a chance here than almost anywhere else online.

YOUTUBE SEO

YouTube can be used as an effective marketing tool, but you must observe the SEO (Search Engine Optimization) techniques outlined later in this book (see Gregory Markel's interview). Before you go live on a video, make sure that you do the following:

1. **Name your video something descriptive.** "Emerald at the Lone Star Club video 1/9/09" is good. "Untitled_bandvideo12.mov" is not descriptive at all, so your video will never get added by the search engines, and your fans won't find it.

2. **Choose your keywords based on your title. In the above case, the key-wor**d phrases would be "Emerald" (you might want to say "Emerald

band" to be more descriptive) and "Lone Star Club." Keep your number of keyword phrases to four or five, since anything more could be construed as "keyword stuffing" (that means using every keyword you can think of in hopes of getting ranked by a search engine), and you might get penalized with a lower search-engine rank as a result.

3. **Make sure that your description contains the same phrase as your title.** For example, "This video features Emerald at the Lone Star Club on January 9, 2011." Something like "Here's our band at the Lone Star Club" wouldn't be as effective, because it omits the keyword "Emerald."

4. **Properly tagging a video can be a major step in being found during a search.** Not only should the artist name be included, but also any similar artists and even the type of music.

5. **Cover songs are a good way to get an artist noticed on YouTube**, but song selection, performance, and proper tagging play a big part in its popularity.

If I had to give some advice, I'd say song choice is number one. Choose songs that are relevant today by using the Billboard *charts as a guide. Select a song that's on the top of the charts today, then post a really good cover, then make sure the video title is appropriate by posting the original artist's name, the song name, then your name. Make sure it's tagged with the original artist's name and the song name, as well as the record label name and anything else about it. If it's a love song or a pop song, put that descriptive tag in. Sometimes people just search for love songs, so they'll come across your video that way. Finally, make sure the video description is complete.*

—Dae Bogan

There are other ways of using YouTube promotionally. You can:

- ▶ Find people making creative videos on YouTube and offer them some original music to pair with their videos.
- ▶ Run a contest to see who comes up with the best music video for one of your songs.
- ▶ Run a contest to see who can do the best mash-up of your existing videos.

Also, the more text the body of your description has, the more likely it will be found by a search engine. A hundred words works well but so could 500.

These are just other ways to get not only your current fans involved, but also potential new fans.

THE HALF-LIFE OF A VIRAL VIDEO

Video distributor TubeMogul's Insider's Report states that a typical YouTube video gets 50 percent of its total views in the first 6 days. After 20 days, it's already received 75 percent of the total views that it will ever see.

You may think that if your video doesn't receive many plays in the first week, it may never get any, but that's just not true. This study obviously applies to the DIY "novelty" videos, and not ones that are meant to extend your brand. Many videos gradually gain an audience and continue to build over time, especially after a mention on a blog or social network. If you maintain a good video SEO practice and your video is aimed at building your brand, you'll quickly prove this study wrong.

MAKING MONEY FROM YOUTUBE

YouTube has gone from a distribution-only platform to one that actually can be a revenue generator for artists and record labels alike. An act can make some revenue from Google's AdSense program simply by selecting the "Monetize" button on each video, but a more favorable income split comes from joining YouTube's Partner Program, which is only open to the most prolific content creators.

To be frank, the income generated through YouTube is not going to make most artists wealthy, as it ranges from around $2.50 to $9.00 per thousand views based upon a 55/45 split with YouTube (55 percent for the artist). The exact number is difficult to determine in that so much depends upon the type of advertisement (preroll, postroll, in-movie banners, etc.), how long it's watched, and the amount paid by the advertiser. Many content creators subscribe to a multichannel network such as Full Screen, Omnia Media, or Maker Studios, as they have more favorable splits with YouTube, often as much as 80/20. YouTube partners are also pushing to increase their share of the split from 55 to 70 percent to come more in line with what a music distribution service like iTunes charges.

That said, some money is better than no money, and in today's Music 4.0 world, every revenue stream, no matter how small, counts. The YouTube payouts may not be as high as artists and labels would like, but they're a vast improvement over nothing at all.

STREAMING VIDEO

While YouTube has been a force in the music community for quite some time now, streaming video from services such as UStream, Concert Window, Justin.tv, and LiveStream is a trend that is just starting to explode. Artists can use real-time streaming to offer live performances, jam sessions, studio sessions, or acoustic "unplugged"-style performances from the comfort of their own homes. It's also possible to directly engage fans through a real-time question-and-answer session, or even allow fans to request songs during a performance. To be sure, live streaming will become much more important to the artist of the future as the services become more widespread.

YOUTUBE MEASUREMENT TOOLS

YouTube has a couple of great analysis tools that can provide a wealth of data. One is called the Trends Dashboard, which lets you see exactly what people are viewing and sharing. The Dashboard also gives you a picture of some of the gender and age demographics of the views. Here's what it shows:

▶ Selection by gender
▶ Views or sharing
▶ Selection by age group
▶ Selection by city, country, or globally
▶ Comparison of any of the above

The trend information only portrays viewer habits over the last 24 hours and videos uploaded over the last 28 days.

The Trends Dashboard can be a great informational tool if approached from the right perspective. If you want to learn what's working in a particular area, you can dial it up to take a look. Even better is that you can then analyze the Top 10 videos to gain an overview of the production techniques that worked in those particular cases.

Because the timeline is only over the last 24 hours, it's best if you watch the trends for at least a week, just to be sure that you're not getting a false impression. Keep in mind that many videos go viral because of their cuteness (cats and babies), weirdness, or just plain outrageousness, which is difficult to duplicate, but this tool can definitely give you a better idea of the types of things that are working or not.

Another excellent tool is the Insight tool built into every video and YouTube channel. It features a variety of demographic details, as well as methods of discovery and audience attention.

For more detailed information about using social media for marketing, check out my *Social Media Promotion for Musicians* book.

Marketing with YouTube

People now consume more music by watching it than by any other means.

Create a dedicated YouTube channel.

Keep the video title descriptive.

Use SEO where possible.

The more text in the description, the better.

Make sure to include a link back to your website or blog in the description.

YouTube views can now be a revenue source.

Live streaming will become more important in the future.

Keep track of your video progress through YouTube Insights and Trends.

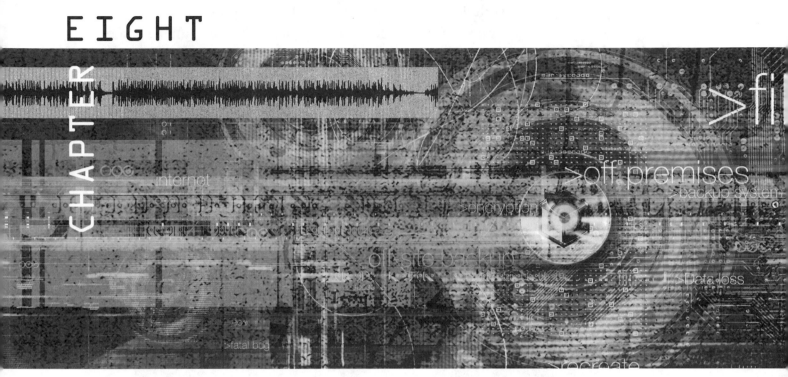

EIGHT

CHAPTER

Social Media Management

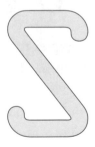

So many areas of social media require attention that it can get a bit overwhelming at times, and that's when you need a social media management strategy.

A common mistake that artists who manage their own social media assets make is to have too many focal points (such as YouTube, their Website, their blog, Twitter, and ReverbNation, for example) all residing in different places and requiring separate updates. You can imagine how tough it is to keep every one of those sites updated regularly! Worse is the fact that it's confusing for the fan, who just wants a single place to visit. Yet another problem is that you may be collecting email addresses from each site, and they may all be going on different mailing lists.

The solution is to use one site (usually your website) as your main focal site and use that to feed daily updates and info to all the others via RSS or social media broadcast tools such as Hootsuite (hootsuite. com), Buffer (bufferapp.com), SocialOomph (socialoomph.com), TweetDeck (tweetdeck.com), or Social Flow (socialflow.com). This means that you only need to do the work of updating a single site, with all the others getting updated at the same time.

The second component of this management strategy would be to have all of your satellite sites (blog, Facebook, and so on) designed in such a way as to feed your social media viewers into your website (see Fig. 8.1). At a bare minimum, the email registration of each satellite site should feed into the same list as your main site.

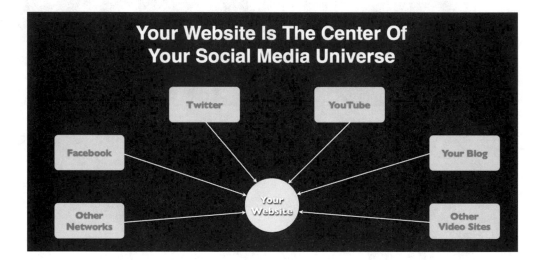

At some point social media management gets too complex for an artist to maintain, and third-party help is needed. This is usually a good thing, since it means you've progressed to a point where the job is so massive that you need specialized assistance. Furthermore, a company that specializes in social media management can keep you current with new tools and techniques that you might not be aware of. Even when outside help arrives, remember that you are still the one that drives the bus. Be sure to take part in all strategy discussions, but leave the actual facilitation to the company you've hired.

Social Media Management

Keep a single site as your main focal point.

Feed all your updates from your main site via RSS or social media broadcast apps.

Develop your satellite sites so they all feed visitors into your main site.

Email-list subscribers from all sites should go to same mailing list provider.

Get third-party help when you get overwhelmed.

Keep driving the bus!

Measuring Your Social Media Exposure

How many people have you reached with your message? How many could you have reached? In social media, there are some measurements about as reliable as a print magazine's circulation, but knowing your potential audience does have value because it represents your potential sales lead pool.

Unfortunately, as of the writing of this book, some of these metrics have to be accounted for manually, so you'll have to balance the level of effort to track the metrics versus the value you'll receive from them to determine their importance to your overall strategy.

A good example of where there can be unreliability in social measurement is when isolating unique users for each of your metrics. You want to avoid counting the same person twice in the list below, but realistically it's difficult to do.

These measurements highlight the number of people you've attracted to your brand through social media. To mitigate the potential for duplication of users, track growth rate as a percentage of the aggregate totals. This is where you will find the real diamonds.

- ▶ **Twitter:** Look at your number of followers and the number of followers for those who retweeted your message to determine the monthly potential reach. You should track these separately and then compare the month-over-month growth rate of each of these metrics so you can determine where you're seeing the most growth. A great free tool to use for Twitter measurement is TweetReach.
- ▶ **Facebook:** Track the total number of fans for your brand page. In addition, review the number of friends from those who became fans during a specified period of time or during a promotion and those who commented on or liked your posts to identify the potential monthly Facebook reach. Facebook Insights provides value here, as does Klout.
- ▶ **YouTube:** Measure the number of views for videos tied to a promotion or specific period of time, as well as the total number of channel subscribers. Check the number of comments and thumbs-ups.
- ▶ **Blog:** Measure the number of visitors who viewed the posts tied to a promotion for a specific period of time. Check the views over a period of time. If it's falling month over month, it's time to adjust either your posting habits or post content.
- ▶ **Email**: Take a look at how many people are on the distribution list and how many actually opened the email, then look at the number of people who actually took action (click-throughs, forwards, general responses).

SOCIAL MEDIA MEASUREMENT TOOLS

Measuring just how successful an artist's promotional campaign is (the artist's buzz) and all the data that surrounds an artist is a top priority in Music 4.0. Precise analytics were impossible in M1.0 and 1.5, somewhat available in M2.0, but now much more widely available and easier than ever to use since M3.0. With so many new avenues available for music discovery and promotion, knowing where the buzz is coming from and how to utilize it is more important than ever. .
Here are eight tools to help track your buzz:

Google Alerts (google.com/alerts)—sweeps the Web and delivers buzz to your inbox.

Mention (mention.net)—newer and more comprehensive than Google Alerts, Mention looks at all of social media and sends an email whenever you're mentioned.

Twitter Search (search.twitter.com)—track your buzz on this popular microblogging service.

Stat Counter (statcounter.com)—statistics about who visits your site and blog.

Tynt Tracer (tcr1.tynt.com)—traces images and text that have been copied off your site.

Next Big Sound (nextbigsound.com)—shows the number of new fans, plays, views, and comments.

Music Metric (musicmetric.com)—provides social network tracking, P2P network analysis, radio and sales data, and fan demographics.

Klout (klout.com)—measures your mentions, likes, comments, and followers to determine your reach and influence.

ADVANCED SOCIAL MEDIA ANALYTICAL TOOLS

As social media becomes more sophisticated, so do the measurement-tool requirements to determine both your impact and branding possibilities. Three updated methods of analyzing social media data are being used more and more by some of the more advanced (and expensive) measurement services.

▶ **Sentiment analysis** is a process that tries to determine the attitude of a speaker or a writer with respect to the topic he or she is writing about. If you actually read a blog or posting, you can tell the writer's sentiment immediately, but this analysis method tries to define and measure it as a point of data.

▶ **Cluster analysis** tries to analyze how certain words are gathering (or "clustering") relative to a search topic. It finds the words that are mostly likely to be associated with your search word, which may provide unexpected insight into what's being said about you and even predict sales before they happen.

▶ **Semantic analysis** is another measurement tool that strives to understand what words mean in context to one another. Once again, it's something that we do for ourselves as we read, but this tool puts a number to it.

All of these tools are trying to measure what we can immediately see for ourselves empirically by just wading into the social media pool. They put a number to something that we can feel.

New measurement platforms such as Sysomos and Radian6 (now a part of SalesForce Marketing Cloud) use these tools to provide a more precise look at how you or your brand integrates with the social world.

If you need data for a meeting, to sway an investor, or appease a boss, these tools are important. If you're a marketer on a very high level, you might find the data immediately useful. If you're a band or artist just trying to make the next sale, the next gig, or make it through the next day of social media management, you'll find them interesting as best and parlor tricks at worst. But while these tools may be cutting edge today, you never know if they'll be an essential part of your marketing toolbox tomorrow. Stay tuned.

The Importance of Measurement

Know where the buzz is coming from.

Know what's working and what's not.

Know who your fans are.

Know where your fans are from.

Know what your fans like.

What Is a Brand?

For an artist, a brand means a consistency of persona, and usually a consistency of sound. Regardless of what genre of music the artist delves into, the feel is the same, and you can tell it's the artist.

Madonna has changed directions many times during her career, but her brand remained consistent. Her persona remained the same even as she changed to and from the "material girl." The Beatles tried a wide variety of directions, but you never once questioned who you were listening to. It was always fresh and exciting, but distinctly them.

On the other hand, Neil Young almost killed his career with an electronic album called *Trans* that alienated all but his hardiest fans, and the well-respected Chris Cornell did enough harm to his long-term career thanks to an electronic album with Timbaland (*Scream*) that he returned to tour with Soundgarden. Why did this happen? For both artists, the album no longer "felt" like them. Both Young and Cornell built their careers on organic music played with a band, and as soon as their music became regimented and mechanical, they broke their brands. After *Trans*, Young returned to his roots and slowly built his brand back to superstar level, but it's too soon to know what will happen with Cornell.

How do you determine what your brand is? It's easier said than done.

In order for you as an artist to successfully promote your brand, you must have a great sense of self-knowing. You must know who you are, where you came from, and where you're going. You must know what you like and don't like, and what you stand for and why. And you must have an inherent feel for your sound and what works for you.

And that differentiates a superstar from a star, and a star from someone who wants it really badly but never seems to get that big break.

THE THREE PILLARS OF A BRAND

Every brand is built on at least one of the following three pillars. The stronger the brand, the more pillars are inherently used. These are:

▶ Familiarity: You can't have a brand unless your followers or potential followers are familiar enough with who you are. They don't even have to know what you sound like to be interested in you if you have a buzz and they've heard about you enough to want to check you out. Amanda Palmer, whom more people know for her social media savvy than her music, fits into this category.
▶ Likeability: Your followers have to like you or something about you. It could be your music, or it could be your attitude or your image.

You could even say how much you hate your fans and do everything to ridicule them, and that irreverent manner could be just the thing they like about you. It doesn't matter what it is, but there has to be something they like. Most artists fall into this category.

▶ Similarity: Your fans have to feel that either you represent them in a cause or movement (like a new genre of music) or that someday they can be you. Female Olympic athletes usually don't do well in this category because their sleek and muscular look is so far beyond what the ordinary girl or women can attain that they can't relate to them. On the other hand, young girls love Taylor Swift because they feel that she could be their best friend from next door.

If you have those three things, along with a product that consistently maintains its quality (your music), you've got a brand. Trying to intentionally manufacture your brand so it absolutely complies with these pillars usually doesn't work (people usually see right through that), but always keep in mind that this is how your audience views you, although none of them may even realize it.

I'M WITH THE BRAND

It seems that as a music star becomes more popular, so too does his or her desire to cash in on his or her fame through nonmusical business moves. This is so opposed to the spirit of what a popular musician used to be that it leaves those of us from that era more and more incredulous. Here are some examples of artists extending their brands into nonmusical ventures.

▶ Rap star Kanye West has his own Internet search engine (it's called *Search with Kanye West*).
▶ Aerosmith guitarist Joe Perry has his own line of hot sauce.
▶ The R&B singer Usher teamed up with Mastercard to launch a range of credit cards.
▶ Justin Bieber has, curiously for a guy, his own line of nail polish called One Less Lonely Girl, named after his hit song of the same name.
▶ Madonna opened 24-hour Hard Candy Fitness centers in Mexico City, Moscow, St. Petersberg, Sydney, and Santiago, which are the first of what she hopes will be a worldwide chain of "first class" gyms.

- ▶ Lady Gaga has released her own range of "Heartbeat" headphones.
- ▶ Beyoncé has her House of Dereon clothing range.
- ▶ Jay-Z has nonmusical business opportunities, including the clothing label Rocawear and the New York nightclub 40/40.
- ▶ 50 Cent, Eminem, and Diddy (Sean Combs) all have their own clothing ranges, while Diddy has also carved out an extra source of income for himself in promoting the vodka brand Cîroc.

Once again, celebrity can mean more to some people than being an artist, but the problem is that the brand soon becomes diluted. Do you know Diddy for his vodka or his music? Do you think of clothing or music when you think of Beyoncé? Many marketers might call this "brand extension," but when you lose touch with your core audience, product, or persona, you've diluted your brand.

SPONSORSHIP

Sponsorship is better thought of as "cobranding," since both the artist and the sponsor's brand image are tied together (a point many times overlooked by the artist). This can frequently put the artist at odds with his or her fan base, with cries of "sellout" in the air and on the blogs.

For that reason, sponsorship is another double-edged sword for the M4.0 artist. While it might be a source of tour support, the artist runs the risk of losing credibility with his or her fans. This credibility gap can come if the sponsor is a large, faceless conglomerate that's difficult to relate to or is at odds with the sensibilities of either the artist or, worse, the fan.

> For instance, if an artist is sponsored by a beer company but everyone in the band is in Alcoholics Anonymous, that can be a problem sponsorship. If sponsorship by a beer company goes with the band's hard-driving, partying image but goes against the mores of its fans, that too can be a problem. However, a biker band that's sponsored by the local Harley dealer, or by Harley Davidson itself, or by the biker bar they play at, could be an effective cobranding.
>
> —Larry Gerbrandt

Ultimately, an artist almost always risks his or her credibility in a sponsorship deal of any magnitude. Consider the risks carefully before entering into such a deal.

Branding

An artist's brand is consistency in persona and sound.

Many artists extend their brands beyond music. Sponsorship cobrands the artist with the sponsor.

Sponsorship runs the risk of losing fan credibility if at odds with the artist's image or fan sensibilities.

Any sponsorship must have perfect image symmetry between artist and brand to be successful.

Other Avenues for Social Media

Many music discovery sites such as Bandcamp, Nimbit, or ReverbNation help your marketing by allowing you to set up a widget with upcoming concert dates, press releases, photos, videos, and stores to buy your music. They also allow you to set up a virtual "street team," where your fans can go out and promote your music for you. Most of these promotional features are provided for paying members of the particular site, but many of the free promotion features are great for someone needing to promote music but who has little money.

Don't Depend on Your Social Network

· ·

It's too easy for today's artist who only dabbles in social networking to get complacent and comfortable with the abilities of a single social network, but that can spell disaster for maintaining your fan base if you're not careful. As those artists who formerly depended upon MySpace now know, what's hot today can become ice cold tomorrow. But other negative scenarios also exist that can be far worse than the network falling out of favor.

Scenario #1: Let's say that you've cultivated a huge following on Facebook. What would happen if Facebook was purchased by Google (a stretch for sure, but a good example), which decides that all it wants is the underlying technology of the network and shuts the rest down? If you didn't capture the email addresses of all your followers, you'd lose them to the nothingness of cyberspace. Don't laugh—something similar with another platform could happen.

Scenario #2: What would happen if Facebook (I'm picking on them because they're currently the big dog on the social block) changes its terms of service, and now charges you $0.25 for every fan past 100? If you've built an audience of 80,000 fans, it's going to cost you $20 grand to continue. They've already instituted something similar in that you now have to pay in order to reach the entirety of your followers (you can reach about 15 percent for free), which means you're now unable to access that large fan base that you've worked so hard to develop.

Scenario #3: This one actually did happen. In June of 2013 MySpace shut down its "classic" platform in order to migrate to a new one with a new feature set. The only thing that MySpace didn't do was inform its members that they were going to lose their entire MySpace following when that happened. Artists that had stayed loyal to the service woke up one day to find that all the fan data that they worked for years to collect was gone, and there was no way of getting it back.

That's why it's imperative that you harvest as many email addresses as you can for your own mailing list so you can keep your social communication under your control. If you rely on an external network, sooner or later you're going to get burnt. It's the nature of the Internet to constantly change, and it's too early to get a feel for the life span of even of the largest sites and networks. So play it safe—develop that mailing list.

THERE'S MORE TO SOCIAL NETWORKING THAN FACEBOOK

When it comes to social networking, the first network we think of is Facebook, closely followed by Twitter. But even though Facebook is still the social giant that dwarfs everything else, there are 28 other social networks worldwide that have at least 1 million daily views, according to Pingdom. Here they are:

1. Facebook: 600 M
2. Qzone: 45 M
3. Twitter: 35 M
4. Odnoklassniki: 17 M
5. Orkut: 11 M
6. Kontakte: 11 M
7. Mixi: 10 M
8. Badoo: 9 M
9. LinkedIn: 9 M
10. Sina Welbo: 8 M
11. Pinterest: 3.5 M
12. Renren: 3.1 M
13. Cyworld: 3.0 M
14. Flickr: 3.0 M
15. Tagged: 3.0 M
16. Nasza Klasa: 2.5 M
17. Douban: 2.0 M
18. MySpace: 2.0 M
19. Tuenti: 1.6 M
20. Hi5: 1.5 M
21. LiveJournal: 1.5 M
22. Hyves: 1.3 M
23. Netlog: 1.1 M
24. Taringa! 1.1 M
25. Kaixin001: 1.0 M
26. Yelp: 1.0 M

As you can see, there are plenty that aren't well known, mostly because they're popular in areas of the world other than North America, but that doesn't mean they're any less powerful in getting your message across. Ask your fans if there's another network that they visit often, and be prepared to jump in if the answer is yes.

Ten Low-Cost, Hi-Tech Promotion Ideas

Never leave promotion to someone else. You must always be actively involved on at least an oversight level to be sure that not only are you getting promoted, but the promotion is something that's beneficial to your image as an artist. This even includes having a publicist, since he or she takes the cues from you. Especially don't depend on a record label, particularly in these days when so few staff people do so many jobs. It's up to you to develop the strategy, or it might not get developed at all.

That being said, here are a number of low-cost M4.0 ideas that you can do to get your promotion started:

1. **Set up a Facebook page, then be sure to stay active.** It won't do you much good if you just set it up and never update it. The only way it's worth your fans visiting is if you keep the updates coming as often as possible.

2. **Every time a Friend request is exchanged between yourself and other Facebook users, send them a note back thanking them, and ask if you can include them in your group of friends outside of Facebook.** Ask them to "Please reply with your email address if that's okay." This is a great way to build your tribe, but make sure they can easily opt out if it's not their cup of tea. It's not too beneficial to have all those Facebook Friends if you can't contact them outside of those sites.

3. **Always have a "Press" section on your Website that contains the following:**

▶ High- and low-resolution color and black-and-white photos
▶ Logos
▶ Biographical information
▶ Quotes from the media
▶ Links to any interviews
▶ Links to music
▶ Links to videos
▶ Social media addresses and links to Facebook, your blog, ReverbNation, and so forth
▶ Scans of three or four of your best press clippings
▶ A press-release section
▶ A discography
▶ A list of upcoming gigs
▶ A fact sheet with bullet points about interesting artist facts
▶ Scans of a promo flyer and poster
▶ Web-ready graphics and banners
▶ Publicist, agent, label, or artist contact info

Having these tools easily available will increase the chances of getting media coverage. It's a fact that the easier you can make it for a blogger, writer, or editor, the more likely you'll get covered.

4. **Backlinks are important.** Anytime you're mentioned in a club listing, on the site of a band you're playing with, or anywhere else, make sure that it links back to your site. People won't do this automatically, so make it standard operating procedure to ask.

5. **Encourage fans to tag you** and your content on sites such as Flickr, blogs, Digg, and StumbleUpon, then make that data available on your site.

6. **Even though you may have a presence on Facebook, you still need a website.** It's still the best place to gather your tribe and communicate with them. Make sure that you follow the "Keys to a Successful Website" sidebar for creating the best website experience for your fans.

7. **Engage your fans.** Ask them questions. Polls and surveys are free (that magic word again) and easy to set up with sites such as PollDaddy and Surveymonkey.

8. **Develop a press-release mailing list of music writers and editors** from all local and regional newspapers, magazines, specialty papers, radio stations, online radio stations, and music blogs (especially) that cover the type of music that you play (you can do national and international later, when you grow into it). Remember that it doesn't do you much good to send something to a blog or magazine that specializes in metal if you're a folk singer, so don't even think about anything out of your genre. Once your list is complete, send out a short email for any major gig, event, or song release, but don't make it too frequent or you won't be covered—ever. Include links to your website and an offer for a free press pass to a show. About once a month is a good frequency. If you get a mention, be sure to send an email or even a handwritten note to say thank you.

9. **Create your own YouTube channel.** Make sure to post new videos frequently, and encourage fans to post as well.

10. **Create a special insider email list** for a few fans, key media, tastemakers, and bloggers for sending preannouncements to those people who love to know things first . . . and like to tell others.

Keys to a Successful Website

Make sure your band's name is in every one of the following: the URL, title, website description, and first paragraph of text.

Keep your keywords to a maximum of five, and be sure that they relate to the content on the page.

Eliminate all Flash animation. It may look great, but search engines can't read it, and it's pretty dated. You want fans to find you, right?

Make sure there's an easy way for people to give you their email addresses. Make sure they know what to expect from signing up.

Keep your content relevant to your keywords. Don't use Katy Perry as a keyword unless you actually have something about Katy Perry in the body text of your page; otherwise Google might penalize you.

A blog tied to your site is a great way for easy updates and a great way for your fans to interact.

Keep the copy of each page to between 150 and 500 words.

Make sure there are no page errors (broken links). It frustrates your visitors and you'll get penalized by Google as well.

But You Still Must Hit the Streets

The Internet provides ways to interact with fans that were unthinkable even back in the M2.0 days, but they're still no substitute for the hard work that goes with being a musician. If you want to succeed, you've got to build and maintain your audience over a period of years, and for that you've still got to hit the streets. This means that you've got to play live, you have to be ready to promote traditionally as well as online, and you still have to sell yourself, your music, and your merchandise one fan at a time. Getting reviews and doing press and interviews will never go away.

All the attributes of M4.0 must be seen as an adjunct to the traditional work that is the business part of the music business. Sure, it's quite powerful and more necessary than ever, but so far, no one has made it as a result of M4.0 only. It's possible to have great visibility, a lot of "friends," and downloads, and still not have anything other than a brief career (remember the turntable hits we spoke of before?) So even as traditional street-marketing decreases in importance, it's still vital for long-term success.

TEN LOW-COST, LOW-TECH PROMOTION IDEAS

Promotion doesn't have to cost money to be effective. Here are some ideas that can be powerful tools that don't even involve a computer.

1. **Don't underestimate the value of something free.** Fans love free items, either as part of a package (for example, buy a CD, and get a T-shirt free), part of a contest, or just being one of the first ten fans to email. Sometimes items of seemingly little value have a wide appeal. Backstage passes, seat upgrades, seats on stage, tickets to the sound check, invites to a meet and greet, and downloads of live songs are all prized by a real fan.

2. It's surprising that this isn't done more since it works so well: **Park a van or truck that has a banner on it across from a show by a similar act.** Every fan entering or exiting the venue will be aware of you.

3. **Free or low-cost entry to show "after parties" extends the show experience and rewards the true fan.** These can be promoted along with the show, and even offered as a part of the ticket package.

4. **Instead of sending a "thank you" email to a promoter, writer, interviewer, or just someone who's done you a good turn, send a handwritten thank-you note by snail mail.** You'll be shocked how well this works. It's unusual, it's sincere, and it's remembered. It's

also very likely to be seen, since we're all getting fewer and fewer snail-mail items these days.

5. **Consider asking your fans to help you with promo.** Ask them to put up flyers or send out emails. Put a PDF of a poster or flyer online for fans to download.

6. Fans always want a chance to meet the musicians. **Consider having a "meet and greet" after every show**. But make sure that the fans know about it in advance.

7. **Find your niche and market to it.** It makes no sense to market to Adele's fans if your music isn't like hers, so don't waste your energy marketing in that direction.

8. **Make everything you do an event.** What holiday is coming up? Is it a band member's birthday? Is an anniversary near? Try a tribute to "Fans that just got laid off" or "Fans that just got hired."

9. **Use the power of your niche to widen your fan base.** Flyer someone else's show in a related genre. Sponsor somebody else's event. Consider trading sponsorships and gigs with another band.

10. **Align yourself with a cause you believe in.** Causes often have a large PR mechanism behind them that can expose your music, but it has to be something you really believe in or it may hurt you in the long run.

Hit the Streets

Traditional marketing can be as important as viral.

Sell yourself one fan and one gig at a time.

Provide your fans with the means to support you.

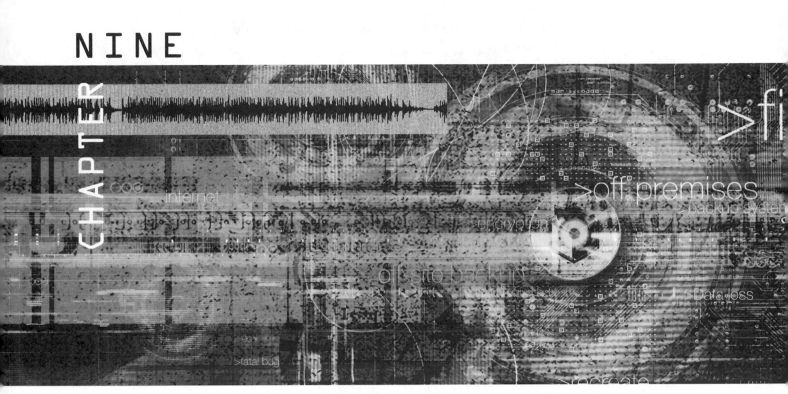

NINE

CHAPTER

The New
Distribution

For the musician, distribution has never been easier or more diverse as in the M4.0 world. There are now numerous ways in multiple areas to get product into the hands of the consumer, but these additional choices also require a new distribution strategy.

In the time prior to M2.5 (before iTunes), distribution was strictly a retail process in which the customer purchased directly from a brick-and-mortar retail store (yes, there were things like record clubs and, later, online CD retailers such as Amazon, but the bulk of the sales were made through retail stores). Starting in M3.0, however, the artist was presented with new possibilities that went beyond the traditional brick-and-mortar retail. These include online digital distribution sites such as iTunes and Amazon MP3, digital, and CD sales made directly to the customer online, and a hybrid of the above, such as CD Baby or Tunecore. Today those distribution possibilities are expanded with online streaming services such as Pandora, Spotify, and iTunes Radio. Let's take a look at some of the current available options, as well as a new way to think about distribution.

Digital, Vinyl, or Bright, Shiny Disc?

In the recent past, there have always been multiple containers (a *container* is the way the music is packaged for distribution) of music that an artist had available for sale. First there were vinyl singles and vinyl albums, then vinyl albums and cassettes, then CDs and cassettes, then digital downloads and CDs. With the recent resurgence of vinyl, an artist has three container options for distribution of his or her work. Let's take a look at the pros and cons of each.

MUSIC FORMAT PROS AND CONS FROM THE ARTIST'S STANDPOINT

Music Container	Pros	Cons
Digital Download	No container manufacturing cost Minimal distribution cost No costs for graphics/liner notes High promotional value Large market Fast release to the marketplace	No collectible value No resale value High rate of piracy Intangible worth Difficult to get reviewed Difficult to get traditional airplay Sales beginning to level off Vulnerable to obsolescence as digital formats evolve
Digital Streaming	No container manufacturing cost Minimal distribution cost No costs for graphics/liner notes High promotional value Large and growing market Fast release to the marketplace No piracy	No collectible value No resale value Intangible worth Difficult to get reviewed Difficult to get traditional airplay Low royalty rates

CD	Tangible worth Potential revenue stream Collectible value Opportunity for added value More likely to get reviewed	Cost of container manufacturing Cost of container distribution Decreasing market size Limited sales outlets Slow into the marketplace due to manufacturing time Difficulty getting paid from distributors
Vinyl	Tangible worth Potential revenue stream Collectible value Opportunity for added value	Cost of container manufacturing Cost of container distribution Hidden costs such as breakage Small market size Limited sales outlets Unlikely to get reviewed Slow into the marketplace due to manufacturing Difficulty getting paid from distributors

As you can see from the chart above, each of the current music containers has an assortment of pros and cons. This is not to say that one container is better than another in our current music world, but it helps to be aware of the benefits and disadvantages of each.

DIGITAL DOWNLOADS

A digital container has no manufacturing costs, so there are few additional expenses after the initial production of the music. Since there is no physical container, there's no need for disc and album artwork or liner notes, so there is no additional expense or time required for manufacturing other than typing in the metadata.

Both downloadable and streaming music makes it easy for numerous services to distribute an artist's digital song for anywhere from a nominal charge (either a yearly or a submission fee, all well under $100) to being free. And it's relatively fast to distribute a digital container, making it instantly available on your website (although it may take two to six weeks to go live for some online distributors such as iTunes). If you want to use a digital song (or songs) as a promotional track, again the cost is minimal, since there are no manufacturing costs to recoup. Finally, the market for digital music is huge and it's growing, a claim that cannot be made about the other containers.

While the digital download was the container of choice in the first era of digital music, it has some downsides to be aware of. The fact that any attempt to monetize digital downloads is hampered by the ease of piracy has been discussed ad infinitum, so I won't go beyond simply making it a bullet point. Much of that problem is actually being alleviated as digital streaming takes hold.

Perhaps a larger issue is that digital's worth is intangible; it's not something that you can physically hold in your hand. This fact has given a whole generation of consumers the notion that music is free, which is difficult to overcome. Indeed, a digital song has no collectible value. It won't be traded or prized, and you can't resell it, which is why the perception remains that it should be free.

Another serious consideration is that digital download formats such as MP3 and AAC are subject to obsolescence as both new formats are introduced and evolve and the world's taste changes to streaming. While today that doesn't seem to be much of an issue in the consumer world, it's become a serious problem in the professional audio world, with early digital masters becoming unplayable as many older formats become obsolete. Digital file-compression formats such as MP3 and AAC were initially used for distribution because bandwidth was both expensive and in short supply. With bandwidth no longer an issue when it comes to music, we're already seeing that files are getting larger because listeners are demanding higher quality. As a result, bit rates of downloads have gradually increased from a norm of 128 kbps when the formats where first introduced to one of 320 kbps and higher. Lossless formats such as FLAC and AAC+ have also gained momentum, which can mean that releases done in the current MP3 format and bit rate will have to eventually be rereleased in a lossless, higher-bit-rate format. In fact, there may soon come a day when bandwidth is high enough that the music doesn't have to be compressed at all, maintaining its original 44.1k or 48kHz (or higher) AIFF or WAV format used during production (musicians, engineers, and producers everywhere will rejoice).

To a degree, that trend has already begun, with sites such as HDTracks.com, acousticsounds.com, iTrax.com, and many more now offering full high-resolution (96kHz/24 bit and above) PCM, FLAC, and DSD files for download. Artist Neil Young is moving forward with his Pono hi-res music service, and iTunes has also stepped up its high-res game by quietly launching its Mastered for iTunes (affectionately known as MFIT by record labels) program, which accepts up to 96kHz/24-bit AIF or WAV files (any file that's 24 bit is technically considered high resolution) master song files. As with standard-resolution files, iTunes does all the encoding to AAC, but the result is a better-sounding digital file, thanks to starting the process using a higher-resolution master. In order to better facilitate the MFIT program, Apple has released a suite of tools for the mixing and mastering engineer to be sure that the file being submitted to iTunes is the highest quality, and to check the encode with a virtual "test pressing" before the song goes live. Go to apple.com/itunes/mastered-for-itunes/ to download the MFIT tools.

Finally and most overlooked, it's still difficult to get digital files reviewed by traditional or even some online reviewers, or to get airplay from a traditional over-the-air broadcaster. At the time of this writing, you still are just not considered legit in the eyes of reviewers unless you present them with a CD.

DIGITAL STREAMING

As stated earlier, the basic premise of Music 4.0 is that streaming becomes the dominant music distribution method as consumers discover that being able to listen to a library of millions of songs anytime and anywhere is much more cost effective than buying it. After all, why pay $10.00 a month to own only ten songs when for the same amount of money (or less) you get an enormously wider selection to choose from, not to mention saving all that storage space on your computer or phone.

Even though streaming is just gaining traction, it's actually been with us almost since the beginning of digital music. Rhapsody can claim the tag of the original streaming service, beginning in December of 2001, actually predating the introduction of iTunes by 18 months. While many other services have come along since then (most notably Pandora), it wasn't until Spotify was introduced to the United States that paid streaming music began to take off, mostly because of its integration with Facebook. The service was already a success in Europe, having begun in Sweden, where it grew to become the predominant distribution method, nearly obliterating the download market. As of the writing of this book, Spotify now boasts 24 million users and 6 million subscribers (they use a freemium model) and is available in 55 countries.

There are more than 30 other subscription services in the world, with Deezer, MelOn, Wimp, Rdio, Sony Music, and Slacker among the most prominent. With iTunes Radio, Google Play, and Beats Music among others entering the streaming arena, there's more competition than ever, but with that also comes the possibility for more growth.

It's now estimated that there are 29 million paying subscribers worldwide according to ABI Research, which now brings in about $1.1 billion a year. That figure is expected to rise to 191 million subscribers bringing in cumulative revenues of $46 billion by 2018 (according to a study by ABI), a figure that could indeed lead to a rejuvenated music industry should it come to pass.

One of the problems for all music services is the cost of the content, as payouts to writers, performers, publishers, and record labels accounts for between 60 and 90 percent of their income, not to mention the large advances paid out to the record labels for the rights to use their songs. This has led to many services appealing for a decrease in royalty rates, only to be met by strong opposition from artists and labels, who feel that the rate is not high enough as is. While this might be an issue today, should subscriber and revenues increase as predicted, these royalty-rate issues may well be a thing of the past. Streaming services and their payouts will be looked at more closely in Chapter 11.

CD–THE BRIGHT AND SHINY DISC

Getting reviews isn't the only reason to consider having CDs in your distribution strategy, since there are still clear advantages for replicating them, even in M4.0. Even though CD sales have fallen off the cliff (CD sales are less than 78 percent of what they were in 2000, and they're declining steadily), they will remain a viable music container for at least a few years to come. Indeed, some music lovers still prefer buying a CD to any other format.

CDs are still viewed as an item of tangible worth by buyers because of their physical nature and the fact that they include graphics and liner notes. For many, there is an added collectible value if the CD is numbered or in short supply, and there is the ability to add value to the unit by including in the packaging something additional such as show tickets or any number of premium items (see the section called "The Wisdom of Trent" in chapter 4). All this adds up to a clear revenue stream for the artist that can surpass anything that a digital download can provide. Of course, that's assuming your music is something the fan wants to buy in the first place, but we're assuming a bare minimum of popularity of the artist throughout this book.

> *We may never get to the point where we don't want to press physical product. In fact, I'm a believer that physical product acts like a souvenir of the band. If bands think of a CD that way and package it as such, they might find some increased success with it.*
>
> —Bruce Houghton

Even with costs ranging as low as $0.60 for a basic CD package (in large quantities, of course), manufacturing still represents a substantial up-front cost that the artist must bear, which is a clear disadvantage. Add the costs of graphic design for the disc artwork and jewel-case trays, with the time the design, manufacturing, and shipping takes before the product gets to market (two weeks minimum but likely much more), along with the difficulty one can have getting paid by distributors, CDs soon become a music container that many artists prefer not to deal with.

THE VINYL RECORD

After the CD was unleashed on the public in 1982, it seemed as though the vinyl disc would soon be headed the way of the horse and carriage, but it never totally went away, and has had a revival of sorts in recent years. In fact, the remaining vinyl mastering houses and pressing plants are busier than ever, running 24/7 pumping out product. And vinyl sales continue to increase, with sales up more than 28 percent over the previous year (2012).

Why has vinyl realized a resurgence despite the recent technological breakthroughs? Many claim that the audio quality is still superior to CDs (although that greatly depends upon the stylus and turntable involved), in spite of the fact that a vinyl record loses fidelity with every play. Others still love the cardboard album covers for their artwork and easily readable liner notes. Vinyl has a substantial collectible value and can be priced as such, giving the artist an additional revenue stream. In fact, a record is often an integral piece of the premium package offered by an artist.

But pressing a record does have its downsides as well. Aside from the obvious graphic design and manufacturing costs and the manufacturing delay to market, there's the additional issue of breakage, or the fact that some records break or warp during shipping. Breakage was normally calculated at 10 percent and deducted off the top of the gross income in a typical recording contract during M1.0. While breakage might have been that high at the time (which is debatable), the actual amount is closer to 2 percent and must be accounted for when budgeting. And finally, a record-only strategy is probably a loser today because the market is so small to begin with and because of the unlikelihood of the record getting reviewed due to the fact that most reviewers don't own a turntable (which are difficult to even buy these days).

Music Containers

Digital downloads are convenient but easy to pirate and have little aftermarket value.

Digital streaming has vastly decreased pirating.

Digital streaming subscription is predicted to quickly grow.

But the content costs for streaming services are enormous.

Digital has the cheapest distribution.

Many buyers still only buy CDs.

Vinyl is undergoing a resurgence in popularity.

Vinyl is subject to breakage during transit.

Collectibles

We've spoken about the CD and the vinyl record as being collectibles, but just what does that mean? A collectible is an item (usually a nonessential one) that has particular value to its owner because of its rarity and desirability. Antiques, paintings, and coins are collectibles because of their rarity, which makes them highly desirable. Do you see the conundrum with a digital song? Because a digital song is so easily transportable and transferable, there's no rarity involved. And it isn't something that you can display, show your friends, or resell, so there's virtually no collectability factor either.

Vinyl records and CDs, on the other hand, are collectible in their very basic form. In a premium package consisting of CDs, vinyl, downloads, DVDs, and so on, everything but the digital download becomes a collectible, especially if it's signed by the artist. With the market for CDs rapidly diminishing, the discs may eventually become as rare as vinyl. With added value content such as concept graphics and liner notes, they become still retain a must-have to true fans.

There are certain music genres (country and metal, for instance) in which fans still prefer CDs to digital downloads. While this might be caused by fans either lagging behind in terms of technical sophistication or being part of an older demographic, it might also be an indication that the fans of these genres have a greater affinity for collectibles, which should not be underestimated.

> ## Collectibles
>
> The rarer it is, the more valuable it becomes.
>
> CDs or vinyl can be collectible.
>
> Digital music is not collectible because it's not a physical product.

Digital Music Distribution

. . . .

Digital distribution is, of course, the backbone of M3.0, whether it's paid or for free, and there seem to be more and more options every day. Since most of these services rise and fall in popularity weekly, I'll mention only the largest and most stable, and how as a genre they might contribute to an artist's success.

PAID DOWNLOADS

While the number of digital downloads is still increasing every year, they have leveled off as streaming has caught on. Paid downloads (meaning a downloadable song that you buy and own) is still a primary revenue stream for an artist in M4.0, as just slightly under 1.65 billion digital downloads were purchased in the United States in 2012 according to Nielsen SoundScan, a sales-tracking system that tracks sales of music and music video products throughout the United States and Canada. What's more, 44 million Americans purchased either a track or album that year as well, despite the rapid growth of streaming options.

Although the payment to an artist for a download varies from site to site, the average is around $.091 per song downloaded (about the same as a mechanical publishing royalty), and $.915 per full-album download when a record label is involved (with a 15 percent royalty rate). This rate grows to around $.70 per downloaded track and $7.00 if an artist or band deals directly with the distributor, before publishing and distributor costs are subtracted. Sometimes it pays to do things yourself.

ITUNES

If ever there were a leviathan in the entertainment room of the music industry, it's the Apple iTunes store. Thanks to Apple iPods, iPhones, and iPads dominating 71 percent of the digital-music-player market share, iTunes holds a commanding 63 percent of the digital marketplace. From its ambitious start in 2003, iTunes has gradually risen to become the largest music retailer in the United States, eventually even topping retail giant Walmart (according to the NPD research group). And even though newcomer Amazon MP3 has garnered its share of users, NPD also states that most of them are new digital users, with most of them never having used iTunes before.

Until April of 2009, all iTunes songs had the same price: $0.99. After much prodding by the major record labels, Apple expanded its offerings and went to a multitiered pricing system, with a limited number of songs available at as low a price as $0.69, and as high as $1.29. Most of iTunes's more than 28 million available songs still remain priced at $0.99. To date more than 25 billion songs have been downloaded from iTunes worldwide.

iTunes has recently introduced iTunes Radio, which uses the freemium model where the service is free with ads, or $24.99 to eliminate the ads plus include iTunes Match, a feature where all of your purchased music can be stored on Apple's cloud and later accessed from any playback device that you authorize.

iTunes is also the largest music distributor, having a presence in 119 countries and 545 million users (over 300 million on mobile), all with credit cards on file.

OTHER DIGITAL DISTRIBUTORS

Although iTunes is the largest digital distributor, there are numerous other choices available. Here are just a few of the online stores that offer paid downloads (limited to services that have a catalog of 1 million or more songs):

► Amazon MP3
► 7Digital
► eMusic
► Zune Marketplace
► Legal Sounds
► Google Play Music
► FairShare Music (UK only)
► iMesh (including 15 million free songs)

AMAZON MP3

Although second to iTunes in market share, Amazon MP3 has made only a small dent in iTunes's dominance, having only risen to 23 percent of the market (compared to iTunes's 63 percent) in 2013, according to the NPD Group. Digital music executives at record labels say the disparity between the two may be even greater, with

Amazon commanding just 6 to 10 percent of the market in any given week, and Apple closer to 90 percent.

But what Amazon MP3 does have going for it is pricing, with a "daily deal" album at $3.99, a monthly promotion of 100 albums priced at $5.00 each, and most of the rest of the more than 14 million song catalog typically at $8. The price levels are broken down like this:

▶ **Front Line:** The highest retail price in the store (good for new releases)

▶ **Midline:** Slightly lower than front line (good for new releases and other current releases)

▶ **Catalog:** Slightly lower than midline (good for older or lower-selling releases)

▶ **Special:** The lowest retail price in the store (good for promotions, old releases, and low-selling catalog songs)

Like iTunes, Amazon MP3 sells digital songs and albums via different stores, depending upon the territory, and also does not use DRM (Digital Rights Management) on music they sell. All music is sold as unprotected MP3s.

SUBSCRIPTION IS THE NEW DOWNLOAD

Music subscription has been talked about to death, but the bottom line is still true—consumers now see the value in subscription music, and their interest will only grow. There's both a lot of hope and a lot of record-label resistance to subscription music. On the one hand, everyone likes the idea of a steady monthly income that subscription might bring. On the other hand, how that money gets split up has labels, publishers, and artists all wringing their hands in simultaneous anxious hope and fear.

But consumers are seeing the value of not condemning 20-plus gigs of hard-drive real estate to a library that provides you no discovery options, and where you only listen to a few hundred songs anyway. An all-you-can-listen-to, anytime, anywhere option that subscription promises is beginning to make more and more sense to more and more people. The "access model" means more variety for less money from a consumer standpoint, but it also means smaller revenue increments for the artist, songwriter, label, and publisher.

While it's nice to have your music so widely distributed and available, the big negative for most artists and songwriters is the paltry payout seen from streaming services. What's more, the rate paid varies, depending upon the type of services (on-demand or radiolike), how the income is derived (paid subscription or ad based), and how long the consumer listens to the song (see Chapter 11 for more details).

The major labels have extracted large upfront advances from every streaming service for the license to use their songs. The problem is that creative accounting has caused most of that money to fall to the bottom line of the companies, with pennies on the dollar forwarded to their artists. Many artists remain suspicious of how this money will be distributed in the future, but as streaming becomes a higher ratio of an artist's revenue, you can be sure that sharp attorneys and managers will make sure that recording agreements provide for a fairer distribution.

SUBSCRIPTION SERVICES

With a subscription, you pay a set monthly fee to be able to listen to as much music as you want during that time without limitation. The music is usually streamed, so you don't actually own it, but since it's available at any time, there's really no need to keep it on your computer, phone, or mobile device anyway. There are some subscription services in which the music you choose is downloaded and stored on your playback device, but if you discontinue the service or are late paying, the files will no longer play. In many ways, it's as though your fans joined a service that lets them rent your music. As soon as they stop paying their monthly rental fee, they no longer have access to listen to your music. Every time that more than 30 seconds of your music is listened to, you get paid a fee called a streaming pay rate.

Other services use a "freemium" model that lets you listen for free in exchange for playing commercials at designed intervals. Still another freemium model caps the free listening at a certain number of hours per month. Upgrading to the paid tier eliminates the ads or lifts the hour cap.

There are typically two types of streams: tethered and nontethered.

▶ A tethered stream means the media player must be connected (or "tethered") to the Internet at all times in order to listen to the music.

▶ A nontethered stream means the media player needs to be connected to the Internet only once a month for the service to confirm that the user has paid his or her monthly subscription fee. After one month, if the person either stops paying the fee or doesn't connect the device to the Internet to verify that he or she has paid, the songs will stop playing on his or her computer or portable player.

The more widely known subscription services include:

▶ Spotify
▶ Pandora
▶ Slacker
▶ Deezer
▶ iTunes Radio
▶ Google Play All Access
▶ Rhapsody
▶ Grooveshark
▶ Rdio
▶ rara
▶ Sony Music Unlimited
▶ X Box Music

Many brilliant business minds both within and outside of the music industry have predicted that all online music business will eventually move to the subscription model. Perhaps that's because a widespread acceptance of subscription services is wishful thinking on the part of the major record labels, as it might solve many of their current problems, thanks to a more predictable monthly income. That's a nice thought, but the vast majority of music consumers must subscribe in order to make up for the lost download income. Most artists signed to a record label are also not convinced that subscription is the way to go. That's because it's likely that the label will get the majority of the income, as many of the royalty splits haven't been worked out yet, and the advances that the services pay to the major labels tend to go to their bottoms lines instead of to their artists.

THE DIGITAL STORAGE LOCKER (CLOUD MUSIC)

Digital storage lockers work on the principle that instead of storing all of your music on one desktop, laptop, phone, or tablet, you probably want the same music available on all of those devices. A big pain is having to copy and transfer all of your music files over to each one, and in many cases, you just won't have the storage space to do so anyway. A cloud music locker such as Amazon's Cloud Player, Google's Play Music, or Apple's iTunes Match allows you to store all of your music on their online servers ("The Cloud"), which you can then access from any of your playback devices, such as your phone, MP3 player, or iPod. This saves you the time it takes to transfer your files to each device, as well as any storage space that might be required.

What's important to an artist is that the user pays for the privilege of using these services. Whether artists signed to record labels will see much of that remains to be seen, since the language of current and past contracts may not cover this technology, but indie artists could see an immediate new revenue stream, however small.

The bottom line is that if music consumers get used to streaming their music from the cloud as predicted, it can become another revenue stream for the artist.

> ## Digital Distribution
>
> Paid download means the customer owns the music.
>
> The Access Model means the customer rents but has access to the service's entire catalog anytime.
>
> Subscription is the new download.
>
> The digital storage locker allows streaming of your own music to any device that you own.

Music Aggregators

There are so many digital music sites that it's become a lot of work to submit a release to all of them, and for that reason, a number of submission services have been created to save you not only the hassle of submission. In addition, the companies will collect the royalties from the various services and forward them to you.

In exchange for these services, the companies (Tunecore, ReverbNation, and CD Baby are the most popular) usually charge either a small initial fee or take a small percentage of the royalties. These companies can also provide bar codes and ISRC codes that identify the song, the album, and the CD that makes it easy for the CD to be digitally tracked. Oneload is a similar service for music videos.

> ### Music Aggregators
>
> Save the hassle of individual submission.
>
> Submit to different digital distributors.
>
> Submit in different formats and bandwidths.
>
> Collect the money from digital distributors.
>
> Take a flat fee or percentage of sales.

License or Distribution?

If you're not involved with a record label, this doesn't apply to you, but if you are, listen up. A recent ruling as to whether a digital download is subject to a license fee or a distribution royalty could eventually mean a lot more money in your pocket from digital download sales.

Traditionally, a license agreement meant that you gave a company the right to make copies and sell your product (this could mean music or merchandise). A distribution deal, on the other hand, gives a company the right to resell the product that you make and sell to them.

This was pretty cut and dried in M1.0 through 2.0, when physical product was the normal sales container. If a distributor sold records or CDs that the record company made, then it was a distribution deal. If the record company gave a copy of the master to a distributor so that the distributor could make the records or CDs themselves, it was a license deal. In today's music world where digital products are the norm, the line between distribution and license deal becomes blurry.

In a test case, rapper Eminem's FBT Productions sued his record label, Universal Music Group (UMG), over what amounted to the definition of ownership of a digital file. FBT claimed that UMG owed the company more money because a digital file sold by either iTunes or Amazon MP3 is actually a license. UMG insisted that regardless of whether it's a CD, a vinyl record, or a digital file, Eminem's music is part of UMG's distribution deal. So the question became, "Is this licensing or is it distribution?"

FBT claimed that since there were no manufacturing or packaging costs (which are covered by the record label), and only a single copy was delivered to the digital download companies, then it should be considered a license, because that's what occurs with other licensing deals. UMG argued that a sale is a sale regardless of how it happens, and that it was therefore a distribution deal, and the terms of the recording agreement should still apply.

A lot of money was at stake here. If the court decided that selling a digital file on iTunes amounted to a licensing deal, then the record label and the artist would split the proceeds 50/50 and the artist would be entitled to about $0.30 per download. But if the court decided it amounted to distribution, then the original recording agreement would be in force, and the artist would make about 15 percent, or about $0.10 on every download instead.

In a very closely watched case, the court initially ruled in favor of UMG, but FBT appealed and had the ruling overturned. Then UMG essentially appealed the appeal and took the case to the US Supreme Court for a ruling. The Supremes refused to hear the case though, and sent it back to the 9th Circuit Court of Appeals to determine the damages, which ruled in favor of FBT. While this reportedly meant as much as $30 million payout to FBT, the irony is that Eminem declined to be part of the lawsuit so as not to make waves with UMG, so he might not see an extra dime.

As predicted, more classic artists have been coming forward to sue their labels, such as the estate of Rick James, Rob Zombie, White Zombie, Whitesnake, and Dave Mason suing Universal; Michael McDonald, The Doobie Brothers, The Cars, Kenny Rogers and Peter Frampton suing Warner Bros; and Chuck D suing Sony, among others.

Although this ruling can change the music industry in that it means major labels could be in serious trouble if big payouts are necessary, the reality is that some artists are afraid to engage in a battle with their labels, especially if they depend upon royalties from their catalogs. There's enough accounting shenanigans that go on with labels already, and many artists are wary about giving them an excuse for more.

That said, you won't see a suit by an artist signed after about 2003, since the labels put language in all their contracts from that time on that clearly specifies that a digital download is equivalent to a sale.

License or Distribution

Distribution deal: the distributor sells a product.

License deal: the distributor manufacturers and sells a copy of the product from your master.

Paid downloads are ruled to be a license, but this may not apply to artists with recent contracts.

Games—Hip or Hype?

For a while music games such as Guitar Hero and Rock Band were hot, and mostly legacy artists made a fair amount of money if their songs were used. With that fad basically dead, another opportunity has emerged for the M3.0 artist instead.

With much of the game business turning to online rather than console games, there's more need for music than ever before. The difference is that the soundtrack to a game no longer has to be baked into the code, and can in fact be dynamic. That means it can easily change or even be selectable by the player, which means that the game now becomes more of a distribution platform for a new artist. The gamer is given a number of selections to choose from, and can even purchase music by his or her favorite artist to be used as the soundtrack. The opportunity for the artist is that he or she can now collect a royalty based on sales rather than a one-time licensing fee as with console games.

If this model is adopted, gaming may soon turn into a significant source of income for many artists, with more opportunity for new artists than ever before.

Games

Music games will live on, but they don't enjoy the same popularity as before.

Console games pay a license fee for music.

Online games can pay a royalty based on sales.

Games may become a new music distribution platform.

The New Brick-and-Mortar

It's been noted in the press and various industry blogs (including my own, which is at music3point0.blogspot.com) that sales of as few as 40,000 units can now get you a No. 1 position on the *Billboard* charts. In M1.0 to 2.0, a No. 1 slot on the album charts would've had at least an additional zero on the end. So why are CD sales so bad today? As stated in Chapter 2, contraction and the death of the major record retail chains, along with the demise of half of the independent music stores, have left a gap in music retail. An enterprising individual or company could take advantage of this gap, but the chances are slim that would happen in the current economy.

That being said, there's still a network of about 2,500 independent retail music stores to service a release. Companies like CD Baby (through Alliance Distribution) make independent CDs available to most of the remaining brick-and-mortar retail stores and distributors, as well as provide additional mastering, packaging, and graphics services, and bar and ISRC codes.

The Many Ways to Ask for the Sale

It's one thing if you're selling through one of the many online distributors, since their prices are set, as are their sales methods. It's another thing entirely if you're trying to sell your music on your website. There, the way you ask for the sale directly affects how many sales you'll actually make.

Amp Music Marketing ran a study regarding "call to action" buy buttons where they decided to test a number of buttons to see which was most effective when it came to selling music. The choices were:

"Get The Music"
"Download The Music"
"Buy The Music"

It turns out that the most effective was the most direct "Buy The Music" (album, CD, etc.), while "Get The Music" was the least. It seems that consumers relate "Get The Music" to a bait and switch in which they're lured into clicking, only to find that there's something additionally asked of them.

When it comes to sales, sometimes the very best technique is the most direct. Ask plainly for the sale. If your fan or customer really wants to buy from you, you're doing him or her a favor by making the process streamlined and easy. If your fan or customer is unsure, you're not helping the cause by being ambiguous.

And another thing. Keep the choices to a maximum of three (two works best). If given too many choices, the customer is likely to throw his or her hands up in the air in frustration and not buy anything!

TEN SALES TIPS

Here are ten sales tips to always keep in mind:

1. **Ask for the purchase.** Never forget that even though you're selling yourself, you're still in sales.

2. **Sell a package.** With a ticket you get a CD, with a CD you get a T-shirt, with a T-shirt you get a ticket. The idea is to make each purchase something with added value.

3. **Sell merchandise at as an affordable price as possible.** Until you're a star, you should be more concerned about visibility and branding than revenue. If you want to spread the word, price it cheaper.

4. **There are other things to sell besides CDs and T-shirts.** Hats, a song book, a tour picture book, beach towels—get creative, but choose well. Too many choices may actually reduce sales as a result of buyer confusion. You can now sell a variety of branded merchandise with no up-front costs using CafePress.com or Zazzle.com.

5. **Begin promoting as soon as possible.** That allows time for the viral buzz (a.k.a. free promotion) to build and ensures that you'll get a larger share of your fan's discretionary spending.

6. **Capture the name, email address, and zip code** from anyone who makes a purchase, particularly ticket buyers.

7. **Always give your customers more than they expect.** By giving them something for free that they did not expect, you keep them coming back for more.

8. **Give it away and sell it at the same time.** In the M1.0 to 2.5 days, you used to give away a free track to sell other merchandise such as the album. Now if you give away a track, that track will help you to sell more.

9. **The best items to sell are the ones that are the scarcest.** Autographed items, special boxed sets, limited-edition vinyl that's numbered—all these items are more valuable because of their scarcity. If the items are abundant, price them cheaper. If the items are scarce, don't be afraid to price them higher.

10. **Sell your brand.** You, the artist, are your own brand. Remember that everything you do sells that brand, even if it doesn't result in a sale. Just the fact that people are paying attention can result in a sale and more revenue down the road.

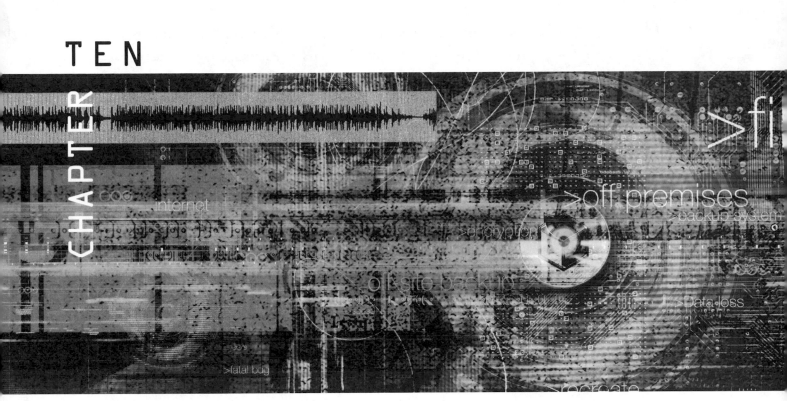

T E N

CHAPTER

The Music 4.0
Rules for Survival

Like just about everything else, the rules to survive and flourish in M4.0 have changed from those rules that worked in the past. In M1.0, the success path might have looked like the following:

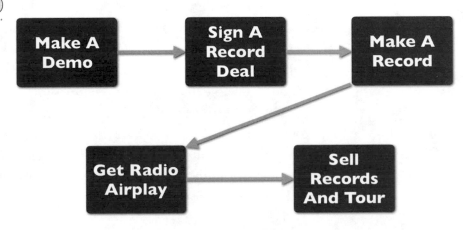

The path in M4.0 is much different; it's shorter than before but at the same time more complex for artists because they must do so much of the work themselves.

While it might seem simple, since the path to the consumer is so direct, each step is much more complicated. Assuming that you've already created your music (if not, check out a few of my other books for tips), let's take a closer look.

Developing Your Audience

M4.0 is totally dependent upon the development, care, and feeding of your fan base. Your core fans or "tribe" is only a piece of your total audience though. Your audience can be broken down into the following two categories: your casual fans and your core fans.

Your total audience, or your fans, are fervent about a particular small niche of music that's usually a subcategory of a larger genre, which means that they love speed metal (as opposed to the much larger metal or hard-rock genres), bluegrass (as compared to the larger country-music genre), or alien marching bands (as opposed to either of the larger alien-music or marching-band genres). If you're an artist in that particular niche, your audience will automatically gravitate toward you, but still might not be your fans. This includes casual fans, occasional listeners, and people who like what you're doing yet aren't particularly passionate about it.

Although this part of your audience can't be ignored, it's probably not a good idea to expend all your energy on it. They're aware of you and will probably give you a try with every release, unless they're disappointed too many times in a row. They can be turned into passionate fans though. One "hit" song or album, a change in image, or a change in general perception, and they become the passionate critical mass needed for the breakout that turns a respected artist into a true star.

In M4.0, your most important core audience contains your most passionate fans, or your "tribe," as described in Chapter 4. They'll buy whatever you have to sell, work for free, recruit other fans, and basically do anything you ask. All they want is access to and communication with the artist, which is the basis of M4.0. But how do you develop your tribe?

Developing Your Audience

Your audience consists of your casual fans and your core fans.

Fans may like an artist but may not be particularly passionate.

Your core fans (true fans, uberfans, superfans, tribe) are very passionate about everything you do.

Most of your energy should be directed toward your core fans.

Establishing Your Tribe

According to Seth Godin, the originator of the tribal concept, a tribe is a group of people connected to one another, connected to a leader, and connected to an idea. In M4.0, tribe members are connected to each other and to the artist via their passion for the artist's music, but the leader is the integral part of the tribe. In fact, without a leader, the tribe is only a self-organized group. As an example, a blog may have thousands of readers who never add a comment, so this makes it a group. The blogger could be the leader, but if she's the only one that posts, there's still no tribe.

Now we're assuming that there are more than three people that are passionately connected to the artist, since this is obviously essential to the creation of a tribe. The music is what connects them to the artist and to each other.

THE LEADER

The most important thing that the tribe needs is a leader. Although the artist is the most logical leader, a representative that speaks for the artist works in that capacity as well. In the old fan-club days, the fan-club president acted as leader, and today he or she still could be the leader of the tribe. But unless he or she directly represents the artist, the tribe isn't as powerful or as dynamic as it could be.

So how does one become the leader of the tribe? The leader initiates contact with the tribe and leads the conversations. For instance, the artist/leader might send or post a tour schedule with a list of "meet and greets" especially for tribe members. He or she makes it easy for everyone to participate and rewards the members that do so. Before the artist makes a new recording, she might ask the tribe what direction they'd like her to go in, then reward the ones that respond by sending them a link to download a special mix of the song. And most importantly, the leader gives projects to tribal members to work on. The artist might ask for people to send suggestions on venues in a certain area or to pass out flyers before an upcoming gig. Remember that tribal members are passionate and truly want to be part of something. Active participation fulfills that longing.

However the leader reaches out, it must be authentic and show true caring for the tribal members. Tribal members can feel in an instant if you're just going through the motions, and the tribe will begin to dissolve. If you're posting just as an exercise because "That's the way M3.0 works, dude," then you're better off finding a surrogate leader.

The next thing that a tribe needs is a place to meet. This is pretty easy as of M3.0, because there are a variety of alternatives that range from blogs to Facebook and Twitter to a custom social network on Ning. Whatever the online technology used, the tribe has to be able to communicate with one another easily, or the glue that holds the tribe together will be weak. That being said, having just a simple mailing list can be enough to connect the tribe.

Establishing Your Tribe

You don't have a tribe without a leader.

The leader doesn't have to be the artist.

The leader initiates contact, leads conversations, and makes it easy to participate.

The tribe needs a place to meet and communicate.

GROWING YOUR TRIBE

Now that your tribe is established, it must be carefully expanded (we'll get into some of the reasons besides the obvious in a minute). While not seemingly a method for expanding the tribe, the way the leader treats the tribe is as integral to expansion as any external methods. Tribes flourish from within. Word of mouth is perhaps the most powerful marketing method, and your tribe will champion you to anyone that will listen if you give them the slightest reason. Therefore, the first and most important way of developing the tribe is by nurturing it.

The easiest way to nurture the tribe is to transfer some of the social standing that the artist has onto them. To you, the artist, it might not seem like much if you have only 10 dedicated members in your tribe, tally a dozen downloads a week, and get only 15 people to your shows. But your tribe feels that you're the greatest thing since Christina Aguilera or Coldplay and that they've discovered you before anyone else. In their eyes, you have a degree of prestige and status that comes with the uniqueness of your music. You must transfer some of it to them in ways such as the following:

▶ If a certain fan has seen you 15 times, call him out at a show. Bring him backstage for a meet and greet or invite him to an after-show party.

▶ If a member consistently posts in a helpful manner for the v of the tribe, develop a personal off-list dialog with the fan, offer her a free ticket to the next show, or post a picture of her on the meeting space.

Any small action, such as the ones listed above, that transfers a bit of status will make the member more loyal and vocal, and will encourage other fans to take more action in hopes of reaping the same rewards.

The leader must constantly check the pulse of the tribe to hear what the members are feeling and thinking. This can be helpful in determining just what the tribe likes and dislikes about you and your music. Maybe there's a direction that you briefly touched upon on your last record that drove the tribe wild, or maybe one that they hated? You might choose to follow your musical instincts instead of listening to tribal feedback, but at least you won't be surprised by the resulting reaction.

Taking the tribe's pulse also lifts the mood of its members, since interaction with the leader is always appreciated and results in more participation. Showing your appreciation for their participation fosters even greater loyalty and participation and gets them invested emotionally and intellectually.

So how do you take the tribe's pulse? You ask them questions or ask them to help you.

▶ Ask them which piece of merch they prefer.
▶ Ask them about the best venues in their area, why they like them, and if they'd prefer to see you there.
▶ Ask them what song they'd love to hear you cover.
▶ Ask them who their favorite artists are (this answer is great for other elements of social marketing, as mentioned in chapter 7).
▶ Ask them to judge the artwork on your next release. Then, when they respond, reward them. Give a free T-shirt to the first ten people who respond.
▶ Send them a secret link to download a track that's available only to them.
▶ Give a personal shout out to some of the best responses.

All of the above makes them feel special and great about belonging, and keeps the interest of the tribe high.

Also remember that the tribe is composed of both leaders and lurkers. These two subgroups usually fall into the familiar 80:20 ratio (80 percent of the participation is provided by 20 percent of the tribe). Leaders are the first to respond and are always eager to participate. Lurkers remain in the shadows—interested, but not enough to engage the tribe. Getting the lurkers to participate is essential in growing the tribe. Let them know that there are benefits (such as free show tickets, after-show party invites, and exclusive CDs or downloads) for being more active. Above all, let them know that they'll be sorely missed if they decide to opt out of the tribe.

Even though you want the tribe to expand, don't focus on the number of members; it's not the numbers that count, but rather it's the quality of the experience. Focus on the members themselves, and they'll bring others to the tribe. Remember that a tribe's rate of growth is dependent upon two things: the level of passion of the members and the leadership's involvement. Have a high level of tribal passion and leadership participation, and the tribe will grow quickly; but have a lower level of either of the two, and the tribe will be faced with slower growth. When the tribe no longer benefits anyone, it will die.

Growing Your Tribe

Tribes flourish by word of mouth.

The way the leader treats the tribe determines how it grows.

The leader must constantly check the pulse of the tribe by asking questions or asking for help.

The tribe is composed of leaders and lurkers.

Getting lurkers to participate also grows the tribe.

MARKETING TO YOUR TRIBE

Be extremely careful about how you market to your tribe. Chances are that your tribe wants everything you have to offer, but they don't want to be hyped about it. Make an announcement about a new release or a piece of swag, but don't oversell it. Members don't need to know that you think your new music is the greatest thing you ever did or that it's better than the Foo Fighters' last release. They'll decide for themselves and then sell it for you in their own conversations if they like it.

The way to market to your tribe is by simply presenting your product to them. Just make them aware that it's available, and they'll do the rest. You can take it a bit further by offering them information about the product—the more exclusive, the better.

Instead of a sales pitch:

▶ Give them a behind-the-scenes story about the making of the product.
▶ Tell them where the idea for it came from.
▶ Tell them about all the people involved, especially other tribe members.
▶ Provide interviews with others involved in the project.
▶ Give them all the trivia involved in the project, no matter how small. True fans will eat it up. If it's a new song, tell them where it was recorded, who the engineer and producer are, how many Pro Tools tracks were needed, how long the mix took to finish, how many mixes you did, how the final mix compared with the rough mix, and all of the hundred other fine details that go into producing a song. If you just produced a new T-shirt, describe where the design came from, why you chose the manufacturer, what the shirt is made of, why you chose the color, and so on. Get the idea?

Giving them insight that no one else has makes them feel special, will keep them loyal, and will show mere fans and lurkers the benefits of tribal participation.

> ## Marketing to Your Tribe
>
> Present your product, don't sell it.
>
> Give them lots of information and trivia.
>
> Absolutely no hype!

Sustaining Your Career

The way to sustain your career in M4.0 has changed significantly from previous eras of music. The formula is simple: *maintain your connection with your audience.* This could mean by putting out frequent releases, blog posts, email blasts, tweets, or anything else in social media, but you've got to keep your fan base engaged on a consistent basis. While long periods of time between releases (such as six months or a year) are not recommended, they can be overcome by constant interaction by the artist. It's only when communication grows cold that the tribe begins to dissipate.

A typical consistent communication schedule might look something like the following:

▶ **Tweets:** a few times a day or every other day
▶ **Blog posts:** once or twice a week
▶ **Email blasts:** once a month with tour schedules, release schedules, or just general info
▶ **Music releases:** once every six to eight weeks
▶ **Videos:** at least two a month, but once a week is best.

Online communication isn't the only way to stay in touch with your fans. Touring will always be a part of being an artist, and it's an especially important ingredient in not only sustaining your fan base but also growing it. The more you have contact with your fans, the more opportunities there are to reach out and touch them. Don't forget some of the items mentioned in chapter 5, such as meet and greets, after-show parties, backstage passes, and the like. Online and offline contact must all be part of the same strategic plan.

THE "1,000 TRUE FANS" THEORY

The "1,000 True Fans Theory" by *Wired* magazine's "senior maverick" Kevin Kelly states that all an artist needs is 1,000 true fans (the members of his or her tribe) to maintain a fruitful, if unspectacular, career, thereby relieving the artist of the need for some of the nastier things in life as a regular job. True fans are sometimes called superfans or uberfans, depending on whose theory we're talking about.

Kelly wrote the following:

> A creator, such as an artist, musician, photographer, craftsperson, performer, animator, designer, videomaker, or author—in other words, anyone producing works of art—needs to acquire only 1,000 True Fans to make a living.
>
> A True Fan is defined as someone who will purchase anything and everything you produce. They will drive 200 miles to see you sing. They will buy the superdeluxe reissued hi-res box set of your stuff even though they have the low-res version. They have a Google Alert set for your name. They bookmark the eBay page where your out-of-print editions show up. They come to your openings. They have you sign their copies. They buy the T-shirt, and the mug, and the hat. They can't wait till you issue your next work. They are true fans

The idea is that if each of the 1,000 fans bought $100 worth of product every year (the figure equals an arbitrary full day's pay), you'd have an income of $100,000, which, even minus expenses, can still represent a reasonable living for most artists. The trick, of course, is how you expand your fan base to that magic 1,000-fans number (providing that you buy the theory, of course).

I also see the rise of the musical middle-class artist that can make anywhere from a store-clerk living to $100 grand a year per band member. There'll be fewer superstars and a lot more mid-level artists as time goes on.

—Bruce Houghton

Like most theories on such things, the detractors of the 1,000 True Fans theory point out several relevant issues. They are:

► **The $100,000 amount is the gross income and doesn't take expenses into account.** Expenses for any creative endeavor can be quite substantial and must be accounted for in any income assumption.

► **Even if you reach the magic 1,000-fan number, that doesn't mean that each will spend $100 per year.** That's true, but remember that $100 is an average number. Some fans might spend $500, while others might spend only $20. Of course, you have to present them with the products and the opportunity to spend money. If you put out a single release and don't tour, it's unlikely that you'll hit your target. If you're touring, and a true fan attends three shows and brings five friends, that could easily account for $100 right there. And if you release two albums, a deluxe box set, and newly designed T-shirts, hats, mouse pads, and coffee cups, there's an even greater chance that the true fan will just have to have whatever you're selling.

► **M4.0 presents a worldwide marketplace, so 1,000 fans don't necessarily have to reside just in the United States.** Again, this is true and can lead you to believe that developing your fan base is a lot easier than it really is. Don't forget that true fans in some countries such as Russia, China, and Mexico might not be paying anything at all and still be enjoying your work thanks to the prolific piracy that those areas are accustomed to.

► **You can expect some attrition of your new fans.** Hopefully, the attrition of your tribe will at least be offset by new members, and perhaps even grow some in the process.

► **Other artists are competing for the same fans.** There's always competition in the marketplace for every dollar, sale, and item. You must differentiate yourself and your product from your competition to make the choice easier for the fan. For sure, you'll lose some fans during this process, but if done well, you'll make that number up, and more.

While the total number of true fans actually required to make the theory work (is it 300 or 1,000 or 4,000?) may be in question, the idea is that you need this hard-core group in order to sustain your career. Whatever the number that you're lucky enough to develop, be sure to take care of and nurture them, because they truly want you to.

Sustaining Your Career

Frequent online communication is a necessity.

Too little or too much communication can be detrimental to the growth of your fan base.

Touring and face-to-face communication are as important as your online presence.

Aim to develop a core audience (the 1000 True Fans theory).

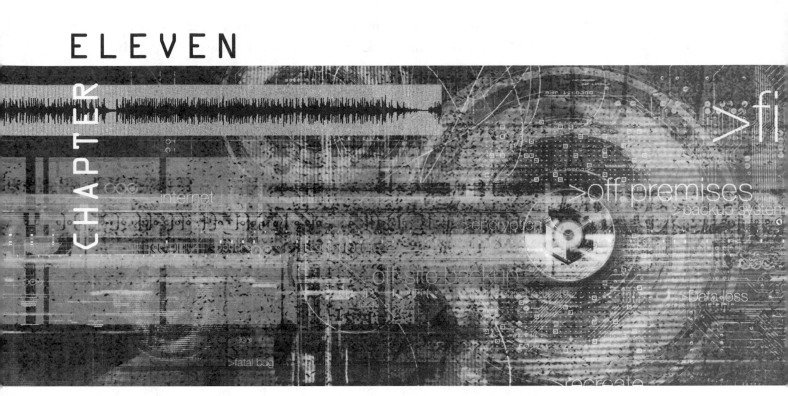

CHAPTER

How to Make Money in Today's Music World

To be sure, making money in M4.0 is a lot trickier than it was in previous stages of the music business. When you're signed to a major label, there's an ever-changing sea of cross-collateralization between accounts, in which big sales by the record label might still result in small royalty payments to you. Yet at the same time, things are in some ways more cut and dried than before. As an indie artist who's without a label and is dealing directly with the fans, you know exactly how much money you're earning and where it's coming from. No longer tied to the fortunes of a record released by a major label and therefore the uncertainty of a royalty statement, what you see is what you get.

Although the exact recipe for making money in today's music world is different, the ingredients pretty much remain the same. If you're looking for a magic formula, however, you won't find one here, I'm sorry to say. It still comes down to talent and a lot of work, same as it ever did.

Hit the Road, Jack

. . . .

As said a few times earlier in the book, from the beginning of time in the modern music business, artists have always made the bulk of their money from touring, *not* record sales. Depending on who you speak to, this figure varies anywhere from 90 to 95 percent of a currently hot artist's total income, and even more for a former platinum-selling heritage act.

This means that for you to make money, you've got to play in front of people, and the more people you play in front of, the more you'll make. The problem is that large crowds hardly ever happen overnight, and if they do, beware. This can be a warning sign that they're interested in the spectacle of a media buzz or something other than the music you create. Any success that comes too fast will probably be short lived, as you've not spent enough time building that core fan base that's been referred to over and over in this book.

Unfortunately, developing an audience on any level is slow and time consuming. You still have to build your audience one show at a time. The formula is always the same: the more you play, the better you get at performing and the more the crowd will notice, generating bigger crowds as a result (see my book *How to Make Your Band Sound Great* for some performance and show tips and tricks). Things can snowball from there if you've got what it takes.

> We often see bands that try to do too much too fast. A lot of indie labels will say, "We want the band to get in a van and we don't want them to get out of it for three years." At some point at the end of year one or 2 that runs its course. Virtually no band can keep on running around the country to try to build an audience indiscriminately. As much as touring is the most important thing, it has to be done strategically, concentrating

on certain markets where you see the beginning of growth, then doing them often enough but not too often.

—Bruce Houghton

Are you playing in front of people and still not making enough money to keep it interesting or to even pay your expenses? Maybe what you're offering just isn't compelling, either musically or show-wise. People will gladly pay to see anything that they're passionate about, so perhaps they don't find you enthralling enough to pay for, or maybe even to come to see for free. Then again, maybe you haven't found your audience yet. If that's the case, use the marketing tools outlined in chapter 4 to build that tribe. Either way, growing your live audience is always a slower process than it seems it should be.

What you still never get away from is that it's still about a song and it's still about a performance of that song. Can you play that song in front of your audience however large or small and create the "WOW Factor?"

—Rupert Perry

Describing just how to go about finding gigs, playing a show, and building your team with management and an agent is beyond the scope of this book. There are plenty of other books that focus on just that part of the biz. Suffice it to say that playing live has got to be part of your strategy for developing your tribe and making money.

Hit the Road, Jack

Most of an artist's income after a certain level comes from playing live.

You've got to build your audience one show at a time.

It always takes longer than you think to grow your audience.

Use social media marketing techniques to find your crowd.

Swag Is Your Friend

Performing live is only one ingredient of the recipe, however. You've got to have merchandise (other terms include *swag* or *merch*) to supplement your income. It's always been a huge part of the income of an artist, but until recently was considered just an ancillary revenue stream. Today it's an essential part of most artist's earnings.

It used to be that merch required a sizable capital outlay in order to get in the game. You had to buy enough to get some sort of economy of scale, but then you also had to worry about storing the inventory. And what if the item didn't sell? What do you do with 4,835 custom key chains or 492 pairs of branded underwear? Luckily, there are now alternatives that make the buy-in easier on the pocketbook than ever.

Today both Café Press (cafepress.com) and Zazzle (zazzle.com) make it easy to provide quality merch of all kinds without worrying about either the up-front money or the inventory. Both companies provide a host of items that they'll manufacture to order, and they'll even allow you to show examples of merch on your website or store. In other words, whenever an order is placed, that's when they'll make the item. They'll even drop-ship it to the customer for you so you don't have to worry about shipping and inventory. All this comes at a cost, and so your profit won't be as high, but it's an easy and inexpensive way to get into the merch business.

So what kind of merch should you have? You can now get a huge variety of items branded with your logo, but typical merch items are:

▶ T-shirts (probably the number one item ever for a musical artist)
▶ hats
▶ lighters
▶ sweatshirts
▶ coffee cups
▶ posters
▶ bumper stickers (a high-profit item because they're cheap to make)
▶ mouse pads
▶ bags (timely now, since people use them instead of paper or plastic at the supermarket)

Surprisingly, the top sales items have the highest profit margin and are also the least expensive to make—stickers and patches. A single color sticker costs around $0.20 and typically sells for $1.50, while a patch costs around $0.55 and typically sells for $4.00, which means both have a markup of over 700 percent! Sadly, most artists and bands overlook these simple and inexpensive merch pieces.

TOP TEN MERCH PIECES WITH THE BEST MARGINS

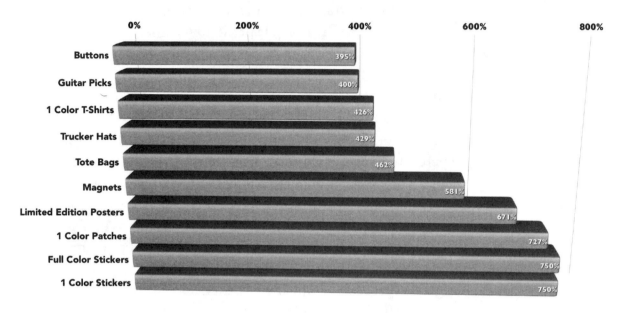

Just about anything you can think of can now have your logo on it. Of course, that doesn't necessarily mean that just because you can make it available, it's a good idea. It's still best to narrow things down, since offering too many types of items can actually prevent willing customers from buying anything because they can't make up their minds. Keep the number of types of items to a maximum of 2 at first, and be sure that they will sell before you add more options.

Another interesting idea is to offer a tour book of photos (available from blurb.com) like the one the Grateful Dead did on their recent tour. Once again, it's on-demand printing, and the company offers a number of professional templates to make the design easy.

Don't forget that in the end, branded items such as T-shirts, hats, beach towels, and Frisbees are for marketing you as an artist, so be sure that the design looks professional. If you're going to spend hard cash, this is the place to do it. Find a pro or an advanced hobbyist to design it for you. Don't forget that the true reason for selling merch is that if enough people see your intriguing logo on a T-shirt, coffee mug, or bumper sticker, some of them will be interested enough to check you out.

PRICE IT RIGHT

Whatever you choose to sell, be sure to price it right. The obvious temptation is to price an item too high to try to make a large profit. Don't fall into this trap. Price things low enough to cover your expenses and make a reasonable profit. Remember, these items are promotional; it's better to sell more at a lower cost than a few at a higher cost.

Above all, be sure that your costs are covered. Make sure that any costing includes the price of shipping, sales taxes (don't forget those), and any labor or sales costs involved (many artists will pay someone 10 percent or more of the sale's gross for manning the merch booth). Also don't forget that some venues will also take a commission of between 20 and 25 percent. A good formula for pricing might be your costs (all of them) plus anywhere from 50 to 100 percent. If you're sure the market will bear a higher price than that, go there, but make sure that you test the price first. Try a lower price at one gig and a higher one at another and see which sells better. Sometimes a higher price sells better because the customer perceives a higher quality.

Make sure you round it up to a reasonable number. If you use the formula of costs plus 50 percent and it comes out to $6.38, round it up to $7.00. Stay away from change. It's easier on everybody.

THE SECRET TO THE MERCH TABLE

Even though merchandise is a major revenue stream for the M4.0 artist, most musicians have a natural aversion to selling it (or selling anything for that matter). Yet one simple act that doesn't directly involve selling can help you greatly increase your nightly take from the merch table.

By just announcing during and at the end of the show, "After our show, we're going to be hanging out at the merch table, so come over and say 'Hi,'" without trying to specifically sell anything, you bring your fans that much closer to an impulse buy.

By getting people the ability to casually chat with you, it becomes a low-pressure way of getting people to look at your merchandise, which is always half the battle.

This one simple act can make a big difference in your merch sales, and that's the one place that you can be assured of making money these days, especially if you're just starting out. Remember, you don't have to physically sell anything yourself, just be there and talk to fans. Can you imagine what the sales would be like if Bono did that after a U2 concert?

CREDIT CARD TRANSACTIONS MADE EASY

More and more we're living in a cashless society. People are more likely to make a purchase with a debit or credit card when they want something, especially if they're short of cash. Of course this can be a drag at a gig when you're selling CDs and merch and have to rely on the Benjamins because of the hassle of taking credit and debit cards.

While the ability to take credit cards for merchandise purchases at a gig can make transactions easier, it can also eat into your profits. First of all, you have to enter into a long-term contract with a bank, then pay for the card reader, and in many cases pay a monthly subscription fee. Then, after a purchase, you have to wait for the money to hit your account, with the bank taking its piece through processing and transaction fees that are like the phone bill—lots of small fees for each transaction that no one can seem to explain.

Transaction costs are frequently overlooked, and they are the secret expense that eats your profit. All credit cards charge you multiple fees. First of all, there's a monthly transaction fee that's a minimum of $20.00 (usually more), a "gateway" fee of between $5.00 and $20.00 for ecommerce, an authorization fee, a customer service fee, and a monthly minimum transaction total. Slip below that total and you're charged a penalty.

Then there's the transaction costs per sale, which can go from $0.20 to as high as $0.35 (it's usually higher for an Internet transaction), plus a charge of between 1.5 and 3 percent of the total of the sale. Add all that up, and it means that if you only make a dozen or so song sales a month, you've actually lost money. Even if you've met your monthly minimum, you still may be only making less than half of a dollar per sale, thanks to the transaction costs involved.

Swag Is Your Friend

Merch is an essential part of your income.

But don't forget that it's promotional too.

Invest the money on a great design.

Use CafePress or Zazzle to avoid
upfront costs.

Limit the number of items to one or two at first.

Make sure that all your costs are covered.

Price to cover your costs plus at least 50 percent.

Meet and greet at the merch table
to increase sales.

Use Square for credit card transactions.

When Music Is Your Product

While your music is your marketing, there are times when it's your product as well. As we've seen, a CD, vinyl record, or cassette, or boxed sets involving one or more of each, can be viewed as highly valued and sought-after collectibles by your core fans. We've also discussed different ways to price these tangible products for either maximum promotional value (free or priced low) or maximum profit (priced high). Even though the world is going more and more to digital, physical products of some type will always be around. There's always at least some demand, and their potential as a money maker is too good to dispense with altogether.

But Music 4.0 is about music in the digital age, specifically when it comes to streaming, so it behooves the artist to know as much about the subject as possible. After all, one day soon it may make up a good portion of your income. Unfortunately streaming is not as cut and dried as a CD (and even how the money is divided there isn't always totally clear when a record label is involved), as there are numerous streaming scenarios today that makes how the revenue is generated and how much it generates a seriously tangled web. Just go online and do a search for "streaming royalties," and you'll find numerous articles proclaiming how little the artist is making against what he or she feels is fair. Hopefully this section can provide some clarity in that regard.

THE DIFFERENT TYPES OF STREAMS

What most artists and bands don't realize is that there are two different types of streaming services, and each operates differently and therefore pays at a slightly different rate.

NONINTERACTIVE STREAMS

The first is called a "Noninteractive" stream. This is either from a platform that acts as an online radio station, such as iHeart Radio or any traditional broadcaster with an online presence (like your local radio station), or a service like Pandora, where the user has a certain amount of control over what plays but can't directly select a song or make it repeat. Streaming platforms in this category include services such as Pandora, Last.FM, and iTunes Radio.

Radio broadcasters with terrestrial radio stations pay $0.0023 (.23 of a cent) per stream. Noninteractive platforms such as Pandora pay $0.0023 per stream from a paid subscriber and $0.0013 per stream from a nonsubscriber, which increases to $0.0014 in 2015.

This money is paid directly to SoundExchange and is paid out at a rate of 50 percent for the owner of the copyright (which could be the record label, or you if you're DIY), 45 percent to the featured artist, and 5 percent to unions that represent the musicians that played on the recording.

If a service such as iTunes Radio also provides advertising, it pays out at a slightly different rate, as a percentage of the ad revenue is added as well (prorated of course). In the case of iTunes Radio, that rate is 15 percent of ad revenue until September 2014, when it increases to 19 percent.

INTERACTIVE STREAMS

Interactive or on-demand streams are treated different from the radio-style streams in that the rate is considerably higher (between

$0.005 and $0.007, depending upon how much the listener pays per month). Services that provide interactive streaming include Spotify, Rdio, Mulve, and Slacker.

The downside here is that if you're signed to a label, the money is paid directly to them first. You'll then be paid based on the royalty amount negotiated in your agreement. For instance, if you've negotiated a 15 percent royalty, then you'll be paid 15 percent of $0.005, or $0.00075. If you're not with a label, the money will be collected by SoundExchange or an aggregator such as Tunecore, Ditto Music, or CDBaby if they've distributed your songs to the online streaming services.

Streaming Type	Royalty Paid
Interactive	$0.005 to .007 (depending upon the tier)
Commercial Broadcasters	$0.0023
Noninteractive	$0.0023 (paid tier) $0.0013 (free)
iTunes Radio	$0.0013 plus 15 percent of ad revenue (until September 2014) $0.0014 plus 19 percent of ad revenue (September 2014 onward)

On top of the royalty paid to the artist and label, there's also a publishing royalty that varies yet again from the above rates, which we'll cover in the next section.

You can see why artists, bands, musicians, and even record labels can be confused about how much they're receiving from streaming. As The Temptations once sang, it's a "ball of confusion."

That being said, every artist should register with SoundExchange, a service created by the US Copyright Office to collect performance fees for musicians featured on a recording and a song's copyright owners. SoundExchange collects money for the actual performers on a recording, not the songwriters. Go to soundexchange.com for more information.

When Your Music Is Your Product

Physical product containing music
will always be around.

There are two different types of music streams.

Each pays at a different rate.

Some include a percentage of
advertising revenue.

The amount paid to the artist is decreased
when a label or some aggregators are involved.

Register with soundexchange.com to get paid
if you're an artist or musician.

The New Publishing Paradigm

Despite popular belief, the ones who have traditionally made the most money on the sale of music have been the songwriters and publishers, not the performers (unless they were the songwriters or owned the publishing companies). The songwriter and publisher make money in two ways: mechanical royalties are paid whenever a digital download of a song or a physical CD is sold, and a performance royalty is paid whenever a song is played on radio, on television, in a film, or streamed over the Internet. This payment mechanism hasn't really changed all that much in M4.0 from previous music eras.

What has changed is that during this period in which music sales are less than half of what they were at their peak, publishing is the one area of the music industry that has held its own. How does that happen when sales, and therefore mechanical royalties, are down, you ask? While it's true that mechanical royalties are not nearly what they used to be now that CD sales are so low, they're offset by the tremendous increase in performance royalties, because music is now played on so many more broadcasts than before. The 500-channel cable and satellite television universe, along with satellite and Internet radio, provides more opportunities for music to be played, and as a result, more performance royalties are generated.

In aggregate, people are still watching as much television as ever if not more, but they are watching it across more channels. They're watching the cable channels more and the broadcast channels less.

—Larry Gerbrandt

As record company sales have been going down since the year 2000, publishing company income has actually been going up. What's happened is that performance income (when a songwriter gets paid whenever the song is played) has gone up because there are many more places where music is played and used. Now you have tons of little cable stations and they have to all pay a small fee. As a result, you have the increase in synch fees offsetting and sometimes exceeding the loss of mechanicals. Publishing is still one of the few ways left to monetize intellectual property.

—Richard Feldman, CEO
of ArtistsFirst Publishing

While publishing is sophisticated enough to easily fill an entire book (and there are many books specifically on the subject), here's a simple breakdown of how the money is paid:

ROYALTY TYPE	AMOUNT PAID
Mechanical Royalty	
Physical product (CD, vinyl)	$0.091 cents per song
Digital download	$0.091 cents per song collected by the record label
Interactive On-Demand Streaming (Spotify, Rdio, Deezer)	$0.005 cents per stream

Performance Royalty	
Radio	Depends on a sample survey of all radio stations, including college stations and public radio. ASCAP, BMI, and SESAC use a digital tracking system, station logs provided by the radio stations, and recordings of the actual broadcasts to determine how much a song earns.
Noninteractive Streaming (iTunes Radio, Pandora, iHeart Radio)	Blanket rate of about 4 percent of total revenue collected by ASCAP, BMI, or SESAC.
Synchronization Fee	
Television	Subject to negotiation of license fee, plus revenue via the survey from cue sheets that program producers provide to ASCAP, BMI, or SESAC, as well as program schedules, network and station logs, and tapes of the broadcasts to determine how much a song earns.
Commercials	Subject to negotiation of license fee, plus revenue via the survey from cue sheets that program producers provide to ASCAP, BMI, or SESAC, as well as program schedules, network and station logs, and tapes of the broadcasts to determine how much a song earns.
Movies	Subject to negotiation of license fee.
Printed Sheet Music	Subject to negotiation of license fee.
Ringtones	$0.24 per sale.

Can you make money from publishing if you're an indie artist? Maybe. If you're the songwriter on your own CD or digital release, then separating the songwriting money from the recording money only makes sense if you're sharing royalties with bandmates and getting paid separately for writing. Otherwise, it's irrelevant.

To receive any kind of significant royalties from streaming or radio airplay, you really have to have a huge hit that gets a lot of plays. So expecting any significant income is irrelevant for all but the extremely lucky indie artists.

Where you can make money is through synchronization fees, although there is less of it to go around these days than previously. Anytime music is played with a moving picture—either on television, in a movie, or on the Internet—it requires a synchronization license. If your song is considered for a movie, you'd negotiate with the producer for a fee, which could be from $0 to $100,000 or more, depending on the placement in the film and its budget. As with everything in the entertainment business, the higher your profile, the more you'll get paid. But if you have a song that uniquely relates to the movie, television show, or commercial (e.g., the hook of your song is the title of the movie), you can usually get a higher rate. You'll also receive performance fees whenever it's played on television.

> *Still there is money to be made in synchs. At the high end, hit shows like* True Blood *can pay as much as $15,000 to $20,000 for a publishing license, and there are tons of cable TV shows paying between $500 and $3,000. If you want to get down in the weeds, it often happens that the music supervisor blows the budget on one big song, then has to decrease the amount for all the other songs on the show.*
>
> —Richard Feldman

Bottom line, your income from digital publishing may remain a tiny grain of sand on a beach of potential income for the foreseeable future. There's real money in synch fees, and that's what you should be aiming for (although keep in mind that there are more musicians than ever trying to do the same thing). The problem is, how do you get your songs to the people that will license them? Unless you live in New York, Nashville, Los Angeles, or Chicago (mostly for commercials) where you can network and sell yourself, your only options are to have either so much airplay or so much online visibility that you get noticed, or you get a publisher. Part of what a publisher does (besides collect the money) is to promote your work. Once again, there are lots of books and articles about this to check out. If you want to self-publish, it's also a good idea to become a member of the Association of Independent Music Publishers, where you can network with other publishers both large and small. It's well worth the $60.00 per year. See aimp.org for more information.

THE PROBLEM WITH DIGITAL ACCOUNTING

Unfortunately, collecting performance-fee money for digital music streams is a lot more difficult than it should be. There is no standard way of electronic accounting yet, which means that online radio stations and subscription services frequently account to publishers in hard copy (though that's beginning to change). This hard copy (usually the size of several phone books for a busy publisher) must then be manually entered into the publisher's accounting system so the songwriters can get paid, which sometimes costs more than the entire amount collected. To make matters worse, it's possible that a publisher is not being paid because it can't be found by the digital broadcaster (or so they say), or it's impossible for the publisher to obtain an accounting of what was played. And after all that, it takes a huge number of streams and an equally large amount of accounting to show any substantial money, because the songwriter is earning only $0.005 per stream from a service like Spotify and then has to split that 50/50 if a publisher is involved.

To complicate matters, streaming is divided into two different categories—the noninteractive webcaster style used by services like Pandora, iTunes Radio, and iHeart Radio, and the interactive on-demand style featured on services like Spotify, Rdio, and Deezer—and they pay different rates.

While new accounting systems are being offered by Crunch Digital and Rebeat Digital, hopefully many of the problems plaguing publishers will soon come to an end, but as of the writing of this book, few publishers have chosen to adopt the new systems.

WHY USE A PUBLISHER?

While many artists feel that they want to control their own publishing and just hate the idea of dividing any income, a publisher can provide a number of useful services that can make that 50 percent (the highest rate that is used when splitting your royalties with a publisher) well worth it.

Besides giving you an advance against earnings if the publisher feels your songs warrant one, a publisher does the following:

- ▶ Registers the copyright for your songs so you don't have to do it
- ▶ Licenses the songs to commercial users
- ▶ Collects money from the licensees
- ▶ Pitches songs to music supervisors for film, television, and commercials
- ▶ Pitches songs to record companies and other potential users of songs
- ▶ Introduces the songwriter to artists looking for material

Having a publisher is just like having someone take care of your social networking: they'll free up your time so you can make more music, and they'll probably do a better job at administering your publishing than you can because they're pros at what they do. What's best is, in the right hands, they can even make some money for you.

The New Publishing Paradigm

Publishing is still making money in M4.0.

The mechanical royalty is the same for a song on a CD or a download—9.1 cents.

Publishing royalties from streaming are growing.

Streaming rates differ depending upon the type of platform.

Everyone wants synch fees.

Making Sense of Streaming Income

By now we've all read the horror stories of the artist or songwriter making what seems to be an incredibly small amount of money from millions of streaming plays. What's more, it seems even more outrageous when you see that the amounts paid look to be random, with not many of the tiny payments at the same rate. Here's a way to hopefully make sense of those payments, based on what was just presented in the previous two sections. What we'll do is look at the potential income from a million streams, and how varied that could be. Let's look at Spotify first.

1,000,000 streams to the copyright owner (hopefully the artist) x $0.005 = $5,000

This could be more, if some of the streams were from listeners in a higher pay tier and with some of the prorated ad revenue added in. It could also be lower if most of the revenue came from listeners from the free tier.

Now if you're with a record label and your deal split is 15 percent of the revenue (it might be more), that means you'll only get around $750, maybe a little higher and maybe a little lower.

$5,000 revenue from Spotify x 15 percent royalty rate = $750 paid to artist

There's still publishing income as well, which in this case is the same amount.

1,000,000 streams to the publisher (hopefully the artist) x $0.005 = $5,000

If the songwriter owns the publishing, then all that income will be paid to him. If the songwriter is signed to a publisher, then the publisher is entitled to half, leaving $2,500.

Total income to the artist = anywhere from $750 to $10,000 or more

For a radio-style service like Pandora in the paid tier:

1,000,000 streams to the copyright owner (hopefully the artist) x $0.0023 = $2,300

In the free tier:

1,000,000 streams to the copyright owner (hopefully the artist) x $0.0013 = $1,300

Once again, this will be augmented with a prorated percentage of the ad revenue, but the fact of the matter is that there will be a certain percentage at each rate, so the average will be somewhere between $.0013 and $.0023.

As before, if the artist is signed with a record label, the label will take their cut. If you use an aggregator like CD Baby, they'll take a percentage as well.

$1,300 revenue from Pandora x 15 percent artist royalty rate = $195 paid to artist

When it comes to publishing, ASCAP, BMI, or SESAC collects the royalties and distributes them to both the publisher and the songwriter, but the amount depends upon the total income of the service, so it can't be predicted.

As you can see, this is a very complex system with multiple rates and potentially multiple fingers in the financial pie. If an artist is signed with a record label, the amount of money paid out to the artist will be a lot lower than the money collected. The same with the publishing income, where the revenue is split if there's a publisher involved. Most of the horror stories that you've heard come from artists and songwriters who have a third party in the middle taking a lot more of the income than the artist is getting, so the income from streaming looks a lot worse than it really is.

Keep in mind that while a million streams sounds like a lot (as it is for most indie musicians), most hit songs get far more than that. Add that up across a catalog of music, and add in the fact that at least a tenfold increase in streaming subscribers are expected in the next five years, and we could be talking some real money that will make everyone in the industry a lot happier about streaming income than they are today.

Crowdfunding

. . . .

One of the most difficult aspects of being an artist is finding funding for your project. Regardless of where you're at along the ladder of success, if you don't have the resources for recording or marketing, you're severely hampered in the process.

A new trend in social media called crowdfunding (sometimes called fanfunding) is becoming a popular way to finance a recording project, thanks to sites such as Kickstarter, MyBandStock, indiegogo, Rockethub, and Sellaband, among others. Regardless of which site you use, the idea is the same—it allows your fans to pool their money in order to fund your project.

The way this is done is that the artist sets the amount-of-money goal, then the length of time to reach it. There are then different levels of rewards that vary based on the amount a fan contributes towards the project, very much like the multitiered product offerings by Trent Reznor and Josh Freese as described in chapter 4.

While this sounds like a great way to fund your project, it does take a moderate amount of planning and effort, as well as a significant amount of time before you see any cash. More importantly, most funding platforms require that the entire goal be hit before the artist sees any of the money. It does work though, with high-visibility artists such as Public Enemy, Jonathan Davis from Korn, Rockwell, and Marillion having been successfully funded.

THE FOUR TIERS OF A CROWDFUNDING CAMPAIGN

In crowdfunding, a funding tier is a level of investment, going for as little as $10 to increments such as $25, $50, $100, $500 and more. One of the most important elements of a crowdfunding campaign has to do with the rewards that an investor receives for putting money into the project. Just getting credit and money back usually isn't enough, but Yancey Strickler of Kickstarter had these suggestions in a blogpost on Hypebot to make the campaign a bit more enticing:

1. **The Basic Reward:** If nothing else, the investor should receive a copy of the recording, be it a CD or a free download, along with a written credit on the project.

2. **Limited Editions:** For either the first 100 investors or the next-higher tier, the investor receives a deluxe edition that's individually numbered and personally signed.

3. **Share the Story:** The next tier investor would receive something even more exclusive, such as pictures or videos from the studio, used guitar strings, or drum heads, the coffee cup used by the artist, or some other personal item.

4. **The Creative Experience:** Bring the investor into the process itself by asking for his or her opinion on which version of a song

or photo to release, bringing him or her into the studio for background vocals or handclaps, or just inviting him or her to sit in on a recording, photo session, or video. The idea is to give an investor at the highest level a once-in-a-lifetime thrill.

None of these cost very much, yet they could mean the difference between someone investing or not, or investing in a more costly tier.

THE FOUR RULES FOR CROWDFUNDING

If crowdfunding is something that you'd like to pursue, here are four rules to help your campaign be successful:

1. **Choose an attainable goal amount.** Everybody would like a $100,000 budget to work with, but unless you have a large fan base to begin with, you're probably dreaming if you think you can raise that amount. Even a once huge-selling band such as Public Enemy had to cut their goal from $250,000 to $75,000, so be realistic in both what you need and what you can raise.

2. **Concentrate on low price-points.** Kickstarter's data indicates that $50.00 is the optimum investment point, closely followed by $25.00. While most artists include amount in the thousands as well, don't count on these being filled.

3. **Make sure the investment reward is sufficient.** Remember that you're not getting a donation, it's an investment, and your investors will expect something in return. Once again, check out the examples of successful tiers by Trent Reznor and Josh Freese in Chapter 4.

4. **Keep the campaign short**. Kickstarter has found that the optimum campaign is 30 days, with longer campaigns performing significantly worse. The largest periods of investment come right in the beginning and right before it closes, with everything in the middle a somewhat "dead period." If that's the case, you might as well make the campaign short, since there's no advantage to dragging it out.

Kickstarter also has some great additional info and data on their website that's worth checking out.

THE CONCEPT OF "FUELERS"

Rockethub has a separate site that provides some insight into crowdfunding and how to take advantage of their service, and on it they introduce the concept of "fuelers." In Rockethub parlance, fuelers are contributors to your crowdfunding project and can be broken down into three categories. According to the site:

The vast majority of your Fuelers will be people you already know. They are your friends, family, and fans. These are people who already know and trust you. For most projects, the number of strangers who become Fuelers is fairly low. That being said, all Fuelers will fall into one of the following three categories:

1. **The Committed**—already committed to supporting you when they arrive

2. **The Inspired**—become inspired to support you after they arrive

3. **The Shoppers**—will shop (and tangentially support you)

Category #1, the Committed, will be populated with your First Degree Network of friends and family. These are folks who will support you every time, regardless of the project, or its quality. Your parents are likely a good example.

Category #2, the Inspired, will be populated with other friends and family members, your Second Degree Network. These are people whom you invite to the project page. They are not committed to contributing when they arrive, but after watching your video or reading your project description, they decide that you are up to something great! They become inspired to support you. Some strangers may fall into this category, but a friend you see occasionally is likely a better example.

Category #3, the Shoppers, will be populated with everyone else (i.e., your Third Degree Network). In order for your project to grab friends-of-friends and strangers, you'll need to grab the shoppers as well. The best way to do this is by creating rewards that are interesting and/or a good value.

If you think about it, the fueler concept also applies to an artist or band's audience.

▶ The **Committed** are your "tribe" (as best-selling marketer Seth Godin calls them). These are your most passionate fans that will go to any lengths to attend a show or buy a product.
▶ The **Inspired** are your "casual" audience: the ones that like you but don't love you. It may only take a single great song to push the casual fan into the committed category.
▶ The **Shoppers** are the part of the audience that really like your genre or even subgenre of music, but either hasn't been properly exposed to you or just hasn't caught the fever yet.

Your first job as an artist is to take care of your most passionate members (the Committed or your tribe) first, since they frequently bring the Inspired or casual fan into the tribe just with their enthusiasm.

Spending too much time on the Shoppers of the audience can take too much attention away from the fans that really matter, and you may never win them over anyway. In short, take care of the fans that are already in your corner first. If treated well, they may be your fans forever.

Crowdfunding

Allows your fans to pool their money to fund your project.

Set an attainable monetary goal.

Make the incentives enticing for investors.

Embrace your "fuelers."

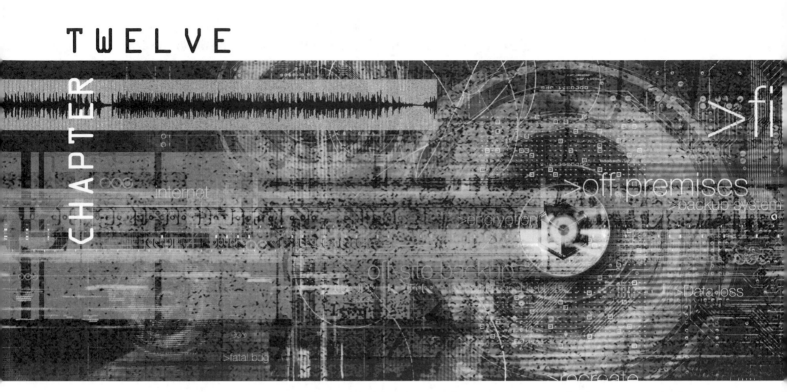

Living in Music 4.0

To many in the business, the future is now. Yes, you can say that we're already in Music 4.0. So what was the barrier that we crossed? Was it a date, a technology, or an event? Yes, it was all of those, but also a change in attitude. Let's look a little into the very near future. Chances are that much of it will have already come to pass by the time you read this.

Making a Living Is the New Success

Musicians and artists will begin to see success in a different way as making a living replaces stardom as the big score. To some degree that was always true. Most musicians are only too happy making a living by playing music, but thanks to the excesses of previous eras, far too many felt that stardom was well within their reach.

This has changed as a new realism takes place

▶ The realism that DIY takes a lot of work and the rewards aren't as great as in the heyday of the major labels. There's not as much revenue in the music industry pie to split as there was before, at least for now.

▶ The realism that social networking has limitations just like traditional marketing, so traditional marketing and promotion can't be completely abandoned. You still need both for effective branding and marketing.

▶ The realism that the touring market is not nearly the gold mine that it once was during better economic times. Fewer venues, less money, and more competition makes gigging more difficult than ever.

▶ And the realism that some things in the music business never change. You still need talent, great songs, lots of hard work, and a little luck to make your mark.

THERE'S NO SUCH THING AS A DEMO

If you're an artist or band recording your own songs, erase the word "demo" from your mind. In these days of increasingly better recording gear at ever lower prices and great information on just how to use it, a demo will always keep you in the "good enough" mindset. Each song has to be approached as if it were a finished master because these days it's easier than ever to make some really excellent recordings, and that's what nearly everyone expects to hear. The days of a producer or publishers being able to "hear through the song" (hear the final product in their head) is over. So forget about demos. They're just an excuse for a recording that's inadequate in some way.

The idea of the demo came out of practicality, since up until about the year 2000, you just didn't have the ability to make a record that sounded like a major release anywhere but in a real recording studio. Yes, it was done occasionally, but the vast majority of songs that you'd hear on the radio had real pros with real pro equipment involved. What would happen is that you'd make a "demo" that was just good enough to get a label or producer interested in taking you to the next level. Because studios were so expensive to record in (typically $100 to $250 an hour, plus engineer, tape, etc.), it was usually impossible to spend enough time to make a recording that was up to snuff with a major label release. And if you weren't located near a reasonably high-end studio, you were forced to use whatever was available, so as a result, almost everyone made a demo before moving on to a deal with a label where they got to make real records in real studios with some real pros who knew what to do.

Most of that has changed with the last few generations of affordable recording gear that are now readily available, and with the fact that the listening public doesn't care as much about audio fidelity as they once did (maybe they never did, but the record companies sure thought so). So now it's easy enough to record for not a lot of money and distribute it for next to nothing, but people expect every recording to be as good as you can make it.

Major Label Deconstruction

. . . .

Among the many recent changes in the music business is the total disruption of the major label paradigm. Where once the music world revolved around six majors, the number has been reduced to just three. What's more, the influence of the majors has dwindled considerably in just a few short years. To most young artists or bands, the majors now represent the idea of indentured servitude rather than the path to fame and fortune.

The path to major label deconstruction has been rather swift. The Big Six of Warner Music Group (WMG), EMI, Sony Music, Bertelsmann Music Group (BMG), Universal Music Group (UMG), and Polygram reigned for only ten years, from 1988 to 1998. The group decreased to five in 1998 when UMG absorbed Polygram, and further consolidated to four in 2004 when Sony Music and BMG merged and became Sony BMG. In October of 2008, Sony acquired Bertelsmann's 50 percent of the venture, and the name returned to Sony Music. Bertelsmann wisely retained many of the publishing elements it maintained prior to the merger and was renamed Bertelsmann Rights Management, understanding that the record business was floundering but publishing still remained strong. In 2009, the private equity firm Kohlberg Kravitz Roberts, also known as KKR, acquired 51 percent of the company, a sign of things to come. In 2012 BMG expanded into administration and management of master recording rights with an unusual arrangement of offering artists a higher royalty rate in exchange for zero advance. The company distributes through the other major labels.

THE SAD CASE OF EMI

In May of 2006, EMI attempted to buy Warner Music Group, but the bid was rejected. WMG then returned the favor and tried to buy EMI, only to have it reject a $4.6 billion offer. Then in 2007, EMI was acquired by Terra Firma Capital Partners, a private equity firm, for £4.2 billion (about $6.8 billion) that was largely financed by a loan from banking giant Citigroup. After buying at the top of the market, EMI began to hemorrhage money almost immediately after Terra Firma takeover, as their sales and market share fell through the floor, and several important artists such as Paul McCartney and Radiohead walked away when their contracts ended. Shortly thereafter, Terra Firma was no longer able to make payments on the debt service, and sued Citi essentially for "forcing them to take the money." Terra Firma lost the court case in short order, and as of February 1, 2011, Citigroup became the owner of EMI, immediately writing off £2.2 billion of the debt. In 2012 Universal Music Group acquired EMI from Citigroup, making The Big Four into The Big Three as a result.

WMG CHANGES HANDS

Warner Music Group (WMG, previous known as Warner/Elektra/Atlantic) was one of the most respected labels by both the music industry and among artists. Once helmed by music-industry pioneers such as Mo Ostin, Joe Smith, Ahmet Ertegun, and Jak Holzman, the label was known to stick by artists it really believed in, regardless of whether the first few albums sold or not, as was the case with Jackson Browne and Fleetwood Mac.

From the time that Seagrams (the Canadian liquor giant) purchased a small piece of the company in 1994, WMG has been in increasing disarray, which was exacerbated in 2004 when a group of investors lead by Edgar Bronfman Jr. (who became CEO) purchased it from the Time Warner group. Since that time, it's been all downhill.

WMG has struggled, with sales, market share, and revenue dropping in spite of excellent digital sales. In a surprise move, WMG recently put itself up for sale and was purchased by Russian billionaire Len Blavatnik and his Access Industries.

Today WMG is known as being the most digitally progressive of the remaining major labels, as evidenced by a 2013 deal with Clear Channel Media that will see Warner artists paid for terrestrial radio play for the first time. In return, Clear Channel will get preferential rates for streaming songs through its iHeartRadio service and other online platforms.

In the end, even though the remaining major labels may lose even more influence, they won't go away. There will always be needed for what they do best—taking successful artists and making them superstars

THE MAJOR LABEL OF THE FUTURE

In Chapter 4 we briefly looked at Azoff MSG Entertainment (AMSGE), the joint venture between Madison Square Garden Company (MSG) and music-business mover and shaker Irving Azoff. What makes this venture interesting is that the company will have four divisions: artist management, music publishing, television production/live event branding, and digital branding. Couple that with the many venues owned by MSG that could host concerts for the company's artists, and you have a look at what the new-world major label looks like.

For the record, Azoff and MSG chairman James Dolan never called this venture a record label, but they don't have to. It's an outdated term for an outdated concept anyway. The traditional record label combined talent scouting, artist development, distribution, and marketing, but each of those operations has changed substantially since the new millennium. Record labels now have fewer A&R talent scouts than ever, and in this one-failure-and-done atmosphere we live in, artist development is merely a nice term with little execution. Couple that with a dying brick-and-mortar music retail business and companies that are still stuck in the past when it comes to marketing, and you can see that something in the way the current music business is run has to change.

Of course Azoff brings his formidable roster of talent (including The Eagles, Christina Aguilera, Steely Dan, and Van Halen among others) with him, but more and more in the future new talent will bubble to the surface through social media (think Justin Bieber from YouTube and more recently Macklemore and Ryan Lewis) that a cognizant digital department could spot. The digital department could also take care of the heavy lifting when it comes to marketing, since the music consumer that a music company wants to reach today is primarily online.

And then there's management. The so-called "360 deal" recording agreement where a label participates in all the revenue streams of an artist is now what major labels prefer, but AMSGE are among the best in the business when it comes to management, which labels are not. As an artist, which would you choose? Today's record labels also have publishing arms, and so will AMSGE, but according to an article in *The Hollywood Reporter*, they will concentrate more on digital performance rights, a place where many publishers are slow to catch up.

One of the ways to expand the revenue stream from concerts is to live stream the event as a pay-per-view, or package the show and sell it to a cable network like Palladia or Fuse, which MSG owns. Consumers are already getting used to live streaming of concerts from sites such as Livestream and Concert Window, and they'll eventually adopt it as they're doing with streaming music. Another win for AMSGE.

So when you step back and look at it, doesn't this seem like a company prepared for music's future? Doesn't it seem like a "label" that artists would kill to be on? It's true that physical product hasn't gone away completely, but putting brick-and-mortar distribution in place shouldn't be a problem in this new era. It can be farmed out to one of the existing major labels, just like BMG now does.

Make no mistake about it: major record labels are not going away. An artist can break online, but to go to the superstar level, you still need the infrastructure that only a major label can bring. The current majors are desperately trying to change, and on some levels they're doing a pretty good job of it, but they're stilled mired in the framework of the past, just like any corporation that's been around for 50 years. It takes some time for that supertanker to change course.

AMSGE offers things that no major can offer, like management, integration with venues and television, and a new outlook on publishing. That's why we're looking at the next-generation record label if they can pull it off.

When You Need a Label

This entire book so far has been about getting along in the new music world without a record label, but there does come a time when having a label is worth considering if you want to jump to the next level as an artist. Record labels are not intrinsically bad; it's just that you have to weigh the advantages versus the disadvantages to determine whether or not the time is right for you to be associated with one.

You might want to consider a label if:

▶ It's offering you a staggering amount of money. If this happens, either you must be hot enough for a bidding war to have broken out or they really, really believe in your future. Just remember that this might be the last money you'll ever see from the label, and it may have a significantly negative impact on any credibility that you have with your fan base. Best to test the notion of signing with a label with your tribe just to see their reaction first, since they won't buy anything from you if they feel you sold them out.

▶ You need money for recording, touring, or any other needs. One of the things that labels do really well is to act like a bank by using your music as collateral. Major labels still do this as skillfully as ever before, but is it worth the price you're going to pay in terms of the freedom that M4.0 offers?

You're spending too much time on certain aspects of a career. A label can take some of the burden of marketing and distribution off your shoulders. You still have to be involved on some level, though, or you run the risk of things getting way off course before it's brought to your attention. If you don't have a manager already, that might be a better association to make at this point than to start working with a label.

▶ You need expanded distribution. If distribution into the remaining brick-and-mortar stores is beyond what a small indie label can provide, a major label can be your friend. Major labels have the relationships, the sales force, and the means to collect the money. If you're distributing by yourself, you'll get paid if and when the stores feel like it because you have no clout. In some cases, you won't even be able to get into the remaining chains and retail stores because you don't sell enough to get on their radar. A major label or large indie sells the stores a lot of product, and they're trusted, so it's a lot easier for them to get the retailer to take a chance. Further, the label has some leverage in that they can always threaten to withhold in-demand product if they don't get paid.

► You want to expand into foreign territories. Let's say that you have a huge following in Germany via your online efforts, but you can't service them properly because you live in Kansas City. A major label can use their overseas resources to promote you and get product in the stores there. It saves you the hassle of reinventing the distribution and marketing wheels.

► You need economies of scale. Sometimes the power of a big label can be used to your advantage since they can cut a better deal with a service (YouTube and MTV come to mind) than you ever could as an indie.

► You need major marketing. Another thing that a major label does well is to market you traditionally. If you want airplay on radio and appearances on television, a label may be your only hope. If you want reviews and articles in mainstream media, they still have the clout to get it done.

► You feel that you've gone as far as you can go as an indie artist. If you need help to push your career over the edge to stardom, then a major label or major label imprint may be the way to go. This is what they do—sometimes well, sometimes not.

Unless you have a specific need for any of the above that you're sure you can't fill any other way, it's best to stay independent for as long as you can, in order to retain as much control over your music and your musical destiny as you can.

Getting Along In Music 4.0

. . . .

As you've read this book, hopefully you've spotted a number of concepts that have continually popped up that directly apply to the music world we live in today. Some of these principles are a change from the old Music 1.0 through 2.5 way of doing things, and some are still relatively the same. Let me leave you with some additional thoughts about making music in the Internet age.

▶ It's all about scale. It's not the sales, it's the number of YouTube views you have. A hit that sells only 50,000 combined units (album and single) may have 50 million YouTube views. Once upon a time, this would have been deemed a failure; today, it's a success. Views don't equal sales, and vice versa.

▶ There will be fewer digital distributors in the future. It's an expensive business to get into and maintain, so in the near future there will be a shakeout that will leave far fewer digital competitors. Don't be shocked when you wake up one day to find a few gone.

▶ It's all about what you can do for other people. Promoters, agents, and club owners are dying to book you if they know you'll make them money. Record labels (especially the majors) are dying to sign you if you have an audience they can sell to. Managers will want to sign you if you have a line around the block waiting to see you. If you can't do any of the above, your chances of success decrease substantially.

▶ Money often comes late. It may not seem like it, but success is slow. You grow your audience one fan at a time. The longer it takes, the more likely it is you'll have a long career. An overnight sensation usually means you'll also be forgotten overnight. This is one thing that hasn't changed much through the years.

▶ Major labels want radio hits. They want an easy sell, so unless you create music that can get on the radio immediately, a major label won't be interested. This is what they do and they do it well, so if that's your goal, you must give them what they want.

▶ You must create music on a regular basis. Fans have a very short attention span and need to be fed with new material constantly in order for it to stay at the forefront of their minds. What should you create? Anything and everything, from new original tunes to cover tunes, to electric versions to acoustic versions, to remixes to outtakes, to behind-the-scenes videos to lyric videos, and more. You may create it all at once, but release it on a consistent basis so you always have some fresh content available.

▶ YouTube is the new radio. Nurture your following there and release on a consistent basis (see above). It's where the people you want to reach are discovering new music.

► Growing your audience organically is best. Don't expect your friends and family to spread the word, as they don't count. If you can't find an audience on your own merits, there's something wrong with your music or your presentation. Find the problem, fix it, and try it again. The trick is finding that audience.

► First and foremost, it all starts with the song. If you can't write a great song that appeals to even a small audience, none of the other things in this book matter much.

There's far more that can be written about what Music 4.0 has to offer and how to navigate it, especially in the realm of social media. For that I recommend you read *Social Media Promotion for Musicians*. That said, I'm sure you'll agree that the music business is both exciting and invigorating in its current form. It's not dying and it's not wilting, unlike what you'll hear and read from the old-school naysayers. It is constantly evolving and progressing, and those who don't progress with it will fall behind.

Hopefully after reading this book you'll have the tools that you need to thrive in our current musical age—the age of Music 4.0.

THIRTEEN

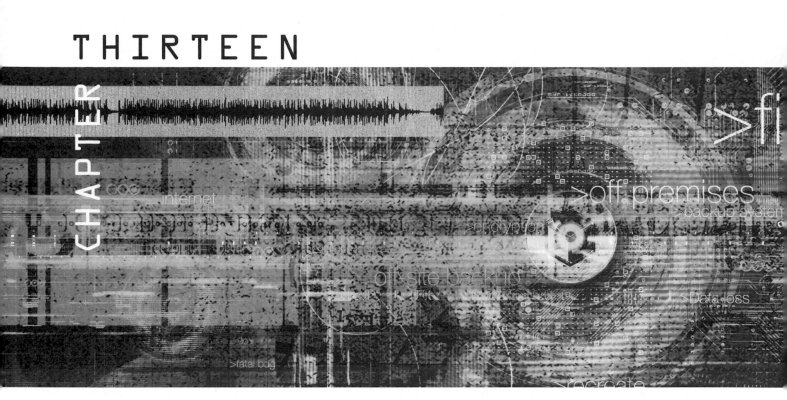

CHAPTER

Interviews

Dae Bogan

. . . .

Dae Bogan has considerable experience in both music and social media marketing, starting out in event production for major brands such as Chipotle, Dell, Blackberry, Virgin Mobile, and Def Jam, then as vice president of marketing for Shiekh shoes and their Shiekh Music Artist program. His current company, Chazbo Music, provides in-store video music entertainment services by programming custom-curated channels for businesses, music, and lifestyle. Not one to rest on his laurels and experience, Dae returned to Rickhurst University to receive a certificate in social media marketing in order to take his expertise to an even higher level. I met Dae when he appeared on a social media panel that I moderated at a conference where he stole the show with his wellspring of knowledge regarding the latest in social media.

In your opinion, what's the most important social network?
There's no such thing. It's not like you can't survive by not being on one of them. In fact, there are successful artists who may not even be on the Top 5.

If we break it down, there are really three levels of social presence. The first is no presence whatsoever on social media, which tends to happen with your older artists.

The second has very low engagement because they have no strategy. These are artists who are signed up all over the place that just go with the flow with engagement. It tends to be organic and could be beneficial, but there's no strategy in place. This happens more with indie artists.

Then you have the social savvy artist who has all his aliases correct from platform to platform, so there's not like "garageband123" on one platform and "lagarageband246" on another. Their image and header are consistent from one platform profile to another and the message is the same. Their hashtags are consistent, and it helps them to reach their audiences on different platforms.

When I consult with an artist, the first thing I do is find out which platforms they're on and make sure that everything across the board is set up consistently. I always recommend Twitter, Facebook, and YouTube at first, but if you're an artist out of Asia, for instance, then there might be a different platform that might be more important for you to be on. Knowing what's the best regional platform is important. For a US-based artist I recommend Facebook, Instagram, YouTube, and MySpace.

MySpace? That's a surprise.
Yeah, I just did a social media panel with the director of artist relations from MySpace where the audience learned what the new platform is all about and the new tools that it offers today versus what it offered in the past. What people don't realize is that most social platforms are still fragmented. For example, you can't upload a hosted video on Twitter, and you don't have the same status updates on YouTube that

you have on Facebook, so there are limitations with all the current platforms that we normally use.

MySpace has essentially put all of the best tools from these other platforms together in one place, and they're more friendly today than other social platforms. You can post status updates on MySpace and then share them on Facebook and Twitter. You can upload and host a video on MySpace and then build some nice-looking galleries. You can create video, music, and picture compilations, which is great when you're trying to tell a story with a campaign. You can have pictures from the tour, video from backstage, and the music video all in one "mix," which you can't do on any other platform. Every artist also has their own radio station, so you can curate your own music to show who you are as an artist. You can have a video that floats with the user as she moves around MySpace. There's also a lot of analytics, which are important for your strategy.

There are a lot of tools that the platform has that are very beneficial for the artist. Unfortunately MySpace hasn't done a great job of communicating those to artists, which is why I've been bringing their staff to some of my workshops. On the other hand, if you sign up and don't have any real followers, then you won't see the impact of the new tools. But in terms of just looking at all the tools of all the platforms, MySpace has the most relevant ones for indie artists at the moment.

Have you seen anything new on the scene in terms of social media marketing?

Yes, Thunderclap.it is a platform in the new field of exchanging social action. It's one thing to follow someone on Facebook or YouTube, but it's another to be rewarded for some sort of social interaction. Thunderclap is a campaign generator. You can set it up so you can have a thousand people tweet a message on your behalf on a specific day and time, which is perfect if you're releasing something like an EP or a new video.

When your fan base signs up, they give permission on their Twitter account for Thunderclap to tweet on their behalf on a particular day and time, so your reach grows exponentially when that happens. Thunderclap will sign in to all their accounts at the designated time and tweet that message because your fans already gave them their approval. It's a way to generate a large reach for your message but also create trending hashtags, because if you get enough people to generate a specific hashtag, it will trend on Twitter so everyone will see it, which will increase your followers as well.

On the panel that we did together you mentioned your cousin, who got a lot of YouTube traction because of some cover songs that he did.
His name is Durand Bernarr, and he started as a teenager doing cover songs in his basement and then posting them on YouTube. He's very talented, first of all, so people would share his videos and rewatch them constantly. Eventually he did a cover of an Erykah Badu song that she saw somehow, and she reached out to him as a result. Within a couple of weeks he became one of her background singers and then one of her arrangers. Since then he's travelled around the world with her, which boosted his international fan base, but it all started from a cover song on YouTube.

What did he do to get the traction?
He made sure that his titles were really appropriate. If you're going to do a cover of an artist, you better have the name of the song and the artist name in your title, because that's what people are going to search for. If the video is really good or really bad it will get shared; if it's in the middle not much will probably happen.

What else would you recommend to help with YouTube SEO?
Today you really have to do optimization for search or it'll be buried with the other 700 million videos on YouTube at the moment. If I had to give some advice, I'd say song choice is number one. Choose songs that are relevant today by using the Billboard charts as a guide. Select a song that's on the top of the charts today, then post a really good cover, then make sure the video title is appropriate by posting the original artist's name, the song name, then your name. Make sure it's tagged with the original artist's name and the song name, as well as the record label name and anything else about it. If it's a love song or a pop song, put that descriptive tag in. Sometimes people just search for love songs, so they'll come across your video that way. Finally, make sure the video description is complete.

Also at the end of the video there should be all the information about your social media; then ask people to subscribe to your channel. Now with annotations you can also embed links in the video as well. Those are ways to optimize the video so that at least some information is carried along with it. What artists forget is that once someone shares that video, a lot of the meta information that you inserted is lost. The description and the tags don't come with it and the title isn't visible. The only thing that you can see is what's inside the video player, so by using annotations there's a way to make at least some of the information available to the viewer.

Finally, release it at the right time. YouTube shows in their analytics what time of day is best. Look at when you have the most viewers or followers.

Does the same advice apply for original material?
Absolutely, except the artist should sign up with the YouTube Partner Program to monetize their videos, or even sign up with a multichannel network like Full Screen, since they offer additional tools on top of what YouTube provides that helps an artist manage their channel better in terms of analytics.

Follow Dae's blogs at daebogan.wordpress.com and daeboganmusic. tumblr.com, and check out his company at chazbomusic.com.

Richard Feldman

. . . .

For as long as I've known Richard Feldman (more than 20 years), he's been trying to get out of the music business to pursue a non-music-business career, only to get pulled back by more success and an enduring fascination with the evolution of the industry. A very successful songwriter and producer who has Platinum and No. 1 records to his credit, Richard's 2005 attempt to leave the business ended with him winning a Grammy award for producing Toots and the Maytals' *True Love*. His latest foray into getting out of the business finds him with a successful publishing venture focused on evergreen music compositions, a music library with Time Warner Cable and Fox Sports, and a successful music placement agency, Artists First Music. As a past president of the American Independent Music Publishers association, Richard brings a unique perspective to publishing as seen from the point of view of a musician, producer, and songwriter and businessman.

What's the difference between music publishing today and the way it used to be?

There are many differences, but you've got to look back at publishing from the beginning to understand them. In the beginning, publishing meant receiving a royalty or percentage from the sale of sheet music, then from other physical products like piano rolls, and as technology evolved, vinyl to cassette to CDs to MP3 downloads. This is called a mechanical royalty and results from a physical sale of a song.

Another source of revenue is for the performance of a song. This started out as a payment for a live rendition of a song, then evolved into payments from broadcasting the song on radio and television. The performing rights organizations (PROs) like ASCAP, BMI, and SESAC collect this money from the various radio and TV broadcasters and distribute it separately to publishers and their writers.

There's another source of revenue that has become a big part of music publishing and has helped offset the decrease in earnings from physical and download mechanicals, and this is called synch income. A sync license is required if anyone uses music simultaneously with moving pictures, and for that there is a negotiated fee which cannot be pirated. So as sales from mechanical royalties from CD sales have gone down, income from sync licenses has gone up.

Why has sync income increased?

There are many reasons, but the most obvious is that there are so many more broadcasters today. Where it used to be only the big three networks (NBC, CBS, and ABC), now it's more like 300 with all the cable networks, so there are more sources of income than there were before. As a result, you have the increase in the number of sync fees offsetting and sometimes exceeding the decrease of mechanicals. You could say publishing is now the "last man standing" in terms of making money in the music business, and still one of the few ways left to monetize intellectual property.

Still, a lot has changed in publishing in the last few years.
That's true. For example, there's been a big rollup of the larger indie music publishers by the majors. Big established independent publishers like Bug, Chrysalis, and Cherry Lane, who have been around for decades, have been gobbled up by BMG (now considered a major) and the remaining biggies: Sony, Universal, and Warner Chappell. There are some major indies left like Peer, ABKO, and Bicycle, but they tend to play in a different sandbox than the majors and tend not to sign the mega pop writer/producers, although they compete fiercely for legacy catalogues that come to market.

The majors do still sign indie bands but focus more on big pop writer/producers. These writers make the mega advances because their work is played by major radio and there are still decent sales. For indie artist/writers, the publishing deals are often combined with recording contracts and other revenue shares like merchandising and concert income.

And there are other challenges. Just like the music industry, film and TV are being tested by new distribution models that produce less revenue, and this results in smaller synch fees. This is exacerbated by the fact that music production libraries and record labels that have publishing rights sometimes reduce or even give away synch fees in exchange for exposure, which is driving down synch fees.

Still there is money to be made in synchs. At the high end, hit shows like *True Blood* can pay as much as $15,000 to $20,000 for a publishing license, and there are tons of cable TV shows paying between $500 and $3,000. If you want to get down in the weeds, it often happens that the music supervisor blows the budget on one big song, then has to decrease the amount for all the other songs on the show.

The king of all earners are still evergreen titles (recognizable songs that have an established earnings history), which still command the biggest fees. There's only one "Purple Haze" and if a TV or film company wants to use that song they will pay a high fee, so the price for legacy catalogues like the Gershwins, Lieber and Stoller, and acts like The Doors have been steadily increasing in value. Interestingly, the jury is still out on many of the current hits. It's safe to say that songs by Adele will be commanding big fees for years to come, but the market is telling us that much of the "hot and trendy" music you hear today may not do as well. For instance, will any Lady Gaga songs become ever-green? We don't know yet.

On top of the pressure on pricing there are legislative challenges created by new technologies that are causing problems, but hopefully will see relief in the courts.

The biggest issue is the amount publishers receive from the digital performance of songs. Why this is so important is that streaming arguably is the future and the deal that has been struck is terrible!

To understand this better you must go back to the '70s. Because radio stations were forced to negotiate only with ASCAP and BMI for performance licenses, these PROs were considered quasi-monopolies and negotiations were put under a consent decree. This meant that every five years a tribunal appointed by the court would rule over the license fees.

This worked okay until digital rates for companies like Pandora were set. Because there had never been a performance income for the labels (think masters) for terrestrial radio, the Copyright Rate Board mandated a fee structure giving labels 14 times what the publishers received.

Where will this end? There are challenges ahead such as more disruptive technologies on the horizon and a lot of pressure for direct licensing by bypassing the PROs entirely, so I believe this consent decree will need to be amended to more properly reflect what the market rates should be.

Has accounting gotten any easier?
No, it's gotten more difficult because there are so many more sources, and these sources are making micro payments. You can have 500 pages of accounting that might be worth only $50.00. Of course publishing

software is meeting the challenge, but it puts more strain on music publishers, and for the self-published artist it can be overwhelming—especially if direct licensing increases. And of course auditing becomes an even bigger problem. How do you trust these guys that are screwing you to begin with.

What will the publishing world look like in a new streaming world?
With the ability to hear what you want, when you want it, and where you want it, there is little incentive to "own it," so in this streaming world there is some sunlight. For one, because it is 100 percent digitally delivered, it can be tracked and there will be software to monitor and calculate this. And the other thought is that there will be more and more sources of income that over time will be enough to keep publishers and more importantly songwriters in the game.

The perception of success has changed in the business, hasn't it?
You bet! The digital revolution has definitely changed the game. For one you don't have gatekeepers from major labels and publishers determining your future. It's a world of self-publishing. This has led to a more democratized landscape and there are many artists and writers who hold onto their publishing, so being signed by a big label or publisher is no longer the endgame.

I recently spoke with a big manager out of the UK, who said he had a list of things that he tries to do for all his artists. Way down at number eight was trying to get the band signed, where it used to be on the top of the list. So far it has not affected the volume of new music, although maybe it has when it comes to the quality, but the bigger question is whether the Chuck Berry of tomorrow will have enough incentive to leave his day gig and become a full-time musician.

What I see evolving is an industry where music is more a social language. Sure there will always be the few artists who make major bank with pop hits but there are literally millions of artists who seem satisfied with the social currency that 10,000 YouTube views can bring. And if that works and they hone their craft over time, they might just become the new Chuck Berry or Beatles that make this world a better place.

The truth is that music that matters is and will always be about passion, not money. People need music like oxygen, and people who make music do it because *they have to make it*. Where this all ends is uncertain as the industry continues to search for its "New Model," but you can bet people will keep making music whether or not that model is ever found.

Check out Artists First Music at artistsfirstmusic.com.

Larry Gerbrandt

An expert on entertainment analytics, Larry Gerbrandt's Media Valuation Partners advises its clients on the economics of media and content on traditional and emerging technology platforms. Formerly a senior vice president with research giant Nielsen Analytics, Gerbrandt provides a wealth of experience in entertainment market research that we're pleased we could tap for this book. Get ready for some interesting and insightful facts and figures regarding sponsorships, branding, and advertising—all the things necessary to monetize M4.0.

Why does television have less of an impact on music than it used to?
What's happening is that the numbers for traditional broadcast television are dropping dramatically. In a 500-channel universe, viewers have a lot of choices and a lot of the programming is simply not compelling enough. Reality programming isn't as compelling as scripted drama, and [yet] there's more and more of it.

Does that mean that the aggregate is going down, or is it the per-channel viewing?
Per-channel viewing. In aggregate, people are still watching as much television as ever, if not more, but they're watching it across more channels. They're watching the cable channels more and the broadcast channels less. What's also happening is that people are using new technologies to increase their overall consumption of video.

What's the digital reality of actually monetizing that?

The problem is that on cable you have a 500-channel universe but on the Internet you have a 5,000- or 50,000-channel universe, and there is no central place to aggregate information as to what all of them are doing. Having said that, sites like Hulu are starting to gain some traction, although YouTube is still the 800-pound gorilla.

It used to be that an act appearing on **Saturday Night Live** *could expect a sales bump of 100K units the next week, but that's no longer true. Why do you think that is?*

First of all, *SNL*'s viewership is down. It used to be that it did a 12 rating, but now it might do a 2 or a 3. What that means is that only 2 percent of the households are viewing it, or to put it another way, it's not being viewed by 98 percent of the available households. So there's been some dramatic drops in viewership, and, as a result, traditional media becomes a lot less effective.

The demo for TV has grown older as well, hasn't it?

The US population is aging, so we as a nation are growing a bit older as a result of the baby boom [generation]. What's happening on television is a bit more complex, however. Young adults watch significantly less television than their older counterparts. They are busier with education, careers, raising families, socializing, and have less leisure time as a result. That's why advertisers are willing to pay a premium to reach the younger demographics—they are simply harder to target. There's also a continuing belief that individuals make lifelong brand choices as young adults.

How do you see television changing in the future?

The first thing is that the DVR is going to have an ever-greater impact. Secondly, we're going to see online content come to the big-screen TV. And third, we're going to see greater consumption of television outside of the traditional sources. You'll see more and more content on mobile devices, for instance, as well as portable display screens connected to wireless broadband. Television will have to adapt to the new zeitgeist: that whatever video content they want should be available whenever and wherever they want.

How will everyone monetize video online as compared to broadcast?
The models are not that dramatically different. The difference is in the commercial loads. Fox has begun to experiment with less clutter [shorter commercials] and charging advertisers more. We're probably going to see a reprising of the program sponsorship model. Part of that is in response to the DVR.

Can the consumer be driven to the network's online shows, and can they monetize it to a level that makes it worth it?
All the online numbers are still tiny compared to broadcast. If you took all of YouTube's views in a 24-hour day, it's equivalent to about an hour of a single prime-time show on any of the four major networks. Now, that YouTube number is growing, and one of the things that makes it so attractive is that the demographics of that viewer tend to be younger and a little more affluent.

You'd think that the prime demo would be the boomers who have more money.
Yes, but what brand advertisers continue to believe is that people make up their brand choices in their 20s and early 30s. By the time you're a boomer, you've already decided that you're a Dove Bar–eating, Chevron-using, Charmin-wiping fan, and that's what you like. So the advertising is really designed to affect the young.

Let's talk about sponsorships. Is the sponsorship spend getting wider or more targeted?
What I think we'll see a lot more is much tighter integration with the program, because then you can control the message. What we're seeing with *American Idol* is incredibly tight integration with the products. They're almost shameless. At every turn they're integrating the show with a sponsor's message. This is still virgin territory, and we're still trying to figure out exactly what works. What they do know is that over time consumers develop advertiser-aversion techniques. For instance, they're increasingly finding that banner ads don't work because we've come to ignore them. Billboards became the same way, so now they wrap entire buildings and use it as a giant billboard and use the new digital signs that are much more compelling and attention grabbing. It's a constant battle between advertisers and viewers in

terms of making the advertising message get through the visual corridor that we're confronted with.

What seems to work online these days, then?

There's a new set of ads that pop up with the content (not pop-ups as a separate window, like before) that take over your screen, as well as mouse-over ads that integrate movement into it. We all hate it, right? But for the Web to continue to be free, commercial messages have to continue to work in some fashion. It's going to continue for the rest of our lives. There will be escalations and different techniques, but it will continue.

NASCAR is probably an extreme example. Every car and every driver is covered head to toe with messages, so affiliating yourself with something that people positively associate with definitely works. It's all branding and identity. The problem is that it's getting harder and harder to tell a story, and there's still nothing like a 30-second commercial to do that.

Two of the emerging forces in advertising are the power of the blog and of social media. Word of mouth has always been critical to spreading brand awareness. With the viral nature of online communications, the near-instantaneous methods for information and opinion dissemination, and the ability to rapidly influence large groups through social media, learning how to harness the power of these new recommendation "chains" of interconnected individuals may be the single most important challenge for brands and advertisers going forward.

You can learn more about Larry's Media Valuation Partners at media-valuationpartners.com.

Shan Dan Horan

· ·

Shan Dan Horan is the director of New Media at Century Media Records as well as the head of Social Media at Standby Records. He's also a talented music video director and photographer for his own company (ShanDanVideo.com), a skill set that's quite in demand in these days when YouTube is the king of music distribution and discovery. Shan Dan was kind enough to provide some insight as to what's required to get the online presence together for a newly signed band.

What's the first thing you do when you get a new act?

It really depends on what kind of act it is and if they're already established or brand new. If they are a new band, it is important to start collecting and developing their networks. Most opportunities that are open for bands really revolve around hype, how many fans they have, and how well organized they are. For instance, if a band gets a huge tour opportunity, most times it's based strictly on how much additional promotion they could bring to the tour.

After an act gets signed, the first and main goal of any label is to get them exposure in every capacity possible, which among other things means uploading track videos, lyric videos, and music videos to YouTube and posting contest campaigns to Facebook. However, it's important to control the time you invest and make sure you aren't targeting ineffective social networks, so that means sticking to the Top 5 most-used networks and focusing on them.

A lot of times what we do is post a full album stream, because when an album hits the street date, you'll see some kids uploading it to their own personal YouTube channels. We still make money because all the metadata tracks back to us, but it's not doing us a favor since it's hosted on someone else's channel. That's why the first thing we do for a new act is to post a full YouTube stream of the album, because it's inevitably going to happen, so we might as well make it happen under our own terms. The benefit for them and us doing so is we can control the quality, promote our channel, and expose them to our 500,000-plus subscribers.

So that's the entire album?

It really depends on the act. If it's one of our bigger acts, we won't put the entire stream up, since we want people to still buy the album, but for newer acts we will for the sake of exposure if deemed appropriate.

The most popular asset that I can't do enough of lately is lyric videos, which are a fairly new phenomenon. They cost hardly anything to create, can be done even if the band is thousands of miles away, and get a solid amount of plays. With YouTube monetization making bands money nowadays, the more plays they get the better.

What are you using as elements in a lyric video?
There's a constantly sliding scale of quantity versus quality. Do you want it to look good and take longer or do you want it to be created quickly and get more assets out there? A lot of time those track videos just have a little bit of movement with like a logo, a CD cover, and an identifier for the song and album and when it's available for the entire stream. In the end, the more exciting and eye-catching the video, the more plays it usually accumulates.

What do you do to promote a video?
While labels will pay for Google AdWords to promote the video on Internet campaigns, a lot of great video promotion is free. For instance, when a big band has a new video asset, most times this can be leveraged for a premiere on a high-traffic, music-related website. So in exchange for having the video asset exclusively for a week, they host it and promote it on their page. Situations like this are usually a win-win. Bands send fans to the premiering website, and they in turn send new fans to the band. It's free cross-promotion at its best.

Are you doing anything special with the video description or tagging?
It's important that you can get all the metadata info plugged in ahead of time, so when the videos get put up, they're actually linked to the iTunes store, so each one will have a link on the song that will say, "Taken from xxx album. Purchase it by clicking here." If the album hasn't been released yet, we'll include all the preorder information and tour-date information as well. Other tactics include adding annotations to "Pick up the new album now" on top of the actual video itself, or even something as simple as adding lyrics to the video description. All of these are great things you can do to boost the effectiveness of your video.

What's the first thing you do with a new act in terms of social media?
I'll dive deep into any analytics to identify their core demographics to make sure that's who they're actually reaching. I have this one band whose core demographic are females from 15 to 18 years old, yet this band was talking about video games and football. Why weren't they getting much interaction from their fans? Well, because 15-year-old girls don't care about video games or football. When I discovered their bad targeting, I had them posting more model-looking photos of the band members talking about how they wish they could find a girlfriend. Guess what? They ended up boosting their interaction by 4,000 percent in one week.

What analytics are you looking at?
I want to see who really likes their pages, so I'll look at the analytics on Facebook to see a breakdown of age, sex, cities, and regions. I'll then do a few posts that target that demographic, or at least what I think they are most interested in, and then watch and see what the interactions look like. If we get a huge spike in users talking about the band or liking the page, then we know we hit our mark.

Do you still feel that Facebook is the most important social network?
I did at one point, but the benefits aren't as great now as they once were, and you never know when it will become "uncool." I always warn people not to put all of their eggs in one basket. The perfect example of that is MySpace. I saw people sinking tens of thousands of dollars into spamming kids or botting pages to boost their plays to compile a huge demographic around their MySpace page. Then when the exodus from MySpace happened, all that time and money that was sunk into that one social network was useless.

The shelf life of any Internet platform is pretty questionable. I do know people will most likely always have a physical address, a phone number, and an email address, so I encourage everyone to diversify how they collect fan info so they don't strictly rely on Facebook.

Facebook still seems like it's the most important tool for the time being, but it's slowly becoming obsolete and expensive. It continues to tighten up on how many fans a band's post is actually exposed to, so if you have 100 fans, each post you create will reach only a fraction (normally 16 percent or 16 fans). If you want to reach your entire fan base that you cultivated, you now have to pay for it, which doesn't seem fair.

If Facebook is declining in influence, what's the next thing? Is it Twitter?

It's hard to follow trends, but I forecast YouTube as the most important tool for musicians in the future. You can interact with fans, upload more engaging content, and you even get paid if you're a YouTube partner. In a day where not as many fans purchase music, how awesome is it that a band can get paid by fans simply viewing a cool, free-to-watch video? I feel like those benefits really aren't something that Facebook and Twitter can offer, even though those sites are awesome tools.

How much do you post for a band?

It's impossible for me to post for every single band, so I show them what to do that's proper, give them the tools, make sure that they're targeting the right demographic, and then I just keep an eye on them.

Sites like Facebook, Twitter, and Instagram are interactive social websites. Having me behind a cubicle making posts for bands lacks that core interaction fans want to see. If the band is at a water park in Arizona, they better be posting photos about it on their networks. Fans will eat it up.

What advice do you give for social posting?

Get creative. Don't post the same rehashed advertisement. Kids are smart and they know when they're being advertised to. Give them some intimate insight into the life of the band. Keep it light and fun, then slip an advertisement in. Bands that are selling all the time see a considerable drop-off when that happens. Do contests! If it's Halloween, do a pumpkin-carving contest. If it's Christmas, do an ugly sweater contest. Just get kids talking, because in the end, the more engaged your fans are, the more money you will make.

What types of videos are useful?

It depends on the band's following. I've seen bands doing long, elaborate interviews with themselves like "Meet a Band Member," and it ends up getting 100 plays because nobody cares about what each member eats for breakfast. You've got to get more creative. Music videos and lyric videos get amazing plays if the band has a following, while other videos are hit or miss.

Another useful video type revolves around cross-promotion. For instance, if you create a video to promote an upcoming tour that's evenly balanced, most of the other touring bands will share that asset. What better way to get more fans than to have another band plugging your YouTube channel?

Keep an eye on views. It's like being your own television station. Just like TV relies on ratings, if you're not getting views, it's not worth doing. If fans aren't digging your acoustic songs but love your full-band songs, then you probably shouldn't be playing acoustic.

How often should they post?
Keep it consistent! On Facebook post no more than three times a day. Always make your posts from 12 pm to 5 pm PST when most people are active.

It's good to be consistent on YouTube, but post at most once a week. A lot of successful channels post at a consistent time every week. Anything less than two videos a month is a waste of time.

If there's one thing that you could recommend (other than writing great songs), what would it be?
Always keep working and don't get complacent, which especially happens with new bands. Most new young bands I meet break up or give up before they really have a chance for success.

Older bands that I work with are professional and tend to know what it's about. They play a show, go to bed and get up early, then do it again because it's their job. New bands think of it as a lifestyle that they've seen on TV and think it's supposed to be about a nonstop party. I've seen too many bands fall apart because they haven't taken it seriously. That's the best advice I can give. Treat your band like it's a job.

Find out more about Shan Dan at shandanvideo.com and facebook.com/shandanhoran.

Bruce Houghton

. . . .

Bruce Houghton started his highly influential Hypebot blog because he wanted to better understand the changes in the music business in order to help educate the clients of his Skyline Music agency. Since then, Houghton's blog has become a must-read for anyone at any level in the music industry. His keen observations come from being not only a highly prominent blogger but also a booking agent working in the industry trenches every day.

Has your booking agency been affected by the digital world we live in today?

We have some problems that we never used to have because there's a fractured media landscape and the major record labels are not as well staffed or well financed as they used to be. The old paradigm was that the promoter bought the band and figured out which radio station to co-promote with, and after that the record label came in and did a lot of the rest. The label was the publicist, they bought additional advertising, and they put up posters in local record stores to help promote a show. None of that happens anymore. The promoter or the artist themselves are left as the promotion machine, and the promoters are, for the most part, pretty ill-equipped to do it. Like the labels, they're also understaffed and don't necessarily understand the digital age. Most of them are starting to try, but overall, there is no formula anymore that they can follow.

So what we see is that it's tougher and tougher to break a band live because too many of the dates are not well promoted. We find ourselves working harder to educate the promoters and the artists so they can figure out how to reach out to their audience directly themselves.

How many artists are equipped to do that?

Honestly, not many—and that's the problem. If they have a really good mailing list, a really active social-networking presence, and some kind of way to mobilize the uberfan to put up posters and that sort of thing, then they have a chance. How many have that or are equipped to use it properly? Probably less than 20 percent. Part of that simply is that there are only so many hours in the day because they're trying to be musicians. Some of it is also that what works is changing so rapidly that unless they really have a propensity to keep up with things, they'll have trouble.

For example, a few years ago MySpace was everything. Now, depending upon who you are and the age of your audience, MySpace may mean nothing, so those kinds of things are very difficult for a band to grasp. If they work really hard to master a craft over here, suddenly the playing field changes, and they have to go over there instead. You see an increasing number of companies trying to deal with that problem on behalf of the artist.

What are the most effective promotional tools that you see?
Right now it's that combination of having a great email list and a great website that's constantly updated and gives the fans a reason to come back. If it isn't updated every day, it's updated two or three times a week with news, pictures, free stuff, and links to other bands they like. Also, some kind of presence on the social networking sites, depending on who you are as a band and who your audience is.

In terms of growing an email list, I'm a big fan of the tools that Topspin and Bandcamp have, where it's something like, "Give us your email address, and we'll give you this MP3," or "Here's an easy way to send this MP3 to your friends." I'm a big fan of anything that encourages viral growth.

Have you seen any huge shifts in the business in the past few years, or has it just been evolutionary?
I think that the end of music retail is in sight, and it really has accelerated in the last two years. What that means is we're only a couple of years away from not caring at all about getting records into stores. That's huge, because it eliminates a marketing opportunity where a clerk in a record store who likes your record will tell people about it, so it's a little sad because that point of contact at the record stores is going to be gone in a few years. On the other hand, it's really exciting, because that barrier where a band feels that they needed a nationally distributed release is gone.

That being said, we may never get to the point where we don't want to press physical product. In fact, I'm a believer that physical product acts like a souvenir of the band. If bands think of a CD that way and package it as such, they might find some increased success with it.

What are the trends in the business that you see today?
I see more and more niche markets finding more coherent audiences. You can be into Hungarian death metal or central Canadian bluegrass and easily fill your iPod with songs of that particular genre. Then in your spare time, you can read blogs pertaining to only that subject.

I also see the rise of the musical middle-class artist that can make anywhere from a store-clerk living to a hundred grand a year per band member. There'll be fewer superstars and a lot more mid-level artists as time goes on.

I also see the marginalization of major labels outside of pop and hip hop.

What do you see happening with venues? Are they healthy or in trouble?
It's really market to market, but in general they're pretty healthy. People still want to go out and have fun and see a band live. The larger the big promoters like Live Nation get, the more it opens up the opportunity for the guys underneath them—and we're starting to see that trend. The venue business took a real hit when the drinking age went from 18 to 21 in 1984, but since then it's been pretty steady.

What's the best way to break an act today?
It depends on the act and musical genre. For hip hop it's entirely about the record and finding a powerful enough team to sort of ram it home on the radio in the mainstream media. If it's not rap or hip hop, it's probably more about touring and doing the work you need to do to build your fan base so that they become your promotional army, telling their friends about you and helping you grow.

It used to be that if a DJ talked about you in afternoon drive time, then there'd be 300 more people at the club that night. Now you need 30 people talking about you on their blogs and to their friends so that each of them will bring 10 more people to the club. So it's doing whatever you have to do to build an audience, which usually includes touring to some degree.

That's how everyone makes money now, right?
Yeah, that's true, but there's also a misnomer about that. We often see bands that try to do too much too fast. A lot of indie labels will say, "We want the band to get in a van, and we don't want them to get out of it for three years." At some point at the end of year 1 or 2, that runs its course. Virtually no band can keep on running around the country to try to build an audience indiscriminately. As much as touring is the most important thing, it has to be done strategically, concentrating on certain markets where you see the beginning of growth, then doing them often enough but not too often.

What's the most effective DIY promotion tip?
It's figuring out what excites your fans and doing more of it, and that means spending some time getting close to them.

I remember going to see a mainstream country act, the Blackhawks, about 15 years ago. They were on their second Gold record, and each of the members had a lot of success apart from the band. There they were at a little county fair in the middle of nowhere, standing in the rain while 400 people lined up to get their autograph and their picture taken with them, and nobody made them feel like they had to buy something. If every band would do that, they would be a lot more successful and have a lot more loyal fans.

To some degree, what we're all trying to do online now is a digital version of that. How can we keep the fans excited? How can we give them the tools to tell their friends about us? Are we worth having them tell their friends about us? [Laughs.]

What do you see as the most important things that contribute to an artist becoming successful these days?
Great music. That's the one thing that really hasn't changed.

Make sure to check out Bruce's Hypebot blog at hypebot.com.

Ariel Hyatt

· ·

A PR person is vital to any artist's visibility, but the right PR person can make all the difference in the world when it comes to an artist's career development. That being said, Music 4.0 is a completely different PR world that few publicists can adequately function in. Enter Ariel Hyatt, one of the few true experts in the field of online publicity and social media, and one of the first publicists to incorporate those tools into her skill set.

Ariel and her socially based Cyber PR agency have been guiding artists, bands, and musicians through the world of Facebook, YouTube, Twitter, and social media since the birth of each of those platforms. As you'll see, her story is as unique as the service she provides.

How did you learn the art of music PR?

I worked at a tiny independent label called What Are Records?, where we were completely DIY. Rob Gordon, the label founder, understood direct-to-fan way before Topspin or Nimbit ever coined the phrase. He understood that The Samples from Boulder, CO, was a band that everyone loved and wanted to feel connected to, and he understood the "1000 True Fan" theory perfectly before it was even coined. There was no social media at the time; everything that we did was with live performances, postcards, and street teams. We created CD carrying cases, beer cozies, and VHS tapes of a documentary we self-produced that took fans on a journey with the band. We had multiple CD releases, cassettes, tons of different T-shirt designs, baseball hats—and it went on and on. What Are Records? grossed that band over a million dollars by having a brilliant direct-to-fan plan in place.

Rob did the same thing with media, and that's how I got trained. He'd say, "We're gonna hit the same market four to six times a year. You go back to the reporter in the local newspaper and don't let up until you get your feature story." It might have taken us four times through a market to get our story, but that was okay. He taught me to go to the Irish or Jewish newspaper or the obituaries or the wedding paper to find the local angle. It's that mentality that still succeeds today. It's leaving no stone unturned and understanding your audience even if your audience is a journalist.

The artists that I see succeeding today have the same mentality. It's that one-on-one model that works. That's how Amanda Palmer does it. She signs CDs until her hand falls off after each show, and so does Taylor Swift.

What would you recommend for a new artist who's beginning to build a fan base, as compared to an artist who's been doing it for while who already has a fan base?
The core message is the same. Unfortunately or fortunately, depending upon how you see things, success lies in engaging your audience. If you are a band just starting out, you're going to need to engage one person at a time. Start with a goal of ten. Most musicians have this really backward-looking concept that you have to engage millions of people on radio or with worldwide distribution. Just go for ten first.

I was on a panel recently where a guy was so frustrated when he asked a question. He said, "I don't know about Facebook. It's the same people all the time. It's only my friends and family." I asked him, "Have you ever gone to listen to other people's music and commented on it? Have you ever reached out to ten perfect strangers or moved them in some way?" Stop thinking about yourself and start asking about how you can help. It will come back in spades.

So that's the baseline. Now an artist who's already established or has "made it" has to reverse engineer that stuff. It's something like, "Oh, I didn't know that Bonnie Raitt was online. I want to be part of her community." She might not be tweeting or doing everything herself, but at least I get to feel special when I see what she's up to. That's okay. It doesn't have to come directly from the artist, although I think that's very helpful. If Britney Spears can tweet, anyone can.

So it's all about engagement. If you can afford someone to help you with social media, hire them to help you with that relationship, but the bottom line is: you still have to care about your audience enough to want to communicate with them.

What's changed in social media since we spoke for the last edition of the book?

There's always some new platform that will pop up and captivate people, but the fundamental piece of social media that hasn't changed is that it's a two-way conversation. It almost feels like it's ridiculous to keep repeating it. Different platforms and techniques have evolved, and we have to constantly be on our feet and aware, but the truth is that engagement is still at the baseline of all that we do online. If you do engage and are willing to participate in conversations with your audience and willing to acknowledge people, that hasn't changed.

I'm acutely aware that everyone now is staring down at their smart phone. It's almost unusual when someone is not doing that. You see it in coffee shops, over dinner, with families—young people, old people—it's almost reached a level where you want to yell, "All right, enough already." But those people are engaging with someone. They're not just staring at a blank screen.

Are you still big on Facebook and Twitter as a tool?

We are, although something that we've practiced here a lot is a blogging strategy. If you really have something to say and you're able to say it, you can use it as a content piece in your marketing strategy. We've been advocating this with our clients, although some are still resistant to trying it.

We're trying to lead our clients to be thought leaders, but from a musician's standpoint blogging can be very tricky. When you think of thought-leader musicians, you've got David Byrne, David Bowie, Amanda Palmer, and not many more. They're few and far between. If I say thought leaders in science or marketing, you can think of lots of people, and most are sharing a great deal of information to an immense audience through a blog. Why can't artists understand this? Mostly because the old obsession of "someone is going to do this for me" is still in their hearts and minds.

I recently spoke with an artist and all he wanted was an article in the *New York Times*. I'm like, "Dude, you have 100 fans on Facebook and 160 followers on Twitter, why would the *New York Times* even look at you?" But there's still this mentality that if someone does this for me, then everything will be better.

What's even worse is that getting the article in the **Times** *probably won't even reach the audience that the artist wants anyway.*
That's right, but there's still some disbelief that all the social marketing that we talk about works.

I just got back from speaking at a tech conference at the O2 Arena in London where I interviewed a number of amazing thought leaders, and the thing that I found fascinating was that every single one of them said that they became a "thought leader" by blogging. Many of them were now six or seven years in and only now are they hitting their stride.

Now that you're branching into helping authors and tech companies, how does what you do differ from helping musicians and artists?
It doesn't really. It's the same strategy: create something that entices people and give it away in exchange for some communication point, whether it be a Like, a tweet, or an email address, and then build your communication with them by creating consistent, compelling content that captivates people.

Are Likes important?
Facebook is the most frustrating platform. I read an article about the way life used to work a hundred years ago where you would have gone out of your house to the community bakery, hardware store (like my grandparents owned), or any local shop to buy your everyday needs. Then the Madison Avenue way of doing business came in the picture by advertising national brands as somehow being sexier and blew much of that model away, and we lost our way of communicating one on one as a result. Now social media brings us back around to where we started, where we only want to buy from people that we like, trust, and have positive engagement with. None of these principles are new, just the medium is.

The problem with Facebook is that it's now placing the Madison Avenue approach on top of a community-based platform, but the two are at massive odds. In the beginning there were all these people that you knew on Facebook that you might've lost contact with, like your school friends, teachers, babysitters, and long-lost cousins. They weren't necessarily on the other social sites, but they were on Facebook. It was all based on community, and it was very personal and very much like the old community bakery or store.

Now Facebook has added a new twist in that no one will get to see your post unless you pay, and now we have a problem. We've been saying for years that it's all about great content and engagement and keeping things interesting, and Facebook has come along and said, "Actually, no. If you pay us, we'll promote something that's not interesting to get you more eyeballs." This is detrimental because it's diluting the whole point of Facebook in the first place. The community is now muddled with Madison Avenue and the "buy a billboard," or "buy an ad" mentality. I'm afraid that just like when Madison Avenue rose in power, the people that don't have the money to buy the ads and billboards are going to get squeezed out. That's why I find Facebook to be a necessary evil. There's still a huge number of active users, so you need a strategy for it, but both the platform and the strategy are rapidly changing.

Do you recommend that a new client be on multiple platforms or just concentrate on one?
Just concentrate on one. I think that it's so easy to get overwhelmed trying to do too much that some people will just shut down. Concentrate on one, and hopefully it's not Facebook.

Which platform would you suggest?
Really it depends on that person's capabilities. Are they visual? Then let's do Instagram. Are they wordy? Then a blog strategy might be better. Are they ADD? Then let's do some tweeting. Let's find the thing that feels like it's the most comfortable. I still struggle with pushing people to do things that they're not comfortable with, because it's not going to work in the long run.

How much do you do for the client, as opposed to what they do themselves?
I used to say that what we do at Cyber PR was to offer education on how to do it. I finally had to stop that after a lot of pain. Now we will

do everything for you. We'll blog for you, we'll tweet for you, we'll write your Facebook post, we'll write and send your newsletter—we are now a one-stop complete community-management firm. I had to change my tune because I realized that there are some people that just will not do it for themselves, no matter how much you show them. I also found that there were predators in this space that were telling clients that they'd do everything for them, then do such a terrible job that they were hurting them instead. After writing 300 articles on this stuff and working with hundreds of artists, we know how this all works. We're nerds and we constantly study the latest updates and techniques. I'd much rather they trust us than some so-called "guru" who talks a good game but then takes the money and runs.

Another of the problems was that we'd get an artist reviewed or blogged, but the artist wasn't doing anything with that. They weren't sharing it, they weren't cross-populating it, they weren't thanking the people, all because of their allergy to social media. If someone does something for you, you cannot ignore it. Actually you can, but it's not a great strategy. We felt that we couldn't effect a change for the artist unless we could participate in the follow-up.

We still need to get to know our client and their voice. We'll spend a lot of time understanding who they are, because it doesn't work unless we do that. But we now do that in its entirety, and it's now one of the fastest-growing areas of our business, because it turns out that people really want someone to do it for them.

At the end of the day, my clients want two things: fame and fortune. But there's two things they usually don't have: time and money. Unfortunately it costs some money and some time to learn all this stuff. The fame part is in their own hands.

You can get more info about Ariel and Cyber PR at arielpublicity.com.

Gregory Markel

. . . .

One of the pioneers of search engine optimization (SEO) and marketing, Gregory Markel's company Infuse Creative touts major entertainment clients such as Gibson Musical Instruments, New Line Cinema, the National Geographic Channel, Led Zeppelin, The Rolling Stones, and many more. As a recording artist and great singer formerly signed to Warner Bros., Gregory has a deep empathy for the plight of today's artist and provides an abundance of good advice in the following interview.

What is search engine optimization *exactly?*
SEO these days has a broad definition. It means optimizing anything and everything that a search engine is going to return. That means a web page, a video, a news feed, a blog, a product, a book, an article; it's paying attention to all those areas.

We have three basic types of clients. The first is a client that wants branding awareness. A good example of that is a theatrical release where they can't measure the number of people who might have visited the website who later went on to buy tickets, but they feel that it's something they have to do in order to get the word out.

The second is a client that does ecommerce, where they sell a toaster or something with a specific fixed cost. If you can choose and effectively set up the right keywords with the right ads, with the right landing pages, and at the right cost, then if your cost is $15.00 and you deliver a sale at more than that, it's a positive outcome.

The next type of client wants lead generation, which can be extremely effective if your product has a moderate to large margin. There are companies like mine helping to generate leads to companies that need them, where they can turn that into $20K to $100K per day.

Turning to music, if your music's good there are so many opportunities available with social media, free technologies, and methodologies that you can definitely get a large number of people to find you. Whether you do these things for yourself or have someone who partners with you as your designated online communicator and extended member of the band, there's lots that you can do now without paying for media. Of course there are a lot of paid options that are very powerful and immediate, but they might not be cost effective for someone who has a limited budget, or even none at all.

What would you suggest to a new artist who's trying to break and who wants to use SEO to get the word out?
Everybody knows to set up a Facebook page. Beyond that, regardless of if you're offering your music for free or not, you want to utilize the rest of the Web that doesn't cost you anything, meaning all the Web 2.0 and social-media stuff like personal profile pages, bookmarking, and tagging, and an official Twitter channel. It's figuring out a way to broadcast to your fans and affinity groups, which are groups of people that like the type of music that you play. For example, if I sound a lot like John Meyer, then I want to reach out to John Meyer fans. You can do all that at no cost by simply putting the time in.

Now the ones that do well with this are either going to have a webmaster as a partner or be a new type of musician. Most musicians are abstract and creative types and don't really have an entrepreneurial or measurement-oriented brain, so a new kind of musician who thinks this way, or has a webmaster, is essential.

What's the advice you'd give about optimizing their website and SEO?
The first thing I'd recommend is research, which means finding some artists similar to yourself and examining their online presence. See how they're communicating, where they're communicating, and what they're offering, then see what appears to be working and what they could be doing better. Look at some obscure acts that you've not heard of but that have a lot of listens, as well as at the better-known acts.

The second step would be to educate yourself on the working of social media, or have someone outside the band as your digital-communications partner so you can address these areas. You have to figure out how to put down some kind of footprint online for people to find you. If you're a serious artist, that might dictate one approach, while if you're kind of pop oriented, then that will denote another kind of approach. So you have to educate yourself about social media and what approaches are available and what approach is right for you.

The third step is to put some thought into being disruptive. There's a constant with a lot of independent artists now in that they've figured out how to do something that gets people's attention. There's online chatter and buzz that will cause the press to talk about the fact that it's different, which is like free advertising. It's pretty easy to realize that the people that are successful do more than just put their CD online: for instance, something like what Radiohead did with the video contest on aniboom.com. For a $10,000 prize, they got these jaw-dropping videos for their songs that were every bit as good as if they'd paid some creative house $100K or $200K. The same thing with Prince and his idea to put a CD in the newspaper over in the UK. You've got to figure out a way to be disruptive.

The last step would be understanding the supply chain and the economics. You have to understand your startup and labor costs, as well as your gross and net profit in order to measure the income you're generating. This has changed a bit from the days when I was an active musician. My eyes would've gone sideways on this last one. [Laughs.]

What did you do for Led Zeppelin?

Believe it or not, Zeppelin never had an official website all these years. When Atlantic was releasing the *How the West Was Won* DVD, we did all the search marketing for that effort. It was a branding-awareness campaign, so it wasn't tied to directly selling the DVD off their website. We were really just broadcasting to the world that this was coming out and was available. We did it through nonpaid search (sometimes called organic search) and website optimization, going after all of the affinity keywords or key phrases, making sure that the website was built correctly and had all the content to address all the keywords that they liked to be found by. Then we helped build links to the site and build up link popularity. We also ran a paid search campaign for all of the obvious and not-so-obvious keywords to get the word out about the DVD and website launch. What was unfortunate at the time was that the site was way too overtly commercial, and there was a minibacklash from the hard-core fans who were initially so excited.

Can we talk about keywords for a bit? I think that's something that sometimes confuses people. You mentioned affinity keywords before. What exactly are those?

That's an ultrageneric phrase meaning the universe of keywords and key phrases that would likely be used by a person or a group that would be interested in your stuff. If the primary phrase was Led Zeppelin, for instance, we'd look all the way out to British blues rock and all points in between, which means every phrase that would have some affinity to the content and to the profile of people interested in the content. I'll bet a percentage of the people landing on a page on ledzeppelin.com who are interested in the blues would find Zep's admiration for old bluesmen interesting. There might be someone interested in Jeff Beck who would enjoy landing on a page on ledzeppelin.com talking about Jimmy Page's time in the Yardbirds when he was playing with Jeff Beck, and so on.

You could come up with hundreds of keywords, so how do you determine which are the most important?

With a branding-awareness campaign, keywords are less mission critical because you're really just getting qualified people to your content. With sales it's entirely different. Let's say that you launch with 500 keywords, to just pick a number. In a very short amount of time, you're turning off whatever isn't resulting in a sale because you're measuring everything within an inch of its life. So in that type of campaign, you know painfully what works and what doesn't because you might've spent $500 on a single keyword and never got a single sale from it.

For organic search it's all about being relevant to your content, so in a sense you're going to be limited by your content. In the Jeff Beck example that I just mentioned, unless you have the content on the ledzeppelin.com page that mentions Beck, then you don't stand a chance in hell in getting a ranking for that keyword. Nothing would prevent you from adding Jeff Beck into your keyword tags on ledzeppelin.com, but it's so irrelevant compared to the content that supports that keyword that you're never going to rank for it organically.

So keywords are joined at the hip with content. Supporting content is as important as keywords and vice versa. In the old days you used to be able to fool the search engines. You could get a ranking for Jeff

Beck without having any relevant content, but it was argued that's not a good user experience since you'd get a percentage of people who resented landing on the page and not seeing anything about what they were looking for. Everything's changed with the search engines, and now you have to have the keyword and supporting content or you just won't rank.

When we have SEO conversations with clients, there's always that surprise in their eyes when we start talking about content. That's usually only a conversation that they have with their developers, but there's a direct one-to-one relationship these days. You have to have the content to support the keywords.

Gregory's Infuse Creative can be found at infusecreative.com.

Rupert Perry

. . . .

One of the most respected and beloved executives in the music industry, Rupert Perry held a variety of executive positions with EMI for 32 years. He went from vice president of A&R at Capitol to president of EMI America to managing director of EMI Australia and, later, of EMI Records UK, to president and CEO of EMI Europe to, finally, the worldwide position of vice president of EMI Recorded Music. During his time at EMI, Perry worked with a variety of superstar artists such as The Beatles, Blur, Duran Duran, Iron Maiden, Nigel Kennedy, Robert Palmer, Pink Floyd, Queen, Radiohead, and Cliff Richard. Such were his contributions to the British music industry that in January 1997, he was appointed CBE (Commander of the Order of the British Empire), a position of British order of chivalry that is just below knighthood. He is also coauthor of the fine book *Northern Songs: The True Story of The Beatles' Song Publishing Empire*.

Despite having worked for one of the "four ugly sisters," as he so affectionately calls the major labels—although it's now down to three—Perry is well up on the latest technology and trends within the music business, and shares some surprising contrasts between the old business and the one we're in right now.

You have a unique perspective on the music industry. In your eyes, how are things different today from the heyday of the record business?

One big thing was that the record labels of that time were making those things called gramophones and record players and radios, and they would also be recording content to play on these pieces, so it all fit together. But in the mid-'50s, the technology got away from the recorded-music business and got into the hands of third parties, and from that time on, everything that happened technologically that affected the music business was driven from outside the business. Record labels were no longer technologists. They understood the recording process, and they understood the manufacturing and distribution process—whether it be vinyl, cassette, or CD. But that was the extent of their technology knowledge.

The other thing is how people consumed content in those days, which was that people mostly listened to the radio. Then the Japanese came up with the transistor radio, which was portable. Suddenly [the idea of] portability meant that consumers didn't have to sit in their living rooms in front of that radio. That was the start of something else from a distribution point of few. You can look at all the things that changed, but then you look at the transistor radio and think, "Gosh, the portability was so important."

Don't we have the same thing today with Steve Jobs and iTunes-driven digital media?

Exactly. And then the other great moment of portability came when Sony came up with the Walkman. It's amazing that Sony let it slip through their hands and let Apple come up with the iPod, which to me is just the next stage of the Walkman. Sony's engineers understood the portability aspect between the cassette Walkman and the CD Walkman, but thereafter they missed out on what became the iPod.

Then when the reel-to-reel tape recorder was introduced, that changed things forever because it had a "Record" button on it. It was that "Record" button that really started to change things.

But what really people forget is that by the end of the '70s, the recorded-music business was in deep, deep trouble. There was a recession and a couple of years of downward trends, and a lot of people thought, "This is the end of it." There was a lot of piracy, thanks to the cassette player and that issue of the "Record" button, and people just weren't buying vinyl records anymore. The issue of people making their own copies was a pretty big one even in those days. People were copying music for free off the radio or from another cassette or a record. We reckoned that we were losing at least 25 percent of our business to home taping. So when people talk about "free" today, there's nothing particularly new about it—it's just a different version of the same thing.

The other big thing that happened was the compact disc. When it came along, there was a big upsurge in the growth of the business, and a lot of large corporations began to take notice. When CBS, which was the king of the business at the time, sold their record business to Sony—that was huge! It was a momentous happening, because CBS decided they wanted to exit the music business, which they had been in for years.

I guess that people forget that there were a lot of big changes and issues in the music industry before the Internet.
Yes they do, but the arrival of the Internet was just as big. If we roll forward to the start of the Internet in 1993, people in the content industry didn't get just how monumental the change was. To have any form of content available through a computer was a totally new form of distribution, but the difference was that the record label had no control over it. Up until that point, any of the media distributors (film, television, or music) were always able to control the distribution, and when you did that, you could decide where it went, who got it, and what people paid for it. With the Internet, that went out the window fast. That's the big, big shift caused by this new form of distribution.

The other big issue that the Internet brought was that everything became global. You could be anywhere in the world and you could access Napster, so all the ways that companies tried to segment the market (the way the film industry did with its regional DVDs) were over.

Yet another issue that was a problem, is a problem, and will continue to be a problem going forward is that the laws that govern intellectual copyright are national, as opposed to global, laws. The US has its own copyrights laws, as does Europe, as does Latin America, and so forth. But the nature of the business now is that it's totally global, so it is going to require a more global approach to copyright law as opposed to the parochial approach.

All that being said, how do you see record labels evolving? How will they evolve into something that monetizes content adequately yet is helpful to both the artist and consumer?

I think that's what we're gradually starting to see now. They're starting to come to terms with the fact that they don't have the same control and that online distribution is not something they're part of anymore. They might become part of it at some point in time, but for the moment they have to resign themselves to the fact that they're not. Who are the new distribution kings? ISPs, telecoms, mobile.

That's not always good for the artist though.

It's not very good for the artist because the other problem with this is the fact that in the physical world, you're selling a CD for $10.00, and in the digital world, you're selling a song for $1.00. If your business was built on a $10.00 model with your overhead built around that, it's very difficult to go to a $1.00 model. If you or I started off with a digital label today, we would build and operate it in a very, very different way. We'd look at each other and say, "Okay, fine. We need a couple of product managers sitting in front of computers instead of a big staff, and we need one or two rooms at the most in an office in North Hollywood instead of Beverly Hills." It's a totally different overhead structure and approach.

So when you think about that, you go, "Wait a minute. That sounds just like in the early '50s when it was pretty much a singles business." People bought a song at a time then, as they do in the digital world. In some ways we have gone full circle.

What's the future of the major labels? Do you think they'll survive?

I think they'll survive because they and a lot of smaller labels have catalogs of recorded music, and someone always wants to consume it.

But they also have to consider what kind of business they're in now. They're not really into artist development anymore or signing lots of new artists like they used to in the past. What they're really involved in is the business of rights management. They're managing the rights in the same way that publishers are managing rights. The music-publishing industry and the recorded-music industry—two industries that grew up side by side—are now coming together a lot faster because it's a business of rights.

If you're an artist, you will decide if you can manage your rights yourself or, if you've become successful, need someone to manage them for you on a global basis. Then maybe you go to one of these entities. Either way, you're going to have a much greater degree of flexibility in how you deal with those rights going forward.

What would be the best way to break an act these days?
It's back to immediately being able to build your website first, then communicating and interacting with your fans. Even if you only have 50 email addresses when you start, if you're any good, that will increase. Create your YouTube channel and Facebook pages, because someone will see you and want to go to your website. When they get there, you want them to be one click from anywhere they need to go. If they want to buy something, it's one click. If they want a ticket, it's one click. If they want to read the bio or see the photos, it's one click. But in the end, it's your songs and your performance that's going to drive the traffic.

What you still never get away from is that it's still about a song, and it's still about a performance of that song. Can you play that song in front of your audience, however large or small, and create the "WOW" factor?

What do you think of the "Economics of Free," where the more you give away, the more you sell?
I don't know if I agree with that premise. People argue the same point about pricing [the lower the price, the more you sell], and it's not necessarily so. Creators need to be compensated for what they create, however that may manifest itself. But in the early stages of a career,

you will find that you have to make your music free to get attention and develop a following.

Is a CD necessary these days?
It still may be. People tell me that they sell 50 or 100 CDs at a show. If you control your content, sell X number of CDs and X number of T-shirts and merch, and stay on the road, you can make a pretty good living. You may not be a household name, but you'll have a really strong fan base, you'll know who they are, and you'll be able to communicate with them. The fan/consumer is the piece of the puzzle that you really need.

Jacob Tell

· ·

Jacob Tell's Oniracom is a new breed of company that provides a full line of digital media services to artists, labels, and management. Starting his career coordinating the merch and running the computer systems on the road for Jack Johnson, Jacob put the big picture into context by watching the interaction between artist, label, management, and promoter in different venues around the world. Helping artists in the digital space before there was a YouTube, MySpace, or Facebook, Jacob has watched the development of social networking and learned how an artist can best take advantage of it along the way. Now 12 years old, Oniracom has branched into branding and design as well as their core business of web development, social media marketing, and community management for artists.

How have things changed since we talked for the last version of this book?
Actually the techniques are somewhat the same but the platforms keep changing. There are new ways for artists to get content out to the world, but that content is now twofold. Where before the content was mainly generated by the band or artist directly in regards to a new single or behind-the-scenes video or something similar, now we're seeing more user-generated content as the other half of the story.

Some of our most effective marketing is based around user-generated content where we might grab hashtags from Instagram photos, throw them on a map based on geo-location, and then visualize the fan base across a geographic region that's posting content around a certain campaign. A good example of that is something we did for Thirty Seconds to Mars called MarsIsComing.com. You can see hundreds of Instagram and Twitter pics and Vine videos from all over the world on a map. This has become an extension of community, and it really helps the artists connect directly with their fans on another level.

What's more important today—Vine or Instagram?

For a minute there we really thought that Vine was going to be the most amazing new platform. There was something needed in the short-form video space and Vine did the trick. I think the format is a winner, and being that they're owned by Twitter, they have a built-in audience right off the bat. That said, because that there are so many Instagram users, as soon as it released its video feature to catch up to Vine, the Vine user numbers started to drag. Now you have this split of really hard-core users between the two, with another small contingent on Viddy. The Instagram people say, "I'm already on it, and since it pastes to my Facebook wall I'm just going to stay there."

We always tell our artists that we don't want them to do things that feel like homework, so if they're already on Instagram, we don't want them to try to learn something else and have yet another social network to track. I don't think Vine is going away, but I think the convenience factor of having both photo and video on Instagram is a huge benefit for artists and managers who have too much to manage already.

How important is Google+?

You ask most people and they'll sort of scoff at Google+, but I'm one of the outliers who really believes in it as a centralized platform. There aren't as many active users or bands or brands on it yet, but those numbers are definitely increasing, and there's a lot of content available if you're following the right sector. I get a lot of new information and news that way personally. There are also a lot of influencers in the music and tech space that I follow on G+, and I find that its mobile and tablet interfaces are very compelling.

The fact that everyone in the business world is now moving to the Google Apps ecosystem and Google+ directly integrates with that is important. And Google Hangouts have been one of the most vital collaborative tools to our business. We started those with managers and artists as much to collaborate with them as to show them the technology and how easy it is to use, so you can plant that seed of "You can do this with your fans."

What's the most important social network to an artist right now?
Personally I think visual content wins, so I'd say Instagram and YouTube. YouTube is ubiquitous across every device, the content is instantly searchable and available, and within seconds it can tell the story of a brand or an artist.

When it comes to the other networks though, personally I'm a big Twitter guy. I'm not so much into the Facebook and Google+ world on a day-to-day basis because of the obligation to connect. For an artist with a busy life, Twitter's great because it's more of a broadcast technology, yet you can still engage with people and stay authentic and true to your brand. There's a little bit more of a wall there, so that offers some protection if that's needed.

What's the first thing you do with a new client?
We have a whole process that we call DNA that stands for discover, engage, and advance. The first step is discovery, which means that we listen, since it's all about hearing the client's story. Marketing is all about storytelling, so I get the client to tell me theirs. They may not even think they have a story, but they always do, even if we might have to coax some of that information out sometimes.

Once we understand the story, then we dive into goals. How to achieve those goals is really based on audience demographic. Without a fan base you're not going to monetize and sustain a business, so you have to proactively listen back to your audience. It's a game of give and take. We've had a lot of success in listening to audiences because we ourselves are indeed fans of art, music, and culture, so that really makes it easy because we're so passionate about the subjects. That means we can explain why it might be necessary to do something that maybe the artist isn't so comfortable with in the social space.

Do you do the social day by day with them? How much do you ask them to engage?

It's a case-by-case basis, but if we're talking about an artist on tour, we absolutely want either the artist themselves or someone with day-to-day access to them like a tour manager, publicist, or assistant to be posting content. Anything that's more from management, like an announcement of a tour cycle, album cycle, or product release, we become more hands-on, crafting the copy to make sure that it matches the brand and voice and goals.

Even with the day-to-day content, we'll work with them to craft their content strategy document. We have a website called New Media Rules of Engagement or NMROE.com that outlines the best practices on every single social network. We take all those practices and filter them down based on their audience and goals. From there we come up with a content-strategy document that says how frequently you should be posting content, how you should be posting that content, how you should be generating that content, how you should be repurposing content from your fan base, and how you should be responding to your audience. That's the blueprint for the artist, the management, and the publicist to stay within the framework.

With wireless bandwidth and speeds enabling us to engage with audio and video content from anywhere we are, it should be easer than ever for an artist to be able to engage with their fan base.

You can find out more about Jacob and Oniracom at oniracom.com.

Michael Terpin

∙ ∙

Michael Terpin is the founder of SocialRadius, a social media marketing company focusing on social media outreach and strategy. The company is a spin-off of his Terpin Communications, which is a high-technology public-relations firm specializing in emerging technologies. The projects that his firm has worked on include the outreach for recording artist Will.i.am's "Yes We Can" video for the Obama presidential campaign (which won Emmy, Global Media, and Webby Awards), social media event marketing for music projects like Live8, LiveEarth, the Green Inaugural Ball, and the David Lynch Foundation, and the social media launch of startups ranging from Software.com to Shapeways. Terpin also founded Marketwire, one of the world's largest international newswires.

PR is really changing, isn't it?

So much of the PR, publicity, and promotional arena have become dependent upon social media that I decided to start another company, called SocialRadius, that just does social media marketing. Social media is different from traditional media in that it still accomplishes the same objectives, but it really reflects the way the world is changing and the way people consume information. It used to be that the most important thing you could do was get written up in *Rolling Stone*, but now it's a very different marketplace. Every year people consume more and more content on the Internet, and more and more of that is social.

If you look at where things were 20 years ago versus 10 years ago versus today, they're totally different universes. For example, we had a couple of clients in a *USA Today* article last week. Twenty years ago that would've been earthshaking in that it would have gotten a lot of people buying their products and sending them mail (10 years ago it would've been email), but now we'll probably get as much traction with a well-placed tweet.

When you say the term social media, do you mean Facebook and LinkedIn and those kinds of sites?

No, most of what we do involves the blogs. That's also social media. Most of the social networks have limited impact outside of one's group friends, so they don't have the same kind of impact on search engines or the same rapid viral growth of more open social vehicles.

Tell me about the strategy for the Will.i.am "Yes We Can" video.

What we did there was not do any traditional media whatsoever. In order to have an impact on the California primary, we started giving it to enthusiasts in the blogosphere on Saturday, shortly after we received it from Will and when the traditional media are pretty much sleeping.

The blogosphere is really divided into a lot of different areas now. Most people know the editorial part of the blogosphere, but a lot of it is technology and it's a form of editorial, too. It's sometimes misperceived as being a lot of angry guys in their pajamas, but *TechCrunch* has more readers than the *Wall Street Journal*. There are 50 times more thought leaders and enthusiasts than editorial bloggers around a specific topic.

There are several hundred bloggers who blog about online video trends and topics; that's a group we've worked with a lot, so we gave them the "Yes We Can" video first. They started posting it and people started picking it up. On Sunday, we started going out to the political bloggers. We wanted to make sure that there was already a lot of stuff on the Web so that the political bloggers would see it as important. By the time Monday came around, we had incoming emails from the *Today Show* and *Larry King*, and the *New York Times* saying "Whoa, what happened over the weekend? How do we talk to this guy?" We ended up getting 47 million views and half a billion impressions on traditional media without even making a single outbound traditional media call.

So that means you go to traditional media after social media?
From the public-relations standpoint, particularly as it relates to the entertainment and music industries, the rules have all changed. You can find and aggregate your audience very effectively online, and then when you get to a certain level, the traditional media looks to the online trends for news.

There's also a lot of interconnection between the two. For example, we did something with the David Lynch Foundation for the Paul McCartney and Ringo reunion at Radio City Music Hall. They have a large, traditional entertainment company that they hired to promote it to about 20 places like *USA Today*, the *New York Times*, *People*, *US Weekly* magazine, and those kinds of things. They hadn't really considered doing anything on the blogs, so we were brought in. We're running an onsite social media pressroom, we're giving access to bloggers who are not able to attend, and we'll be managing those bloggers who are onsite attending. We're going to be doing live streaming of interviews in ways that they can pick it up and post it on their site, and we're going to be doing a Twitter feed and live blogging of the event. Those are the things that we find go over well on the larger entertainment events.

Depending upon the client, would you identify different blogs as being important?
Yes, the same way as in traditional PR, where you would identify different publications as being important. If you've got an automotive product, you're going after a different part of the media than if you have a computer-based product.

How do you identify the blogs that are important?
We have a research department. In traditional media there are directories that have been out for years, and every PR firm subscribes to at least some level of these databases and directories. In the blogosphere you have to build your own, since there's no commercial directory of bloggers out there yet. There are some open-source things that we track and aggregate, but for the most part, we just interact with bloggers and add them to our own database.

We follow about 15,000 bloggers to where we know what their likes and dislikes are and what types of things they're interested in. It's a lot more one on one than with the traditional media, where you can say, "These 30 publications all kind of act the same way," and then send them a press release. It's so much more fragmented and specialized. A lot of bloggers don't even consider themselves journalists. The thought-leadership and enthusiast sites don't take advertising, and all they want is to be tipped off early. For example, with the Paul McCartney concert, there are a number of very large Beatle-fan blogs that are read by tens of thousands to hundreds of thousands of people, so we made sure that we got information to them early and often, which is great for the people that are reading the sites.

So you don't send out a press release to the blogs? You're doing more personal contact?
Correct. It's kind of ironic, since I started a press-release newswire. They've been saying for 20 years that the whole phenomenon of the press release is dying, but it keeps on getting larger every year. Right now most press releases are not put out to get written about; they're

put out with the idea of getting into search engines. There are a lot of easier and more impacting ways of getting into search engines by using social media instead of press releases. There are 30,000 press releases that are issued a month on the major wire services, but maybe 5 percent get picked up by anybody in terms of actually getting written about. It's funny: there's less and less media every year, yet there are more and more press releases.

Then what's the best way for an artist to approach a blogger?
Quite frankly, if you're trying to court a blogger who covers your space, the best thing to do is to first start reading them. The nice thing about blogs is they all have RSS feeds, and most of them link their most important posts to their Twitter account, which is mobile and a lot easier to deal with than a large RSS aggregator. You can follow all these bloggers on Twitter, and it'll be on your iPhone, Blackberry, or anything that has a Twitter client, and they'll sort of recognize you as you become a Twitter follower and are watching what they say. You can comment on some of their posts, and all of a sudden, you have a bit of a relationship, so that when you come out, you don't come across as a salesman who's trying to spam 50 sites with the same information. It's better to come out and say, "Hey, I read your site frequently, and here's what I'm doing."

I know you're high on Twitter.
It's very effective right now, even thought the number of users is a lot less than Facebook. A typical Twitter user is going to be posting several times a day, because you're only posting 140 characters at a time. The beauty of Twitter is that you don't have be "friended" by somebody. You can follow anybody you want (thousands of people if you want), and they can follow you unless you're blocking your profile. And if you're following each other, that constitutes a friend relationship, and that means you can direct message them. It becomes a very sophisticated way to search and have conversations with a wide array of thought leaders. It's a very sophisticated crowd now, but it's starting to expand to the masses. It's not real big in music promotion yet, but it will be.

How would you use it to promote a client?

We'll be following people that we want to contact, and we'll also advise our clients to have their own Twitter accounts and do the same. We'll have certain things that we'll do as an agency, and we'll have things that we'll have the client do on their own. You're both involved in the conversation.

Do you have any advice for an artist who wants to get ahead in this space but doesn't have enough money to hire a firm like yours?

It's something that you can absolutely do yourself if you put the time in. Follow the top bloggers, read a few books on social media marketing (although the books are outdated as soon as they come out), follow guys like Seth Godin and Malcolm Gladwell, look at artists who are Twittering and have blogs, go to some conferences, and experiment and see what works.

Find out more about Michael Terpin's Social Radius at socialradius.com.

Dan Tsurif

· ·

Dan Tsurif is head of digital strategy and an artist manager at Mercenary Management, where he handles the day-to-day management for The Casualties, Nekroantix, and Black Label Society. While I was checking the company out, I noticed that there wasn't much of a presence for the company online, to which Dan replied, "We don't focus on the company brand because fans of a musician don't care about that. I love Metallica, but I'm not buying them because of who their management is. Industrywise, we do have a pretty cool LinkedIn profile." Spoken like a true manager, caring for the client more than himself. That said, Dan has some pretty serious social chops as well, which he was kind enough to share.

What's the first thing you do for a new act?

The first thing we'll do is audit all of their social media pages and website. We'll see what's working and what's not and determine what we can fix and make better, which could be anything from installing a merch store on their Facebook page to making sure that their name is the first one that shows up when you do a Google search. You treat each social network differently, but we'll go through them all and determine what's missing. There are always things to fix, especially when a musician has never had a manager before.

Do you fix it yourselves or just tell them what to do?
We'll get in there ourselves depending upon what it is. If it's an already established brand like Zakk Wylde from Black Label Society, where he runs his own Twitter and Instagram, we show him things like how to use hashtags, which he wasn't doing—little things like watching grammar and spelling, and tagging other people that he's talking to. When I go into a YouTube account and set up the advertising partnerships or Facebook merch stores, that's all us.

It's interesting that you would do this much socially, since that's not traditionally a big part of management.
It absolutely is now because social media is where your audience is. There are other ways to connect with a large group of people, but when it comes to niche genres, the only way to talk to people all over the world that are into that genre is socially.

Do you farm this out to a third-party company?
We do it all in house, because a third party is just going to charge us if we farm it out and it'll be no better than what we can do. Honestly, if you're creating posts on behalf of a client, you have to be able to fit that artist's personality. The fans want to get the experience that they're actually speaking to Zakk Wylde or their favorite musician over Facebook, and for that you have to know the artist. I've never liked that record labels typically take this over, because they do what's in the best interest for them, where we do what's in the best interest for the artist.

Do you charge the artists more for this?
No, just the regular commission. It's part of our service. We do have a separate company (Mercenary Marketing) that just does marketing and digital strategy for clients that we don't manage, and we do that for a fee. We can bring in an art department, video production, and

two publicists, so it's a full-package deal, but our management clients get all of those services for free.

What's the most important social tool right now?

For what I'm currently doing it's YouTube. It's the single most important tool for a musician, because you can distribute your music, monetize it, use the description to promote tour dates and the merch store, and it has the social aspect so people can go and talk and share comments with their friends. For most artists, I tell them to pick just one social network and get really good at it, but if they ask me which one, I'll tell them that YouTube is the single most important tool that an artist has at their disposal.

Do you recommend that your clients post more than just their music videos?

Absolutely. Typically the record label owns the masters to their songs, so the artists won't make anything from posting them, and the label will want to do that anyway. That shouldn't stop them from making their own videos. I tell them not to just focus on music but to put out videos on everything that you can. You can make a guitar lesson, show some cool backstage antics or webisodes, or even a rehearsal video. People love that. It's very interesting for fans to see. That's what we have a video team for.

What's the one type of video that fans relate to the most?

Our most popular videos are webisodes of the artists on tour. Recently we had one with Black Label Society where a videographer followed them everywhere on the tour, and every day we'd put up a new tour recap. That was wildly popular.

We had one with *Alternative Press* magazine for Black Veil Brides where they followed them around on the Warped Tour. It was a similar concept, but those videos had the most impact because it gave the fans a chance to see what the band members were like offstage, then see the transformation to going onstage and performing, so they could see what's it's really like to be in a touring band. Especially now that it's so easy to pick up a guitar and get into music, they want to know what it takes to get to be a professional touring musician. They get access to that world and learn that it's not all just parties and girls.

Do you do anything special for video SEO?

Proper tags and descriptions are wildly important. I see a lot of companies spending thousands of dollars for search engine optimization, and I agree to a point that you need that boost, but so much could be done just on your own with YouTube by properly tagging and using the descriptions. You should be tagging similar artists, having full lyrics in the descriptions, as well as the name of the director if it's a music video. Just these little things that people can do have a huge impact on the visibility of the video.

How much are your bands involved in social media? How much do you do?

It depends on the band. It might be 10 to 50 percent of the time, depending upon who we're working with. We might give them a class on how to do something, but most acts do most of it themselves. For the personalized things it's always the band members, but if they don't know what they're doing, then we'll show them the ropes. We can try to put ourselves in the heads of the band members and maybe post like they would, but nothing beats the actual member doing it.

How important is the album these days?

Very important, but you can't put out an album and have only one good song on it anymore. For the bands that I'm working with, they have these cultlike followings, but they can't get away with having only one radio hit while the rest of the album is lukewarm. You need a lot more than one song that resonates with your audience. It's a great feeling when I can travel to any part of the country to see Black Veil Brides and hear everyone in the audience singing every word to every song. We're talking a thousand to two thousand people a night. That's a huge deal. Fans really appreciate it when an artist does go all out and produces a really great album.

Are CDs still important?

Yes, they're important in that you have to keep your retail numbers up, but it's up to the buyer to determine what's best for them. There's a lot of things in rock music that you can't get away with that you might in pop or hip hop or EDM, like a purely electronic product. Vinyl sales are going through the roof these days, but I think it's more of a collectible, the same as the CD. It helps if you package the physical product with something else that makes them want to buy it, like a poster or sticker.

In general, what is the one thing other than writing good songs that you'd advise a band to do?
Save money. You see a lot of bands breaking up because they can't make it work financially despite their talent. Save for a rainy day. You're going to need it. That $10,000 insurance to get on the Warped Tour is not cheap.

For social media, find the one tool that you like and become an expert at it. Learn everything you can about it and apply it all.

Appendix 1: Online Tools

Below you'll find all of the sites, tools, and applications mentioned during the course of this book.

Band-Oriented Platforms

. . . .

ReverbNation (reverbnation.com)
Bandcamp (bootcamp.com)
Sonic Bids (sonicbids.com)
Nimbit (nimbit.com)
RouteNote (routenote.com)
Ning (ning.com)
The Ultimate Chart (ultimatechart.com)
Ditto (ditto.com)
CD Baby (cdbaby.net)
Tunecore (tunecore.com)
Topspin Media (topspinmedia.com)
A&R Registry (musicregistry.com)

Blogs

. . . .

Blogger (blogger.com)
Typepad (typepad.com)
WordPress (wordpress.com)
Tumblr (tumblr.com)

Crowdfunding

. . . .

Kickstarter (kickstarter.com)
Indiegogo (idiegogo.com)

Rockethub (rockethub.com)
Sellaband (sellaband.com)
Pledge Music (pledgemusic.com)

Facebook

. . . .

BandPage (bandpage.com)
My Band App (facebook.com/rn.mybandapp)
Facebook Insights (facebook.com/help/?search=insights)
Fanbridge (fanbridge.com)

Mailing Lists

. . . .

Fan Bridge (fanbridge.com)
Mail Chimp (mailchimp.com)
Constant Contact (constantcontact.com)
iContact (icontact.com)

Measurement

. . . .

PeopleBrowsr (peoplebrowsr.com/)
Sysomos (sysomos.com)
Radian6 (radian6.com)
Google Analytics (google.com/analytics)
Who's Talkin (whostalkin.com)
Google Alerts (google.com/alerts)
Band Metrics (bandmetrics.com)
Google Alerts (google.com/alerts)
Twitter Search (search.twitter.com)
Stat Counter (statcounter.com)
Tynt Tracer (tcr1.tynt.com)
Next Big Sound (nextbigsound.com)

Music Metric (musicmetric.com)
Star Count (starcount.com)

Merchandise

....

Zazzle (zazzle.com)
CafePress (cafepress.com)
Blurb (blurb.com)
Square (squareup.com)
QR Codes (qrcode.kaywa.com)
Kunaki (kunaki.com)

Music Blogs

....

Hypebot (hypebot.com)
Music Think Tank (musicthinktank.com)
Seth Godin (sethgodin.typepad.com)
Ariel Hyatt/Cyber PR (Arielpublicity.com)
Big Picture Music Production Blog (bobbyowsinski.blogspot.com)
Music 3.0 Blog (music3point0.blogspot.com)

Publishing

....

Association of Independent Music Publishers (aimp.org)
Sound Exchange (soundexchange.com)

Social Media Management

....

Artist Data (artistdata.com)
Amp Music Marketing (ampmusicmarketing.com)
Ariel Hyatt/Cyber PR (Arielpublicity.com)

Streaming Video

· ·

UStream (ustream.com)
LiveStream (livestream.com)
Justin.TV
Google+ Hangouts on Air

Surveys

· ·

Survey Monkey (surveymonkey.com)
PollDaddy (polldaddy.com)

Twitter

· ·

Search.twitter.com
Twellow (twellow.com)
Klout (klout.com)
Blast Follow (blastfollow.com)
Tweepi (tweepi.com)
Gremln (gremln.com)
Tweetdeck (tweetdeck.com)
Tweetchat (tweetchat.com)
TweetWhen (tweetwhen.com)
TweetReach (tweetreach.com)

YouTube

· ·

YouTube Trends (youtube.com/trendsdashboard)
YouTube Insight (available on each video and channel)
OneLoad (oneload.com)

Appendix 2: Glossary

360 deal. A record deal that enables the record label to share in the income of other aspects of an artist's career beyond recording, such as ticket sales and merchandise.

A&R. An abbreviation for *artist and repertoire*. A talent scout at a record label.

AAC. An abbreviation for *Advanced Audio Coding*. A standard compression encoding scheme for digital audio used exclusively by Apple's iTunes store.

Adsense. A Google service for supplying advertisements to a website based on many factors, such as the website's content and the user's geographical location.

access model. Where music consumers prefer to access their music through subscription platforms instead of owning their music by buying downloads.

after-show party. A party directly following a show that is for the band's friends and associates.

airplay. When a song gets played on the radio.

Arbitron rating. A measurement of the number of people listening to a radio station.

art. A creative endeavor that you do for your own personal satisfaction.

artistic control. Control of the creative aspects of a recording. Artistic control usually lies mainly in the hands of the producer, with input from the artist.

backlink. An outside link on another website that's connected to your page.

bar code. A series of vertical bars of varying widths in which the numbers 0 through 9 are represented by a unique pattern of bars that can be read by a laser scanner. Bar codes are commonly found on consumer products and are used for inventory control purposes and, in the case of CDs, to tally sales.

bootleg. An unauthorized recording of a concert, a rehearsal, an outtake, or an alternate mix from an album.

brand. A name, sign, or symbol used to identify the items or services of a seller that differentiate them from their competitors. A brand is a promise of quality and consistency.

branding. The promotion of a brand.

breakage. In the days of vinyl, a certain percentage of records would break in transit. This number was subtracted from the artist's royalties.

brick-and-mortar. A physical retail store usually composed of building materials such as bricks and mortar.

cache. Temporary storage of online digital data like a website on your computer, phone, or tablet.

cobranding. Two firms working together to promote a product or service.

catalog. Older albums or recordings under the control of the record label.

collectible. An item (usually nonessential) that has particular value to its owner because of its rarity and desirability.

conglomerate. A multi-industry company or a large company that owns smaller companies in different businesses.

container. With regard to music, the package that allows the listener to consume it. Vinyl records, CDs, and MP3 and AAC files are all containers.

consultant. A person who advises a radio station about what to play, when to play it, and what on-air personalities to use.

craft. A creative endeavor that you do for someone else's approval.

cross-collateralization. Royalties from one agreement used to cover the losses or advances of another agreement.

crowdfunding. A method of raising money for a project by offering incentives for fans to pool their money.

DJ. An abbreviation for disc jockey. A term used in the early days of radio for the on-air radio person who played the records that the station was broadcasting. Later replaced by the term *on-air "personality."*

distribution network. The various retail sales outlets or, in the case of M3.0, digital music download sites.

DIY. An abbreviation for *do it yourself.*

DRM. An abbreviation for *dgital rights management.* An antipiracy measure that limits the number of legal copies that can be made.

FLAC. An abbreviation for *Free Lossless Audio Codec.* A lossless file format used to make digital audio files smaller in size.

four-wall. When one management individual or company uses the clout of a larger management company in return for a percentage of the income. The manager of the smaller company sometimes shares an office with the larger management company, or is "four-walled" within the company's offices.

freemium. A business model where a product or service is offered free of charge, but the customer is charged for advanced features or functions.

fuelers. Contributors to a crowdfunding project.

gatefold. An album cover that folds out.

heritage artist. A superstar act that is still active. Madonna, Tina Turner, the Rolling Stones, and The Eagles are examples of current heritage acts.

IFPI. An abbreviation for the *International Federation of the Phonographic Industry*. Represents the recording industry worldwide, with some 1,400 members in 66 countries and affiliated industry associations in 45 countries.

imprint. A project, division, or custom label of a record label, usually given to an artist or producer.

independent promoter. A person or company not employed by a record label, but hired by the label to persuade a radio station to play a record.

ISRC code. An abbreviation for *International Standard Recording Code*. An international standard code for uniquely identifying sound recordings and music-video recordings. An ISRC code identifies a particular recording, not the song itself. Therefore, different recordings, edits, and remixes of the same song will each have their own ISRC codes.

jewel case. The standard plastic case that holds a CD.

kbps. An abbreviation for *kilobits per second*, or the amount of digital information sent per second. See also **bandwidth.**

leader. Initiates contact with the tribe and leads the conversations.

loss leader. An item priced at a loss in order to entice people to buy another more costly product, usually at full retail price.

lurker. One who reads a blog but doesn't participate or post him- or herself.

meet and greet. A brief meeting with an artist to say hello, answer a few questions, and take pictures.

metadata. Data about other data or content.

micropayment. A means for transferring very small amounts of money in situations where collecting such small amounts of money is impractical, or very expensive, with the usual payment systems.

millennial. A member of the generation of children born between 1977 and 1994.

MP3. The de facto standard data-compression format used to make audio files smaller in size.

M0.5. See **Music 0.5.**

M1.0. See **Music 1.0.**

M1.5. See **Music 1.5.**

M2.0. See **Music 2.0.**

M2.5. See **Music 2.5.**

M3.0. See **Music 3.0.**

M3.5. See **Music 3.5.**

M4.0. See Music **4.0.**

Music 0.5. The time before recorded music, when sheet music was the only form of music distribution.

Music 1.0. The first generation of the music business, in which the product was vinyl records, the artist had no direct contact with the record buyer, radio was the primary source of promotion, the record labels were run by record people, and records were bought from retail stores.

Music 1.5. The second generation of the music business, in which the product was primarily CDs, labels were owned and run by large conglomerates, MTV caused the labels to shift from artist development to image development, radio was still the major source of promotion, and CDs were purchased from retail stores.

Music 2.0. The third generation of the music business, which signaled the beginning of digital music. Piracy ran rampant because of P2P networks, but the industry took little notice, since CD sales were still strong from radio promotion.

Music 2.5. The fourth generation of the music business, in which digital music became monetized, thanks to the online dig-ital-distributor iTunes store and, later, others such as Amazon MP3. CD sales plunged, the music industry contracted, and retail stores closed.

Music 3.0. The generation of the music business in which the artist was first able to communicate and interact with, and market and sell directly to, the fan. Record labels, radio, and television became mostly irrelevant, and single songs were purchased instead of albums.

Music 3.5. The generation of the music busi-ness in which YouTube became the principle way that music consumers discover music, and as a result, became more comfortable with streaming digital music instead of downloading it.

Music 4.0. The generation of music that we're entering into, where streaming music becomes profitable for the entire supply chain of the music industry, as consumers change completely to the access model of consuming music.

one-stop. A company that buys from major record-distributors and sells to small retail-ers who buy in quantities too small for major distributors to bother with.

paid download. A downloadable song that you buy and own.

pay-per-click. An Internet advertising model used on search engines, advertising networks, and content sites such as blogs, in which advertisers pay their hosts only when their ads are clicked on.

paid search. A type of contextual advertising in which website owners pay an advertising fee to have their websites shown in the top placement on search-engine results pages.

payola. Payment in exchange for airplay. The payment could be in cash, illegal substances such as drugs, or products such as televisions or paid vacations. The practice is illegal.

pay to play. In order to play at a club, the owner demands that the band buy a certain number of tickets, which they then sell or give away to their fans. The club owner is guaranteed a minimum cash presale, while the band usually ends up losing money.

peer to peer. A type of transient Internet network that allows a group of computer users with the same networking program to connect with each other and directly access files from one another's hard drives.

performance fee. A fee paid to the performer (as opposed to the songwriter) each time a song is played on the radio, over the Internet, or on television.

performance-rights organization. An organization that collects performance royalties from broadcasters or Internet streaming and distributes it to songwriters. Performance-rights organizations include ASCAP, BMI, and SESAC. See also **PRO.**

P2P. See **peer to peer.**

pirating. The sale of an illegal copy of a digital file, CD, CD artwork, or any other creative product where the record label, artist, and songwriter never take part in the profit or are provided royalties.

PRO. An abbreviation for *Performance Rights Organization.* Some are ASCAP, BMI, and SESAC.

producer. The person in charge of recording, from managing the budget to creatively guiding the project to completion.

promoter. A person who organizes a concert or show, including booking the venue and talent; arranging for advertising, security, and insurance; as well as a host of other duties. The promoter usually uses his or her own money to finance the project in the hopes of making a profit.

QR Code. A graphic code similar to a bar code that provides a link to a website when scanned. An analog web link.

rack jobber. Someone who leases floor space from a retail store (such as a department store or car wash) and puts in "racks" of CDs or other types of recorded music.

record. A generic term for the distribution method of a recording. Regardless of whether it's vinyl, a CD, or a digital file, it is still known as a record.

record club. An outdated way of obtaining prerecorded music at a discounted rate through the mail. Usually used by the consumer because there is no retail music store in his or her area.

RIAA. An abbreviation for the *Recording Industry Association of America*. A trade organization for record labels.

rotation. The playlist of a radio station.

RSS. An abbreviation for *Real Simple Syndication*. A family of Web-feed formats used to publish frequently updated works (such as blog entries, news headlines, audio, and video) in a standardized format.

SEM. An abbreviation for *Search-Engine Marketing*.

SEO. An abbreviation for *Search-Engine Optimization*.

shed. A large outdoor-concert facility.

SKU. An abbreviation for *stock-keeping unit*. The number allotted to every item in a store for the purpose of inventory control.

SoundScan. The company that measures record sales. Whenever a CD or a DVD is sold, the bar code on each unit is scanned and recorded by SoundScan.

superfan. A fan that is more passionate than the average fan. See also **true fan; uberfan.**

subscription service. A download service for which you pay a set monthly fee and listen to as much music as you want during that time without any limitations.

swag. Another name for merchandise, such as T-shirts, that is sold at a concert or on a website.

technology expense. A clause in a recording agreement that subtracts a portion of the artist's royalty if a certain new technology is used in the production or sale of product.

torrent. The latest form of Internet P2P (peer to peer) file sharing. Since 2006, Bittorrent sharing has been the most popular means by which Web users trade software, music, movies, and digital books across the Internet. *Bittorrents* (a term that is synonymous with *torrents*) work by downloading small bits of files from many different Web sources at the same time. See also **peer to peer.**

true fan. A fan that is more passionate than the average fan. See also **superfan; uberfan.**

turntable hit. A song that receives massive airplay but has few actual sales.

tweet. A Twitter posting.

uberfan. A fan that is more passionate than the average fan. See also **superfan; true fan.**

vertical. A particular marketing or sales niche or demographic group.

WMA. An abbreviation for *Windows Media Audio*. An audio data-compression format created by Microsoft.

Index